I1006073

ALSO BY PETER FENTON

Truth or Tabloid?

I Forgot to Wear Underwear on a Glass-Bottom Boat:
Real People, True Secrets
(cowritten by Susan Fenton)

Monterey Public Library

PETER FENTON

EYEING

≩ *the* ≨

FLASH

THE EDUCATION OF A

CARNIVAL CON ARTIST

SIMON & SCHUSTER

NEW YORK   LONDON   TORONTO   SYDNEY

364.163
FEN

SIMON & SCHUSTER
Rockefeller Center
1230 Avenue of the Americas
New York, NY 10020

Copyright © 2005 by Peter Fenton
All rights reserved,
including the right of reproduction
in whole or in part in any form.

SIMON & SCHUSTER and colophon are registered trademarks
of Simon & Schuster, Inc.

For information about special discounts for bulk purchases,
please contact Simon & Schuster Special Sales:
1-800-456-6798 or business@simonandschuster.com

Designed by Dana Sloan

Manufactured in the United States of America

1   3   5   7   9   10   8   6   4   2

Library of Congress Cataloging-in-Publication Data
Fenton, Peter.
Eyeing the Flash : the education of a carnival con artist / Peter Fenton.
p. cm.
1. Fenton, Peter. 2. Swindlers and swindling—United States—Biography.
3. Carnivals—United States. I. Title.

HV6248.F24A3 2005
364.16'3'092—dc22
[B]   2004056485

ISBN 0-7432-5854-1

Names and certain identifying characteristics of the Alibi agents, Ride Boys, lot lice, Flatties, marks, schoolteachers, compulsive liars, gamblers, police, Hanky-Pank degenerates, outraged citizens, sideshow operators, friends, and others mentioned in this book have been changed.

ACKNOWLEDGMENTS

Thanks to Brian DeFiore and Amanda Murray for rolling the dice on an author who was as real to them as a 13-Inch Foot-Long. Much appreciation to Kate Garrick for reading her email, to Victoria Meyers and Aileen Boyle in the Simon & Schuster publicity department, and to Christina Richardson for her help and assistance.

And thanks in advance to every bookseller who shelves this book face-out or hand-sells it with evangelical fervor at the risk of career and sanity. To you I owe one Free Game Pass.

For Susan

CHAPTER ONE

Why You Should Always Leave the Mark a Dollar for Gas

1967

I had my back turned to Jackie when he said, "You'll never get rich with your hands in your pants."

I whirled around. "Where'd you read that one, a fortune cookie?" It was hard to breathe, let alone come up with a decent retort. I had twisted away to adjust the sweat-soaked roll of cash in my black silk briefs and Jackie was no more than three feet from me, watching my every move. I couldn't let him spot the mysterious lump on my right hip—because, after all, it was his money I'd stolen.

"No, I saw it in a friggin' Oreo. Anyway, who cares? I've got to have lunch with the county sheriff in ten minutes. Can I just show you how to work the Swinger?"

My throat felt like it was being constricted by kielbasa-size fingers. I had struggled to convince Jackie that I deserved a shot working one of the best money-vacuums on the Party Time Shows midway, and now I couldn't get a word out except "Sure." I was anxious about the money slipping down my pant leg. I was sick from the cold corn dogs, pizza crust, and flat Coke I had for breakfast after waking up, fully dressed in my new blue sharkskin pants and white satin shirt with western-style fringe, under a Party Time Shows semitrailer. I couldn't safely sleep in a room, because spending the night in a Motel 6 might have tipped Jackie off that I had a source of income beyond my official cut of the action.

Jackie, on the other hand, was clean and calm, his auburn hair smelling of Vitalis. He was absently cutting a deck of cards with one soft, manicured hand while palming the croquet ball with the other. Then he dropped the cards into the breast pocket of his white, short-sleeved cotton shirt.

"See my pinkie finger?" Jackie asked, holding it in front of my face. "On the Swinger, your pinkie is the gaff, so don't get it chopped off in a bar fight."

"How so?"

"You see, even though it was probably invented in Alabama by some guy with three teeth, the Swinger is based upon a fundamental principle of physics, which is that the angle of reflection always equals the angle of refraction. Or maybe it's the other way around."

"Yeah, I did a science project on that in the fourth grade."

"Let me show you how it relates to the Swinger." Deceptively stripped down and simple in appearance, the Swinger was an "Alibi joint" that required the adult customer to knock a bowling pin down with a croquet ball. The bowling pin stood in the crux of a wooden coat hanger that had been nailed flat on a chest-high plywood counter. The croquet ball hung from a chain directly above the pin. Jackie turned and faced the counter. "In order to win a prize on the Swinger," he said, "the player needs to swing the croquet ball forward so that it misses the bowling pin as it travels past, yet knocks the bowling pin down on the return trip."

"So where does my pinkie finger come in?"

"When you want some moron to win, for publicity purposes or whatever, you wrap your pinkie around the back of the bowling pin so that when you seem to place the pin in the crux of the coat hanger, it is actually slightly off center. Which will result in the croquet ball knocking the pin down on the return trip."

"Because of the angle of reflection equals the angle of refraction thing."

"Like every game on the midway, the Swinger is all about science and the unchangeable laws of nature," Jackie joked. He glanced at his watch, then the neon-lit hot dog stand, where he was due to buy the county sheriff a foot-long and probably hand over a popcorn box full of cash, so that the sheriff would order his deputies to ignore every loser's complaint. Jackie was wise to every carny scam in the book even though, like me, he was seventeen and just a week short of graduating from high school.

"What's a good call?" I asked about the line of patter I'd use to attract a mark's attention.

Jackie shrugged. "Whatever feels right. Like if it was some biker with a tattoo of a Harley on his shoulder, you might say, 'Hey bro, park your scooter and let me show you how to profit by playing a little item we call the Swinger.' Something to get him ticked off. Because when you insult a biker, he'll want to beat you at your own game. And that's not humanly possible."

"So I wind up with his money."

"But don't forget to leave him with a dollar so he can buy gas, drive home, and kick the mailbox instead of you."

For a brief moment, I forgave Jackie for all the tricks he'd played on me over the course of our friendship, how he'd conned me into this, manipulated me into that. With his help, I might soon be earning hundreds of bucks, maybe a grand a day, on the Swinger.

I'd have pockets bursting with cash, a girl under each arm, and a beer in each hand.

Then the $1,253 in my underwear once again began to descend. My sweat and the accumulated grime of thousands of hands had turned the bills into a slimy mass that was slipping from the grasp of the elastic band. I stole a look at Jackie, who was now a few feet to my right, leaning against one of the tent poles that held up the Swinger. Why was he staring at me, I wondered? His opaque gaze was fixed on me just slightly off center, so that he was neither meeting me eye to eye nor looking away. Did he know I was skimming money because I'd discovered that he was paying me far less than my fair share? Hey, we were best friends. How could that happen? Maybe I was paranoid. Maybe at seventeen I was already far too suspicious of my best buddy's motives, not to mention those of the common folk who were currently slogging down the midway through the thick stew of mud, sawdust, and elephant turds the size of bread loaves.

Jackie pushed his black, horn-rimmed glasses back up his nose. Perspiration dotted his quickly reddening face. "Now," he said, "I have a question for you."

"What's that?"

"Did you just shit cash?"

I peered down at my feet. There, peeking out of my right pant leg, was the soggy roll of bills I'd held out from Jackie. "That couldn't have come out of me. All I ate for lunch was nickels and quarters."

Jackie responded by wrapping his hand around the skinny end of the bowling pin. Impulsively, I grabbed the croquet ball, not the best defensive move because it was tethered to a chain.

Far away, from the direction of the Ferris wheel I heard a voice scream, "Please, oh please, let me down from here." That frantic wail was quickly obliterated by a screeching loudspeaker and the announcement that the Greased Pole Climbing Contest was about to begin.

I asked myself: If Jackie was me, what would he say next to hack his way out of this thicket?

CHAPTER TWO

The 108-Pound Future All-American Quarterback

1963

"Crawl through that mud puddle and you're my starting quarterback," Coach Strampe said.

"Which puddle, coach?" I asked. "There are a lot of them."

A gust of wind tugged at the bill of Coach Strampe's Notre Dame cap. His taut gray face remained stoic. "You figure it out, Fenton. In fact, I'm going to add that to the requirement. Crawl through the mud puddle of your choosing and if it's the one I believe presents the appropriate challenge, you're the Big Team's new QB. Plus, you get this new plastic helmet."

It was mid-September and we were on the unpaved corner of the playground at Rose Junior High School in Mineralton, Michigan, a town of 15,000. It was a classic Indian summer day. Behind us, a homeowner burned leaves in his yard. The sky, what little I could see of it through the smoke and branches of the towering hickory nut trees, was a vibrant blue. Yet the black leather helmet I wore muffled every sound, and I felt one step removed from my surroundings, partially encased in my own little world.

I was faced with a choice: Do as Coach Strampe ordered and become the Big Team quarterback, with a new blue plastic helmet; or decline and be relegated to the Little Team and the black, Red Grange–style model that hundreds of kids had sweated in before me. The prestigious Big Team was limited to players weighing 108 pounds or more. The Little Team was composed of everyone below that. At 108 pounds, I was considered "on the bubble" and thus allowed to make my own decision, bearing in mind the coach's desires.

It had rained heavily overnight, and puddles crisscrossed the bumpy field. Hedging my bet, I dropped to my knees, planning to crawl through each and every one. The water was cold and cloudy, and I had to gingerly feel my way through the muck to avoid hidden rocks and broken glass. By the time I squished through the third puddle, I was enjoying myself, fantasizing that I was a World War II Marine, snaking forward on my belly to stay below heavy Nazi fire.

Coach Strampe's voice returned me to the playing fields of Rose Junior High. "Okay, Fenton. That's enough."

"You sure?" I asked, looking up.

"Remove the leather helmet. You passed the test. You covered all your bases, which is what a quarterback needs to do."

I rose to my feet. My fingers could hardly move, and my palms were bruised and dented. My knees were wobbly, and my padded football pants were water-soaked and sagging. The leather helmet grasped my head like a suction cup. After a struggle, it came off with an audible pop. I exchanged the tattered relic for the blue plastic model with the white plastic face guard. I was jubilant.

"Can I take it home and show my dad?" I asked Coach Strampe.

He thought for a moment. "What the heck. Spence will love it. Just wrap it up in something, 'cause that beauty's straight out of the box."

"I'll cover it with my jacket."

"Good. Now hit the showers. And don't run off after that, 'cause I've got a speech to make about Friday's game."

The locker room was a cacophony of towel fights and shouting. I clumped across the concrete to my favorite corner locker, where I could conceal myself somewhat as I disrobed. Admiring a painful raspberry on my right calf, I was suddenly boxed in by three mounds of jiggling adolescent flesh.

The tallest mound said, "Wow! Pete's got a blue helmet like us. Does that mean you're our starting quarterback?"

"Coach Strampe just said so."

The other mounds yelped "Cool," and "Great."

Aaron Solomon, Mike Karpinski, and Zem Kelch were the core of the Big Team's offensive line—or "500 Pounds of Steel," as Coach Strampe had dubbed them. I'd grown up with the guys, and to me, they were three fat kids who hated to run. As was his nature, Coach saw them more favorably. The 500 Pounds were going to form an impenetrable wall in front of me at quarterback, resulting in a winning season that Coach could parlay into a job with the "Magnificent Minerals," the Mineralton High School team.

Aaron, the largest component of the 500 Pounds of Steel at five feet, five inches and 175 pounds, placed his hand on my shoulder and vowed, "Pete, we've known each other since the first grade, and we won't let a single linebacker touch a hair on your head. You know that, don't you?"

Before I could answer, Coach's voice caromed off the moldy tile walls, "Shower fast, guys. I've got an announcement to make in the gym."

Afterwards, dressed in tan pants and a shirt covered with Roman numerals that I thought looked cool, I joined the rest of the team on the gym floor in a circle at Coach Strampe's feet. My new helmet was secured inside my jacket with nearly an entire roll of Scotch tape.

Head bowed, Coach obsessively toyed with the silver whistle that hung around his neck. The impatient janitor had doused the gym lights, and Coach was already growing murky in the dusk. "Gentlemen," he began, "based on the two weeks we've been in training since the school year began, I have a firm belief that you can go the year undefeated. And most of my confidence has to do with our offense, not to disparage you guys on the defensive side. Put simply, on offense I have 500 Pounds of Steel to protect"—he drew out his words—"a future . . . All-American . . . quarterback. Let's hear it for Pete Fenton!"

It had become so dusky that it was difficult to see how many of my teammates applauded, although it sounded like half a dozen at least. I was embarrassed, yet thrilled. No one had ever clapped for me before. I wondered what Coach knew about my talent that I didn't. I'd never played football anywhere but on the empty lot next to my parents' home, and that field was only sixty yards long.

Coach continued, "Pete is a student-athlete in the tradition of his great-uncle Ted Pembroke. You may be too young to know this, but in 1947 Ted brought great honor to Mineralton by being named to several college All-American teams when he was University of Michigan's star quarterback. Like Pete, he studied hard, played hard and wasn't afraid to get his little-bitsy toes wet. And that's why I've invited the entire high school coaching staff to watch us smash Livonia Junior High this Friday. Pete, and the rest of you, are the future of the Magnificent Minerals. Dismissed."

No one congratulated me, which was a relief; I'd had enough of the spotlight. The gym was now pitch dark, and I assumed everyone was preoccupied with trying to find a way out. I escaped through a side door.

The cool night air was a welcome change of pace from the sour sweat socks and Pine-Sol smell of the gym. Unfortunately, the boost I'd received from Coach's overblown praise was undercut when one of my teammates playfully tackled Mandy, a raven-haired beauty I'd had my eye on since the fall term had started. She'd transferred to Rose from a school in Indian Hills, a newly developed area of Mineralton with a racy reputation as far as my parents were concerned— because, as my father put it, "There isn't a single house out there more than two years old."

Mandy had short hair that ended in a curl on the side of each cheek, dark freckles and flashing black eyes. She wore lipstick and had a habit of chewing on her pencil. Once, when collecting tests for the teacher, I noticed an impression of her teeth near the eraser, which made me wonder what it would be like to share a box of popcorn with Mandy and then kiss her. Yet I was so shy I did nothing more than stare at Mandy for an hour of English class each day, and think.

I sprinted down the covered walkway that led to the street, dodging imaginary tacklers, hopefully conveying that I had too much on my plate to have noted Mandy's delighted screams. Yes, my responsibilities were grave and manifold. The fate of the upcoming season, not to mention Coach Strampe's future, was a mighty weight upon my shoulders.

Mineralton was only twenty miles west of Detroit, yet it retained an aura of rural isolation. Few locals took the relatively short drive to Detroit, even though the city had yet to begin its precipitous decline. I'd traveled there only once with my grandparents and still had vivid memories of the massive gray buildings whose true height I couldn't measure from the back seat of a Chrysler Imperial.

Prior to that, the tallest structure I'd seen was the ten-story Mineralton Building, where I'd ridden my first elevator all the way to the top. Yes, Mineralton was all the city many residents needed; in fact, it was the "City" part of "Farm-City Week," when downtown was closed to traffic, the farmers sold fresh produce, and every retail store held a sidewalk sale.

Self-satisfied, parochial Mineralton held a secret, however, one known only to long-term residents. It had once been a glamorous destination, dubbed "Spa City." As one story told it, an early twentieth-century entrepreneur who'd been drilling for natural gas had instead tapped a gusher of healing, sulfurous ooze. Hotels had sprung up citywide, catering to the health-conscious affluent who flocked to bathe in the thick, smelly stew. Each hotel owned its own well and provided a tub with a mud-spewing faucet in each private guest room. The town flourished. In Mineralton money had smelled like sulfur, a rotten-egg stench difficult to escape in any neighborhood.

Eventually, advances in medicine had forced the baths to be shuttered and the wells to be capped. One by one, the fabulous hotels had been converted to weekly residence halls. Still, some old-line Spa City women doused themselves lavishly with perfume to mask the lucrative though offensive odors that were no longer really there.

The Fenton family name was well-known to old-timers. My grandfather, Baker Fenton, had owned a coal and oil supply firm that ran the length of a city block, an ice company, and one of the best mineral bath hotels, The Fenton. An unyielding pillar of Mineralton society, he never missed a Rotary Club meeting in twenty-five years of membership. But when routine-obsessed Baker had been killed by a freight train that arrived at the fuel yard two minutes early, my grandmother Nell sold the businesses and invested the proceeds in stocks and bonds. When Nell died, my father and aunt split the estate, leaving Spencer Fenton with a handsome nest egg that allowed him to indulge in his twin passions for beer and sloth.

We lived on a street named Buckland, in a solid brick house on a modest lot that was a considerable step down from the sprawling property that my grandparents had owned. The view from their sandstone-and-brick home was spectacular by Spa City standards. The Williams River made a hairpin turn there, weaving a brown ribbon between the high, grassy slope upon which their house perched and the low, mud-flecked peninsula known by locals as Kibbee Flats. My grandparents' fifteen-acre property began at a narrow, tree-lined road, then dropped abruptly to an algae-covered pond that was summer home to a complex, ever-in-motion community of water bugs, black flies, mosquitoes, leeches, shy ring-neck pheasants, and migrating greenhead ducks. I spent most family visits there, avoiding the adults.

The Buckland residence offered no such escape from family tension. It was a two-story brick structure with one bath upstairs and a half-bath down. The house was so small that it reminded me of a scaled-down facsimile: too big for dolls and too small for humans unless they were midgets or munchkins. But five of us—my parents, two brothers, and I—resided there, squeezing past each other in the hallways, banging on the bathroom door and squealing "Hurry up," and otherwise smelling, hearing, and observing each other like clipped-wing hawks. I felt like I was shrinking every time I carefully opened the front door and hip-faked into the living room.

On this night, Coach's praise echoing in my head, I stopped first on the front porch, ripped my blue helmet from its Scotch tape cocoon inside my jacket, and pulled it on. Then I raced inside and shouted, "Mom! Guess who was just named the Big Team's starting quarterback?"

Mom was sitting on the edge of her favorite wing chair where, every night, she read murder mysteries in the quiet hours after my father had gone to bed. Getting an early start this evening, she was sucking on one of the Gelusil tablets her doctor had recommended to calm her nervous stomach. An open box of them lay atop her stack of books.

"That friend of yours, Aaron Solomon, I'll bet," she answered, preoccupied.

"No, me!"

Mom frowned slightly, creating a furrow between her arched brows. "But, Pete, aren't you too small?"

"Coach gave me this new helmet," I said, tapping it insistently. "That makes it official."

"Isn't that school property? Can you get into trouble for bringing it home?"

"I don't know . . . What's for dinner, anyway?" I mumbled.

Mom smiled and said, "Liver and onions. Of course, they'll be too cold by the time Dad gets home, but we can't wait for him every night. That wouldn't be fair to the rest of us, now would it?"

Brown-haired, petite, and with a mole on her cheek, Mom took her styling and behavioral cues from sweet 1940s B-movie actresses June Allyson and Deanna Durbin, whose framed glossies sat on her vanity. Mom often smiled at odd times, as if she was guessing when it was appropriate to do so. The same seemed true of her other displays of emotion.

"Hey, I'll eat Dad's share," I said, trying to lighten the mood.

"You can have mine. My digestion is bothering me again."

I trotted into the kitchen, which was as undersized as the rest of the house. My younger brother, Bobby, was making sugar toast. I snatched a piece away from him and stuffed it into my mouth in its entirety, silently defying him to do something.

"I'm going to get you when you're not wearing that helmet," Bobby vowed. Guarding three other slices with his arm, he stalked past me to his designated chair in the kitchen nook. At ten years of age, Bobby had rusty red hair and a bulbous nose that he was ashamed of. My father considered him slow, even though his grades in school were perfectly fine. He was obsequious with Dad and always angry with me, but in the traditional manner of older brothers, I didn't much care what he thought.

My cocky attitude dissolved quickly as I shuffled to my own chair in the breakfast nook, where we took all of our meals. A round, Formica-topped table barely fit into the nook, leaving little room to maneuver. There was only one narrow exit if you sat by the kitchen window, where my brothers and I were assigned, and that route was blocked when my mother and father were in their chairs. During every meal I was trapped, unable to flee unless I crawled under the table or forced my parents to stand and push their chairs in, which they hated to do.

"Where's Harry?" I asked my mother as she slid a platter of fried liver and onions to the center of the table. It was surrounded by bowls of mashed potatoes, gravy, green beans, soft rolls, and a mushy stick of butter.

"He's staying overnight at college to study for an exam."

Harry was nineteen and had been commuting to a nearby school for the past year and a half. Because of the age gap between us, I barely knew Harry, other than that he read engineering texts for entertainment. Recently, he'd grown an Abe Lincoln beard and had begun smoking an ornate Scottish pipe. He had also purchased a black Model T Ford that he'd taken apart piece by piece but had not been able to reassemble. The remains were gathered behind the garage under a canvas tarp that no one could touch because Harry was planning to get back to the task someday.

I was salting my liver when a purple Lincoln Continental lurched into view and finally came to rest against one of the forsythia bushes that lined the driveway. The car idled there for several minutes as my father, Spencer Fenton, slapped the dashboard to the beat of a song I couldn't hear.

I cinched the chinstrap of my helmet tight enough to make me wince, but that didn't prevent familiar emotions from waging war inside my head. Although I desperately wanted to show Dad my new blue plastic trophy, I dreaded his response. I had no reason to expect he'd be gleeful and carry me triumphantly through the neighborhood on his shoulders. But hope won out and I eagerly awaited his entrance, crossing both fingers that this time my real dad, and not his buffoonish impostor, would stride into the kitchen, lift me high, and declare loudly, "My son is a 108-pound All-American quarterback."

"Why is Dad so slow?" Bobby asked as he finished his last piece of sugar toast.

"Drum and bugle corps takes a lot out of you," my mother said, smiling.

Dad was a member of Amvets—like the VFW, a fraternal organization for veterans of overseas conflicts. He'd been a bookkeeper behind the lines during World War II, with a desk in the wine cellar of a French chateau. My older brother called the Amvets meeting hall an "endless keg party." Dad had taken up the snare drum in order to spend more time there. Beating the drum had become his passion.

The Lincoln's engine shut down. Laughing mightily, my father emerged and zigzagged toward the back porch, raising his wobbly legs high as if he was still marching in formation. He stopped just short, shook his head, and held a corner of the house for balance briefly before turning back to the Lincoln to retrieve his shiny, silver-flecked snare drum. This was a reliable sign that the grueling hours he'd practiced band in the dusty Amvets Post 31 parking lot had been leavened with many long breaks inside the log-cabin-style meeting hall. I could see him in the lounge, speed-drinking Stroh's beer, tapping the polished pine bar to whatever played on the jukebox.

I'd once looked at a photo of my father from his Howe military school days. He was clean-cut, trim, and handsome in his buttoned-up uniform. Since then, I'd often thought of the man in the picture as my real, true dad, who'd tragically tripped and fallen into a vat thick with hops and barley, never to be seen again. Instead, something else had been fished out—a monster movie creature, bloated, squishy, and red.

By the time Dad entered the kitchen wearing Bermuda shorts, he had strapped on the snare drum and was beating an awkward tattoo on it. His face was pink with sunburn. The khaki Amvets shirt he wore with its tails out was dusty and here and there soaked through with sweat. The snare drum rested on the curve of Dad's protruding stomach, which seemed too great a mass to be supported by his bandy legs. His pastel blue eyes had a teary sheen and were focused on a point over our heads. A secret smile creased his lips. One ear was cocked as if he could still hear the brass and drums of his band mates.

Heedless, I interrupted: "Dad, I made quarterback. Coach gave me this new helmet to wear." I was surprised that he stopped playing instantly; when he was in this state, it often took him a while to respond.

Sighing, my father unhooked his drum and placed it carefully on the yellow linoleum counter. Clasping both drumsticks in the palm of his right hand, he looked down at me and asked, "What was so wrong with the black leather one?"

"Coach took it back. This is better."

"According to who?"

"Coach."

"Did he actually say, 'Take this blue helmet, it's better?'"

"No, but—"

"That answers my question. You can't on good authority tell me that the blue helmet is better."

"Coach gave it to me as a reward. It's made of hard plastic. It has a face guard. This is the kind the NFL uses."

"Listen, Red Grange wore a leather helmet. Ted Pembroke, your great-uncle, wore a leather helmet. They were both All-Americans. It seems like you're trying to say that these bona fide football legends were no good because they didn't wear plastic helmets."

"But Dad, they didn't make plastic helmets back then."

My mother shrilly intervened. "Stop arguing with Dad, Pete. You're making my stomach act up. You always get so excited about these things, for goodness sake!"

"That's 'cause I'm right. Plastic helmets are better."

"Shush, shush, shhh," said my father. Steadying himself with a hand on the yellow counter, he moved to the small Sylvania table radio that was kept near the sink. The unknowable smile once again spreading across his face, he twisted the volume knob all the way to the right. "Colonel Bogey March," the stirring theme from the World War II movie *Bridge on the River Kwai,* blared out. It was the version by conductor Mitch Miller and His Boys, who in truth were grown men. All three or four dozen of them whistled the tune. At the time, there wasn't a marching band in America that didn't include the theme in its repertoire.

My father hurriedly strapped on his drum, flexed his fingers, and began beating fiercely in time to the music. As he marched out of the kitchen, he hollered over his shoulder, "Follow me, fellows, and start whistling. We're going to put a show on for your mother."

Bobby scrambled under the table and joined him. Furious, I remained seated.

"Oh, Pete, you're such a sourpuss," my mother chastised me. "We aren't going to die of starvation if we have a little fun first."

"But you were so worried about dinner getting cold," I protested. Without further word, I crawled beneath the table and raced upstairs to my room. As I left, I heard my father loudly agree, "Pete's just a grumpy old grump."

I slammed the bedroom door loudly, then leapt onto my bed and began beating the overstuffed pillow I customarily used as my father substitute. I didn't stop pummeling it until the "Colonel Bogey March" and the drumming ended. Still, I felt like a rubber band stretched to the limit. I pulled off my helmet and laid it out of harm's way under the bed. The air smelled like perfume, talcum powder, and lipstick. Because of my parents' estrangement, I now slept in my mother's room with its lavender walls, vases of dried flowers, twin beds with purple coverlets, and a pearl-white vanity with a gold-rimmed oval mirror.

Pieced together from tidbits of information I'd gathered from Harry, I had a rough idea of the trajectory of my parents' relationship and how that had led to my embarrassing sleeping arrangement. Mom, one of four children belonging to Polish immigrant butcher Melvin Tyscho and his wife, Gertrude, had considered Spencer Fenton quite a catch when they'd met in their early twenties on the campus of Ferris State Teachers College. Dad, who'd flunked out of the University of Michigan, was a dashing young man with pockets full of cash and the keys to his father's luxurious

Packard. Occasionally, he sported a silk scarf that fluttered in the wind as he and Jane, downing champagne and beer, sped across the western Michigan countryside. Their wedding had been a fantasy, paid for by Spencer's parents, who couldn't bear the humiliation of the modest ceremony that the Tyschos could afford.

My parents' first years together had been one long party. This must have been a happy relief for my mother, who had endured a severe Catholic upbringing, complete with razor-strop spankings and lurid paintings of the suffering Christ peering down from every room. But when my mother, for never-revealed reasons, stopped drinking and Dad continued merrily along, their romance crashed fatally. Ice-cold mutual disdain became the norm, despite Mom's weak protestations to us that Dad's drinking himself into a stupor was his way of relaxing—even when, at dinner, she was forced to cut his steak into bite-size pieces and feed him because he was incapable of doing so himself, or when he urinated in a bedroom closet thinking he was standing over the upstairs toilet.

Eventually my parents decided that the solution to their relationship problem was to stop sleeping together. That way, they'd have a guaranteed eight hours apart each day. My father moved into the room I'd been sharing with Bobby, and I began sleeping in the master bedroom, separated from Mom's bed by a nightstand and a lacquered Chinese screen. Only Harry, on those nights he came home, had a space of his own.

Soon the house grew quiet. About an hour after the drumming ended, I heard my parents in the hallway outside the bedroom door. Irked at the sound, I swore softly, "Shit," then quickly snapped up a book I'd been reading on the greatest drivers in the history of the Indianapolis 500. The strained tones of their voices made it impossible to concentrate. It was only 8 o'clock, but they often separated early—my mother to continue reading, my father to listen to big

band music while he admired the collection of duck decoys he kept
atop his clothes dresser.

"Janey, can I have a kiss?"

"Why?"

"Why? Because I like kissing you."

"Your clothes stink and your breath smells. Let's put it off until
tomorrow."

"That's a promise, and I'm going to hold you to it." There was a
pause before he started in again. "Janey, remember when I used to
serenade you in college? Remember, 'Janey, Janey, give me your answer, do . . .'?"

"Go to bed, Spence."

"Oh, hell."

"Don't keep Bobby awake. He needs his sleep."

"I always turn the radio low. You know that."

"Goodnight."

"Nighty-night."

Mom entered the bedroom and sighed. Turning to me, she said,
"You took off like a streak of lightning. What was your hurry?"

"I can't stand it when Dad drinks," I said, perhaps a little too
forcefully.

She bridled. "Do we have to go into this every time he comes
home late? You act like he's some sort of alcoholic."

"Don't you think so?"

"That only happens to people who drink wine and whiskey.
You can't become an alcoholic with beer, because the liquid exits
your system so quickly."

This was my mother's stock answer. I always had a yearning to
believe it, and even tonight felt the pull to agree. But I said, "Is that
why he pees on the floor?"

My mother, who was now sitting at her vanity, replied, "Everybody makes mistakes. That's why we keep that little mop around, to clean up Dad's mistakes. You know, your father loves us and we love him."

"Do you?"

"Of course. We're married."

Later, I didn't answer when she said, "Goodnight." I just lay there, tense and angry, my thoughts skating off in all directions. There had been countless evenings like this, and they all ended for me in the same way. I was humiliated by my father's infantilism and frustrated by my mother's denial of the truth. Most of all, I agonized about not knowing how to extricate myself from the game that they'd created and had trained me so well to play.

Eventually I exhausted my fury and fell asleep by mentally running through the new plays Coach Strampe had diagrammed for my quarterback debut. My last blissful vision was winning the game with a rifle-shot touchdown pass and being carried off the field by my exultant teammates.

"Everybody, I mean everybody, shut up and listen up," Coach Strampe intoned. The entire team was in a circle around him on the sidelines of a bumpy football field in Indian Hills. It was a few minutes prior to kickoff, and Coach wore what I had come to call his "game face"—severe, verging on despondent. He rolled a toothpick back and forth across his chapped lips while chewing gum, a stunt I had attempted but could not master. Coach wore high-cut football shoes, pressed blue jeans, and a blue nylon windbreaker. His wife had stenciled "HEAD COACH" across the back of the jacket in defiance of the school principal, who had refused to allocate the $87 needed to print the team name on all of our equipment. Spectators, largely friends and family members, were scattered in lawn chairs and the three rows of bleachers immediately behind us. On the top row sat several intense men wearing Magnificent Minerals red and gray; as promised, the entire high school coaching staff had shown up to observe and take notes. I was jumpy with excitement.

Our attention gathered, Coach said, "Okay, crew. Each of you place your right hand on top of mine." Coach thrust his right hand into the middle of our circle, which led to a lot of pushing and shoving as each of us tried to follow suit. Ultimately, it was impossible for thirty players to compress themselves tightly enough to stack each and every hand. The result was a lot of arms dangling in midair as Coach bowed his head and prayed: "Dear Lord, give these thirty young men the strength to excel on the football field today. Amen."

"Amen," we chimed in.

"Beat Livonia!" he shouted.

"Beat Livonia," we agreed, then clapped and began milling about aimlessly, not sure of the next step.

After supplying footballs for the rest of the team to toss around, Coach pointed at me and the three members of the 500 Pounds of Steel. We followed him behind the bleachers, where three little girls were playing with Barbie dolls in the sand. Coach shooed them away, then motioned for us all to crouch down so we couldn't be seen above the bleachers. In a conspiratorial whisper, he said, "Listen, men. You're the core of this team. Whether we win or lose today is up to you. Got me?"

We all nodded.

"Good. Now, as you know, we won the coin toss. We'll be receiving the kickoff, and on the first play from scrimmage I want you to throw Livonia a curveball to keep them honest."

"Curveball?" I asked.

"Yeah. On the first play, go to the Missing-Teeth Offense I showed you."

"The one where we spread across the field like it's a kickoff and only Pete is in the back?" Mike Karpinski asked.

"That's the one—a modified shotgun. We'll throw them off balance, and they'll never recover. Got that, Pete?"

"Sure," I answered, although I wasn't. I didn't like the idea of standing alone in the backfield on my first play ever as a junior high quarterback.

"Livonia is dog meat," Aaron Solomon growled.

"We'll protect you real good," Zem Kelch added.

Their reassurance was calming. Mike, Aaron, and Zem might not have been much as athletes, but I knew they'd do everything in their power to keep the fierce Livonia defense at bay.

Well, it didn't work out that way. On that Friday against Livonia, Rose Junior High did not score a point. The 500 Pounds of Steel were more like a sieve, and the Missing-Teeth Offense was a fiasco. On the very first play, I fumbled the snap and was driven into the ground by a 217-pound Livonia linebacker. My collarbone broke instantly. I had not moved more than one foot in any direction.

As I was carried away on a stretcher, nauseous, my collarbone burning, face after face appeared above me. I saw my confused teammates vowing revenge; an auburn-haired guy in horn-rimmed glasses, draping his arm around a smiling Mandy; and most vividly, my tearful, sodden dad, asking, "Why, Pete? Why?" before stumbling from view.

That night, Dad ground his teeth as he slept, as he always did when in deep psychic pain. Strangely, sitting upright in bed, plaster cast hugging my shoulders, I had a thrilling epiphany: *It pleased me to make my father unhappy.* With that in mind, I declared my football career over, kaput. Never again would I chase the legends of Red Grange and Ted Pembroke, a decision that I knew would cause Dad continued distress.

Three days later, when I returned to school, I gave the blue helmet back to Coach Strampe. He silently checked it for damage before returning to his office and pulling down the shades. I walked away whistling, and when I realized it was the "Colonel Bogey March," I laughed—but not too hard, because it made my broken collarbone throb.

CHAPTER THREE

Enter the Space-Age Bachelor Pad

"Take my business card."

"That's a twenty dollar bill."

"Very observant. My name and address are underneath the White House. Makes me easy to remember, don't you think?"

I turned over the twenty and written on the back was, "Jackie Barron: Fun, Concessions, and Games. 555-4444."

"It would be even easier if this was a hundred."

"Nice answer. Listen, if you want to fill your pockets with twenties, hundreds, whatever, meet me in the cafeteria in fifteen minutes." Jackie slid the monogrammed money clip into the breast pocket of his short-sleeved shirt and walked down the staircase leading to the Mineralton High School cafeteria.

So ended my first exchange with Jackie, also known on other denominations he carried as the World's Youngest Elephant Trainer. It was a good beginning to what would be a tumultuous friendship: I was already twenty bucks on the plus side.

Jackie and I had just exited sophomore geometry class, and I remained in the crowded hallway, beaming. It was the second week of school, and I was ecstatic. Most kids hated leaving summer behind, but I relished returning to the classroom—opening books musty from the heat and humidity, raising my hand first because I knew the answer. I enjoyed multiple-choice tests, pop quizzes, written essays, and oral exams. During the summer I'd been admitted to Mensa (the high IQ society), so I was now a "genius," thanks primarily to my affinity for tests. Tests were clean and pure, a respite from the stress of being fifteen, deeply shy, and still beleaguered by my father and mother.

"Say, Brain, where'd you get the loot?" Aaron Solomon asked, tugging playfully at the twenty. Aaron had been the last of my friends to start dating, and without him I had no one to hang out with on Saturday nights. The only other teen stuck at home was "Keith T-Bone," a retarded guy who patrolled the neighborhood on a bicycle he claimed was a police car.

"He gave it to me," I replied, pointing out Jackie's name.

"Whoa! Return it now. Anything from Jackie Barron has millions of strings attached."

"Who the heck is he? I never saw him before geometry class, and he hands me this twenty because he says he's looking for someone good with numbers, like me."

"Man, down in Kibbee Flats Jackie's a legend. He started training elephants when he was six. His dad owns a traveling carnival, which is why he wasn't here freshman year. He was on the road and had a tutor or something like that. And get this—he's owned a Corvair since he was fourteen and drives it to Detroit to get drunk."

"Give me a break."

"It's true, man. He has a fake driver's license that says he's eighteen. And you saw how tall he is. He can get away with acting that old. Listen, this guy did it for the first time when he was twelve. His older brother, Chip, set him up with a streetwalker."

I was so naive about the nitty-gritty of life that I had only a vague idea of what a streetwalker did, other than look sexy as she paraded up and down the street. My entire formal sex education had consisted of a single hour-long seminar conducted by a nervous, blushing Coach Strampe. I'd never seen a photo of a woman naked below the waist, not even in the photography magazines I thumbed through at Penzien's Pharmacy in downtown Mineralton. And it got even worse: I refused to eat crème de menthe ice cream because I heard it had alcohol content. My musical tastes ran toward the big bands and aging crooners my parents enjoyed, and my entire net worth was tied up in a passbook savings account.

Which made Jackie's interest in me all the more puzzling. I was good with numbers, but so what? Why would Jackie, a sophisticate experienced in the ways of money, booze, and women, want to meet with an inhibited abstainer like me, whose greatest sin was my bottomless hunger for the fat trimmed from a sirloin, fried until black in a skillet? Did Jackie spot something in me that other people didn't? Suddenly, it was vitally important to know. I said good-bye to Aaron, who shrugged and told me, "Good luck. You'll need it."

Oddly agitated as I headed downstairs, I looked at my shoes twice to make sure my laces were tied. I played most emotions close to the vest, unwilling to run the risk of being hurt by anyone. Yet Aaron's warning about Jackie had had an unexpected effect; it was propelling me toward the cafeteria. Despite possible humiliation, something about the nature of Jackie's alleged transgressions made me want to enter his orbit.

"How would you like more money, more broads, and more booze than you can handle?" Jackie greeted me when I arrived at his table. He sat alone in a darkened corner of the hall near the kitchen. The wisps of steam that swirled around when the stainless steel doors swung open made it feel like we were in a smoky nightclub rather than a noisy, bustling high school cafeteria serving today's boiled Polish hot dogs and sauerkraut.

I battled to come up with an appropriate answer. Desperate, I blurted, "I don't drink."

Jackie smiled and waved me toward a chair on the opposite side of the gray, picnic-length cafeteria table. "So you go for two out of the three . . . that's a good percentage."

"Yeah, sure. I guess."

"'Yeah, sure. I guess,'" Jackie mimicked. "Say, you were talking a blue streak up in geometry class. What happened?"

"I don't know. Hungry, probably," I answered, fumbling again. The tremendous buildup that Aaron had given Jackie intimidated me.

"Hey, Mabel," Jackie hollered toward the kitchen.

Moments later, a moon-faced, heavily made-up cafeteria worker poked her head through the swinging doors.

"Another special for my friend here," Jackie told her, casually pointing a finger at me. Mabel eyed Jackie sourly for a beat, then withdrew.

"I thought Polish hot dogs were all they were serving."

"That's what makes the special so special."

"How'd you become friendly with a cafeteria worker?"

"Mabel and I have a mutual interest in horses," Jackie said, yawning.

He appeared bored. Was I dull? Yes! But what to say to a guy who could say anything a thousand times better than me?

I'd read once that concentrating on a single bodily feature of a person who made me nervous could help calm me down. I focused my attention on the feature of Jackie's that was nearest to me: his nose. It was long and sloped precipitously, so much so that his black, horn-rimmed glasses had slipped halfway down. With his height, he seemed to be peering down, in judgment. Rattled, I rapidly shifted my attention from one aspect of Jackie to another, trying to find a safe haven.

Jackie's skin was a study in gradations of pink and white. His face was pale and unblemished, the top rim of each ear slightly inflamed—probably from the sun, which he otherwise appeared to avoid. His forearms were also pale and hairless, ending in soft hands unmarked by manual labor and neat fingernails that I learned later had been manicured by my beloved Mandy. His lanky auburn hair was combed into a slight pompadour, held in place by what smelled like Vitalis. Even in the soft light he squinted, his hazel eyes unrevealing. He reminded me of a mole that had just broken through to the surface, sniffing sweet air with its proboscis before diving back into its underground home to dig for grubs with soft, restless paws. On the heels of that alarming insight, I abandoned the calming technique as useless. I was hopelessly tense.

The kitchen doors swung open, and Mabel ambled toward us in her crisp blue uniform, carrying a large tray heavy with food and drink. She deposited the tray between us, then drew a ten-dollar bill from her sleeve, slid it to Jackie, and said, "Warrior Lad in the third to show."

"Did she just make a bet?" I asked when Mabel left.

Jackie ignored my question as he rolled the ten into one of several packets of cash, each wrapped in a rubber band, that he pulled from the pocket of his khakis. "Eat," he said. "Mabel's only a sideline."

The tray was filled with aromatic barbeque sandwiches oozing out of wax paper wrappers, along with curly fries, hot German potato salad, cole slaw, and chocolate shakes in fountain glasses.

"You mean eat anything?"

"Sure. Some of the sandwiches are beef barbeque, some are pork, so take your choice."

I was starving—and so, it seemed, was Jackie. There was silence until I was midway through my second sandwich, when a fidgety, balding teacher I didn't recognize approached and handed Jackie an unmarked envelope.

"Who's this?" the teacher asked, nodding at me as Jackie examined the envelope's contents.

"Don't worry. It's Peter Fenton. He's good at math," Jackie answered without looking up. "'Bye now."

The teacher shuffled a bit, then scurried away. I studied the swinging kitchen doors, munching a ketchup-dipped curly fry.

"He's—" Jackie started to say.

"I know. A sideline," I finished his sentence for him. Already I knew not to ask for more explanation.

Jackie eyed me with a half-smile, seeming to make a mental note. "You going to eat any more of this shit?"

Swallowing one last curly fry, I shook my head no.

"I'll clear the table," Jackie said, then swiped several uneaten sandwiches and the empty fountain glasses into a green plastic garbage can at the end of the table. That made quite a noise and I shot a look at the kitchen doors, worried that a cafeteria worker would race out and bust us. But none did.

Then Jackie leaned back and asked, "Are you as good with numbers as you seemed upstairs in class? I'm not talking about that abstract geometry crap—just adding, subtracting, dividing, multiplying in your head."

"Yeah. It comes without trying." And it really did. In grade school I'd discovered I could work numbers mentally, quickly calculating the answers before other kids even picked up their pencils. It was a quirk and nothing more. I actually had no taste for math; I hated algebra and dreaded geometry class.

"Okay . . . how about this one: If Warrior Lad can run at a pace of 18.3 seconds per furlong, how much time will it take him to run 3,973 furlongs over his career, provided he isn't turned into glue before then?"

"Seventy-two thousand, seven hundred five and nine-tenths seconds."

"Correct. How many minutes is that?"

"One thousand, two hundred eleven. Rounded off."

"Hours?"

"Twenty. Rounded off."

"Correct."

Feeling cocky, I asked Jackie, "How do you know I'm right?"

"I have the same talent. The only difference is I've turned my ability to count faster than other people into hard cash. What have you done with it?" Jackie stared hard at me.

"Well, actually nothing," I admitted.

"How would you feel about making money like me?"

"Great. Without a doubt." What else could I say?

Jackie drew his chair close and lowered his voice. "Listen, I'm planning to open a Las Vegas–style casino in my basement. How'd you like to be my partner, 50-50 split, less the expense of mopping bitter tears off the floor every night after the last roll of the dice?"

"I don't know. I can barely play poker."

"I don't care if you can barely play Fish. All that matters, see, is that we rig the odds in our favor. That's where the math comes in. Our classmates—who will be our customers—won't know the difference between good odds and bad. They'll just be excited by the chance to play blackjack or throw dice."

"So we're going to cheat them?"

"We'll be teaching them a valuable lesson in life."

"Like what?"

"Like learn how to fucking count, you dumb asses. Learn how

to calculate odds. Losing fifty bucks to us may prevent them from losing five hundred bucks in Las Vegas somewhere down the line. So you might say we'll be saving them four hundred and fifty dollars apiece."

"That's one way of looking at it."

Jackie pushed his glasses back up his nose. I was now enveloped by the smell of Vitalis. "Listen, Pete. A long time ago, a wise man named Chip, who just happens to be my piece-of-shit older brother, laid the world out for me like this: In life, there are two kinds of people—ulcer givers and ulcer getters. The ulcer givers make sure they have the house advantage, whether it's a casino owner screwing with the odds, a bartender watering down drinks, or your parents screaming at you because you came home too late."

"What's my parents' advantage?"

"You should know that one."

"They own the house?"

"Correct. On the other hand, the ulcer getters are the patrons, the customers, the players, the people who buy cotton candy, shoot dice, ride the Ferris wheel, and all that fun stuff."

"I get it."

"Do you, Pete? Let me ask you a question. And think carefully before you answer. It's your life. Which side are you going to be on? Are you an ulcer giver or an ulcer getter?"

I thought about my mother and her Gelusil tablets. I considered Coach Strampe and his gauntlet of puddles. My father's drums. Then, filled with swirling emotions, I answered, "I want to be an ulcer giver."

"Good decision. Listen, I've got to run to another appointment, and I'm short a business card. Could you loan me the one I gave you?"

"Sure. Okay." I gave the personalized twenty dollar bill back to Jackie.

"Thanks."

"So when do we start?"

Obviously in a hurry, Jackie glanced at his watch. "I'll call you. So stick close to the phone."

Two months crept by until he made the call. Which should have given me plenty of time to discard the unseemly conclusion that I came to after Jackie left, as I sat alone at the cafeteria table, waves of kids strolling past, their lips glistening with the remnants of Polish hot dogs and sauerkraut: I had no qualms about screwing my classmates.

Here's how my reasoning went. My classmates were skilled in the social niceties of contemporary youth, like dancing the boogaloo, throwing Frisbees, and making out in secluded spots along the meandering Williams River. On the other hand, I possessed none of these important social skills. But I knew math well, thought fast on my feet, and was generally a level or two more intelligent than the kids who parked, barfed up beer, and measured the length of the rubber patches they laid down when they spun the wheels of their parents' Oldsmobile station wagons.

So it was a matter of natural selection, or destiny, or what have you, that my classmates and I would be drawn to our strengths, where we could employ our unique abilities to our greatest personal advantage. For example, handsome Rennie Pickering, who claimed to have gone all the way with ten girls, had never, out of the goodness of his heart, shared with me the secret of his success so that I could enjoy the same pleasures. If I set up the casino with Jackie, then, and Rennie became a regular customer, why should I pass along to Rennie details on how we'd fixed the odds and the truth that, in the long run, he would lose everything?

In a way, Rennie and I—in truth, the entire sophomore class of Mineralton High School—were simply finding our niche, and wasn't that what healthy adolescents were born to do?

"Meet me on the corner of Buckland and Hawkins in ten minutes," the urgent voice on the phone said. It was snowing and I had just returned to the kitchen from shoveling the walk, still wearing my wet jeans, slush-covered galoshes, and a sweatshirt.

"Jackie?" I asked, trying not to show too much interest.

"Yeah. You forget what I sound like already?"

"Sort of. It's been two months since I last saw you."

"I had a bunch of dates to play with the elephant."

"So you dropped out of school?"

"No. My brother Chip tutored me, if you can believe that. The guy grew up thinking one plus one equaled snake-eyes. So I ignored him and did the studying on my own."

"What you want to meet about?"

"The casino. What else?" Jackie said, sounding incredulous. "You're still in, aren't you?"

"Uh . . . sure," I answered, even though I'd given up hope that I'd be able to put my new theory of life into play, the one I'd been refining ever since our lunch meeting.

"Good. Because you have just seven minutes left to get your butt out to the corner," Jackie added, then clicked off the line.

"Mom, I'm going out for a while," I shouted to my mother, who was reading Agatha Christie in her armchair, a box of Gelusil at her right hand. It was late afternoon, my father had yet to arrive home from Amvets, and Mom had been complaining about him, which was why I'd fled the house with my shovel.

"Don't be gone long. Dad will be home soon, and I want all of us to eat dinner together. We're having beef tongue and it's only good hot," she hollered from the living room.

"I'll be home as fast as I can," I answered, then ran outside without changing clothes, without giving her time to persuade me to stay. My parents adored beef tongue. To them, it was the pinnacle of organ meats—better than the calf's liver, beef heart, chicken heart, duck heart, kidney of assorted species, "sweetbreads," and, on rare occasion, calf's brain that my mother fried, stewed, or boiled as a treat. I, at first, had followed their lead, popping heavily salted chicken hearts like they were Milk Duds. Slowly but surely, though, organ meats began to repulse me. This aversion had peaked at the frightening sight, on my mother's most recent birthday, of a two-inch-thick beef tongue newly hacked from the steer, steaming on a platter in the center of the kitchen table, surrounded by new potatoes, carrots, and delicate sprigs of parsley.

It was snowing lightly when I reached the corner. As I stamped my feet to ward off the chill, I dismissed as inconsequential the two months Jackie had made me wait for his call. Good things were worth waiting for, sometimes beyond reason. And becoming an ulcer giver was a good thing.

A white Thunderbird with a black landau top splashed through the slush, then turned sharply and stopped in the slop that lapped over the curb. A fogged electric window hummed down, revealing Jackie in aviator sunglasses and a quilted ski jacket.

"Get in, partner," he said, pointing his thumb toward the back door.

"I thought you owned a Corvair."

"Traded it in. Bought this."

I opened the door and leapt over the slop, tumbling into the driver's side back seat. I was surprised to find that the car held two other passengers. Alongside me in the back, trying to act as if I wasn't there, was Ricky Hancock, fifteen, another transfer student from sordid Indian Hills. Handsome and compact, Ricky was part of the hip sock-hop crowd that smoked cigarettes and loitered near—but never entered—any building where a dance was being held. He owned a surfboard that he never used and his father, a member of the private Western Golf Club, was infamous for landing on the eighteenth-hole fairway in his Piper Cub one Sunday ("just for kicks," as he told the cops). Today, perhaps in solidarity, Ricky wore a lime green golf shirt, lemon yellow Arnold Palmer sweater, powder blue pants, and off-white golf shoes with stainless steel cleats.

Mandy was curled up in the front seat next to Jackie, and that made me almost jump from the car. I now realized that Jackie had been the tall auburn-haired guy hugging her when I was carried off the field in humiliation after the first play of the Livonia game. Mandy knew that I liked her yet had been too shy to do anything about it. So there, side by side, were the guy who was going to make me cool and the girl who already knew that I wasn't. I was mortified.

"Hi, Pete. Fancy meeting you here," Mandy said, in a sly way that seemed to me both seductive and taunting. A curling smile dimpled her cheeks. Her midnight black eyes were painted with instinctive, dramatic flair. She used royal blue eye shadow beneath her slanted black eyebrows and had touched her lashes with the same shade of mascara; they fluttered like the hand-lacquered Japanese fans I'd once seen in a downtown novelty store. She wore a black corduroy car coat and a red beret hair-pinned at a saucy angle. Both were dewy with snow that the car heater had melted.

"Mandy, hi, nice to see you," I mumbled.

"You two know each other?" Jackie asked as he snaked away from the curb.

Mandy eyed me, again with that taunting gaze. I mentally begged her not to reveal how I'd stared at her wordlessly day after day.

"Yes, we had English class together in junior high school," Mandy said, winking at me. "Pete received A's on all his exams." She then turned away and curled her arm around Jackie. I was surprised and grateful that she'd kept my foolishness to herself.

"So you two have a long history together. All the way back to junior high. That's something," Jackie said.

"Oh, stop being so sarcastic all of the time," Mandy protested, punching Jackie's shoulder playfully.

"Want a smoke?" Ricky asked, looking at me for the first time. When I shook my head no, he lit up a Salem, lowered his window, and blew out the smoke. Then he coughed, glared at the cigarette, and tossed it into the street.

"Now that you've ended your smoking break, would you close the damn window? It's cold in here," Mandy scolded him. Silently, Ricky did as she asked.

"Anyone want a hamburger before we go to my place? Vera can't cook worth a shit," Jackie asked as he drove past the What-A-Burger drive-in on the edge of Kibbee Flats. It was just two summers before that I'd watched the famous 750-pound wrestler Happy Humphrey eat fifty hamburgers there as the main attraction at the grand-opening celebration. He'd washed the burgers down with ten chocolate malteds.

"Not hungry," I answered.

"Me either," said Ricky.

"Who's Vera?" I whispered to Ricky.

"His mother," he replied in a low voice, "the crazy carny."

Darkness was falling. As the Thunderbird spiraled down from the bluffs to the unkempt Kibbee flatlands, with each turn the headlights revealed more and greater disarray: rotted, uprooted trees, abandoned refrigerators peppered with shotgun pellets, wrecked jalopies, shattered beer bottles, bubbling pools of sub-mineral bath-quality mud filtering odious steam through dead snarls of poison ivy and rusted bedsprings. Occasionally, a human figure staggered into view, dressed in rags or threadbare summer sharkskin. I'd never been to Kibbee Flats in my life, and as the scene became more weird and fantastic, I had to fight the urge to jump from the car and head back home.

Jackie angled off the road in order to avoid a downed willow that blocked both lanes, and when he returned we were in the middle of what passed for Kibbee Flats' main drag. A short row of two-story clapboard buildings was on each side of us, all of them painted a blistered and peeling bright orange. Fifty yards further, we passed a mound of paint cans, brushes, beer bottles, and tarp, stuck together at odd angles by a stiff mass of orange paint. It appeared that the futile urban renewal project had run out of steam here, because from this point every storefront was boarded up, gray, and weathered. A faded, ice-sheathed orange banner flopped overhead, reading, "Welcome To Downtown Kibbee Flats. Paint Generously Donated By Party Time Shows." The sidewalks were empty, except for a cat that was either sleeping soundly or frozen solid.

We passed a scattering of tiny homes and abandoned farm equipment. A sliver of light escaped from beneath the drawn shades of Monty's Fix-It Shop, and I thought I heard the dull commotion of people having a wild time inside. I was completely disoriented. Beside me, Ricky fingered the door lock of the Thunderbird, obviously as tense as I was.

When Jackie turned left on an unmarked dirt road, the landscape became almost overwhelmingly surreal. There was an elephant buried to its haunches in the snow. A giraffe lying helplessly on its side. A baby hippo with its head torn off. Then there was a rusted iron disk lying at an angle, with brass spokes extending from its base to a rotted circular awning. Shattered mirrors and an overturned, bright orange ticket box were resting nearby. Further on, I realized that we had just passed a junked merry-go-round.

The detritus continued to flash by: a sagging Port-A-John melted by fire; a battered bumper car; a half-dozen ticket booths topped by grinning clown heads; a mound of teddy bears, each with one or more limbs cut off; and much, much more that I couldn't identify.

Jackie broke the silence. "And now, here's what you've all been waiting for. Home, sweet home." He used the bumper to push aside a wobbly front gate made from plywood and chicken wire, then eased the Thunderbird into the heated garage of his parents' modern, sprawling brick house.

"We made it," Mandy sighed, unwrapping herself from Jackie. So she'd been worried, too.

"What's the surprise?" Jackie asked as we exited the car. "Hey, I've been driving since I was twelve, when I took a truckload of skinny-neck chickens to a Tennessee geek." Pocketing his keys, he led us down a hall stacked high with carnival posters, reams of ride tickets, and fifty-pound bags of sugar.

"Skinny-neck chickens?" Mandy inquired.

"They were a special breed the geeks preferred. They could bite their heads off easier."

Mandy recoiled. "Ugh. Sounds awful."

"Why? That's how geeks make their living," Jackie continued, amused by her discomfort. "Some people sell stocks and bonds, others bite chicken heads. Anyway, geeks have been sloughed—which means banned—in just about every state. The only guy buying skinny-neck chickens these days is Colonel Sanders, so the Barron family has quit that business."

I smiled for the first time since I had been picked up on the corner, amused by the peculiar commingling of people, chickens, and money. I wanted to ask Jackie how the geeks had been paid: by the neck or the day? But I decided against it. I didn't know him well enough yet.

Jackie bounded up a short flight of stairs, and the rest of us hurried to keep up. We burst into a spacious kitchen, where Jackie's progress was halted by a fierce-looking woman in a silver, slightly askew wig seated in a battery-powered wheelchair. Wearing a pale, flowered housecoat, she had Jackie's nose and a long face dragged down further by sagging jowls. Her bony, sun-spotted hands clutched the arms of the wheelchair tight.

"Hi mom, I'm home," Jackie said to her with false cheeriness, then thrust his middle finger between her eyes.

"Don't make me madder than I already am. I've had your dinner waiting for two hours, you albino bastard," his mother grimaced, pushing his hand away.

"You should know, Vera," Jackie yawned.

"Four-eyed loudmouth." Vera turned and frowned at the rest of us. "And who are these little degenerates? Do you expect me to spend the rest of my evening burping them when I'm not cleaning up their drunken vomit?" Vera flipped a toggle switch near her right hand and whirred to the oven, where she extracted a TV dinner, burned beyond recognition. "Here's your supper," she said, heaving the dinner at Jackie, the carbonized meal wafting to the floor in ashes. "You can get your own catsup."

"I'm not hungry now, but why don't you sweep it up and I'll have it for breakfast," Jackie said. He guided us down the stairwell into a field of laundry hanging from clotheslines.

Vera pushed herself out of the wheelchair and stood erect at the head of the stairs. "I'll have you arrested if you gang-bang the girl on the sheets I just washed."

Jackie pulled one of the drying sheets from the clothesline and blew his nose in the center.

"You—" Vera shrieked and started down the stairs.

"Not another word," Jackie interrupted loudly.

Vera hesitated mid-step, her bottom lip trembling. "You're turning my beautiful home into a skid-row slum," she said, then retraced her steps and slammed the door behind her, the shock wave buffeting the laundry.

"I didn't know Vera could get out of that wheelchair," Ricky said.

"It's a prop she uses when she wants sympathy," Jackie replied, then led us toward a wall of bamboo blinds that seemed to cut the long basement in half. I wove through the hanging laundry, trying to understand the exchange between Jackie and his mother. What lay beyond the bamboo curtain required another major adjustment.

"Make yourself at home," Jackie told me, winking, as we ducked under the blinds. "And don't take Vera seriously. She probably skipped her Thorazine."

I entered Jackie's half of the room, which I guessed was how Hugh Hefner would have redone his parents' basement if he'd created *Playboy* while he was still living at home. The centerpiece was a full-size slate pool table, lit by a hooded overhead lamp that threw the room into wavering dark shadows. A half-dozen barstools with black vinyl seats lined a wall-length counter covered in thick black velvet. Scattered randomly atop the counter were a dusty stereo, piles of LPs, and a row of cut-glass decanters filled with what appeared to be colored water. Several of the records were out of their covers, littered with ashtrays and overturned soda-pop cans. Other albums were unopened, their plastic wraps crinkled and already showing signs of age. A pile of expensive-looking rubber monster masks featuring the highly detailed faces of Dracula, Frankenstein, and the Creature from the Black Lagoon, among others, were heaped on the floor alongside neat stacks of issues of the *Racing Form, Barron's,* and the *Wall Street Journal.* A pinball machine nestled in a corner alongside a small, knotty-pine-paneled enclosure se-cured by a padlock on the door. And the shadows hid other trea-sures, I was certain.

I emptied the contents of an ashtray into my cavernous jacket pocket. If the two cigar butts, a Coke bottle cap, and three broken Necco wafers were still there when I woke up tomorrow morning, this evening had really happened.

"Hey, Pete, put on a record," Jackie called out as he and Ricky gathered the balls for a game of pool.

My heart began beating double-time. My personal favorites were Jack Jones and Gogi Grant, two singers I often heard on my chief source of music, the AM station in my parents' kitchen. But there was no Jack or Gogi as I hurriedly shuffled through the LPs. "Lenny Bruce?" I mumbled, holding up an album with a picture of a man with slick hair picnicking in a graveyard. The other perform-ers were equally alien to me: Redd Foxx, Rusty "Knockers Up" Warren, and Moms Mabley.

"Can't decide?" Mandy purred behind my back.

I forced myself to turn around and face her. Mandy had re-moved her car coat to reveal a pleated plaid skirt, a black velveteen vest over a white blouse with a round collar, along with flat black shoes and black stockings. She'd put fresh color on her cheeks and smelled wonderful. She looked at me with soulful eyes. "I don't see any Jack Jones," I sputtered.

"Why don't I choose something that will help you relax," Mandy said, her eyes remaining fixed upon mine. She slid onto the stool beside me, her skirt rising slightly above her knees.

"I thought I already was."

"You're funny," Mandy giggled. "How about this one?" She picked an album off the counter and handed it to me.

I glanced at the cover: a cartoon of a black man wearing a sport coat over baggy boxer shorts and socks held in place by garters. The title was *Laff of the Party,* and the artist was Redd Foxx. I guessed he was the guy in the underwear.

"He's a singer?" I asked.

"No, no. Put it on. You'll see," Mandy answered, still meeting my eyes.

Laff of the Party was warped. The needle skipped a few grooves, then I heard the drunken laughter of a sparse audience and a gruff voice saying, "So the sick drunk says to his buddy: 'Marvin, when I die, would you pour a fifth of wine on my grave every day?' The other drunk, he stops for a minute and then says, 'Yeah, but you don't mind if it goes through my kidneys first, do you?'"

Mandy doubled up with laughter. Intent upon their game, Jackie and Ricky didn't react. Redd Foxx continued.

". . . So this young couple was getting on their honeymoon train, and the husband was nervous and he had his marriage license in one hand and the train tickets in the other. He was so nervous, in fact, that he gives the conductor the marriage license by mistake. The conductor, he looks down at it and says, 'That'll get you a whole lot of rides, but not on this train.'"

Mandy laughed so hard that tears welled up in her eyes. Sweat trickled down my neck. I was embarrassed: Mandy got jokes about s-e-x.

". . . And then to top that, there's a mess-up when the newly-weds board the train. They're given double berths, but on opposite sides of the aisle. In the middle of the night, the husband starts feeling in the married way. He says, 'Baby, baby, come over here.' And she replies, 'How am I going to get over?' He answers, 'I got something you can walk on.' Then the passenger in the berth below them pipes up and hollers, 'Yeah, but how is she gonna get back?'"

"I'm going to pee," Mandy gasped. "That joke makes me hysterical every time I hear it. Turn off the record, please," she begged, grasping my hand with hers. Mandy's palm was damp and the tips of her fingers were cold. Then, too quickly, Mandy was uncorking a cut glass decanter filled with bright green liquid. She took a swig, a line of green curving down her neck and spotting her starched white collar.

"Go easy. That's 90-proof vodka," Jackie said, removing the bottle from her grasp. He gave Mandy his pool cue. "You're up anyway. Ricky won."

"You lost? You never lose." Mandy couldn't believe it.

"By two balls," Ricky answered, drawing proudly on a newly lit cigarette. Mandy danced her way to the pool table while Ricky chalked and blew off his cue.

"Not your night, I guess?" I said to Jackie.

Jackie tilted his head toward me and whispered behind the flat of his hand, "You have to let the marks win sometimes. Keeps them coming back for more."

"The marks?"

Jackie flipped over the Redd Foxx record, turned the sound up deafeningly high, then indicated that I should follow him to the far corner of the room, near the pinball machine. Extracting a key from underneath it, he told me, "A mark is a chump, like Ricky, a sucker who believes other people always have the best of intentions." Jackie inserted the key in the rear of the pinball machine, then in one move flipped over the entire top half so that it leaned against the knotty pine wall. Inside were hundreds of girlie magazines. "Welcome to stroke book paradise," he said, clapping me on the shoulder.

Gent, Topper, Wild!, Nude Girl, Topless, Sea 'n Sand—the titles were new to me and enthralling. "Dig in," Jackie encouraged me, then grabbed several and began flipping through them.

At first my hands shook, but then I took a cue from Jackie in his leisurely contemplation of gatefolds and exclusive two-page pictorials. The pleasures were many. There were photos of topless women getting tans, husking corn, washing dishes, breaking bread with Jesus at the Last Supper, arguing with umps, hammering rivets, hanging laundry, and hugging Santa Claus in his sleigh.

I wanted to spend the rest of the night in the company of large breasts. But I knew I was here for a more important reason—for business—so I forced myself to say, "So do you want to talk about, you know, the casino?"

"Relax. This is a social occasion," Jackie smiled as if I amused him. "But here's some homework." He dragged a cardboard box from under the pinball machine and handed me the contents, item by item. First was a deck of cards. "Assignment number one is for you to figure out how these playing cards are different from others."

I shuffled through the deck. The cards were diamond-backed and unexceptional. "These are like the kind kids use to play War and Fish."

Jackie shrugged. "Maybe, maybe not," he said, then dug a pair of dice from the box and gave them to me.

"You want me to find out how these are different than normal dice?"

"No. Your assignment is to learn how to throw them so that you can control what numbers come up."

"You mean like two or six or twelve?"

Jackie nodded, then presented me with the last item in the worn-out cardboard box: a green hardcover book entitled *John Scarne's Complete Guide to Gambling*. "Do you own a Bible?" he asked me.

"I won one by memorizing ten psalms in Sunday school when I was eight." Except for my grandparents' funerals, I hadn't been inside a church since. My mother had been raised Catholic, my father

Presbyterian. They had resolved their religious differences with the unspoken pact that Mom could serve fish every Friday night if Dad could drink Stroh's on Sunday mornings. After I'd won the Bible, they hadn't asked me to attend church again. I usually played baseball instead.

"Throw it out. John Scarne is your new god, and this book is your new bible. I want you to study it as closely as you did the good parts in *Peyton Place.*"

"Oh my God, I don't believe it," Mandy raised a sudden outcry.

"Shit," Jackie yelled with equal alarm.

Vera had pushed through the bamboo blinds and dumped steaming spaghetti noodles onto the pool table. "I made you another dinner to share with your friends," she announced, her voice brimming with sarcasm. She began spreading the noodles around with the empty plastic colander. "See what a good mommy I am?"

"You've ruined the felt," Jackie said, leaping to his feet. "That's a two thousand dollar table." He snatched a pool cue from near the stereo and raised the heavy end over his head.

Vera laughed uproariously, then stopped abruptly and said to Mandy, "Ohhhh, look at your big fat hero with his big fat pool cue. Go ahead, tell Mr. Big Shot to hit his mother."

Jackie, arm already cocked, threw the cue stick, toppling the stereo, stopping the booming voice of Redd Foxx mid-joke. "You owe me," Jackie replied, "for the repair of the pool table and a new record player."

Undaunted, Vera shuffled toward him in her ragged slippers. "I gave birth to you, needle-nose, so it's you who owe me. For pain and suffering, for cleaning diapers, for everything. I want a hundred a month for starters, and I want it in cash." She thrust her palm forward, then quickly withdrew it, saying, in a trembling voice, "Double-O. I didn't know you were home."

I turned to see a gigantic man enter Jackie's lair. Double-O was taller than Jackie, perhaps six foot five, and must have weighed nearly three hundred pounds. His bristling gray crew cut was cut to the skin on the sides and shaved in a high circle around the ears.

There was something awe-inspiring about Double-O's presence. It wasn't his red suspenders or orthopedic sandals. Or his strong, bald-eagle nose, his tinted, horn-rimmed glasses, or his soft, hairless arms, like Jackie's. No, it was his face, the most extraordinary I had ever seen. His face was pale and so deeply weary it was as if every wonderful, sick, magnificent, awful human trait had manifested itself before him and Double-O would never experience anything new again. With that had come total peace.

Double-O surveyed the pasta strewn across the pool table. His breath came in rasps. "Did I miss dinner?" he asked, and without waiting for an answer, he unlocked the door to the knotty-pine-paneled room and sealed himself inside.

Mandy burst into tears as Vera silently thumbed her nose at the door and the rest of us before retreating upstairs. Jackie disappeared for a moment, then returned with one of Vera's sheets. Wadding up a corner, he dried Mandy's tears and wiped away her runny mascara.

"Why is your mother like that?" she sniffed.

"She was born in a carnival tent," Jackie answered. He seemed his composed, controlled self again.

Little was said as the Thunderbird climbed out of Kibbee Flats. Jackie and Mandy sat close together in the front. Ricky busied himself counting the cigarettes that remained in his pack. Before exiting the car on the corner of Buckland and Hawkins, I asked Jackie, "Our business deal . . . is it still on?"

Jackie chuckled. "Why wouldn't it be?"

I shrugged and leapt over the slush to the curb. The Thunderbird sped away.

The next morning when my mother left our bedroom, the sun dazzling through frosted windows, the kitchen radio already playing loudly downstairs, accompanied by the dull sound of hands thumping rhythmically, I emptied the contents of my cavernous jacket pocket onto my chest. There, amongst the pungent cigar butts, the Coke bottle cap, and the three broken Necco wafers were a pair of dice, a pack of diamondback playing cards, and a green hardcover book. I ate the wafers, hid the dice and cards in the drawer of the nightstand, and kept the cigar butts and bottle cap to flush down the toilet. Then I turned to the first page of *John Scarne's Complete Guide to Gambling,* grateful that the previous night had not been a hallucination.

CHAPTER FOUR

Welcome to Fun Village

"Polacks fart more because they put lower quality meat in their sausage..."

I was mulling over a point John Scarne had just made, so it took me a while to realize that my father had initiated one of his white-paper pronouncements, at which time I was required to drop everything, listen, and learn. Irritated, I marked my place in the *Complete Guide to Gambling* and shoved it under my jacket. It was a few weeks since I'd heard from Jackie, but he'd just made another of his surprise calls and asked, "How'd you like to become an assistant elephant trainer?" I'd said sure, and he was now on his way over. I hoped he was ignoring the speed limit.

"Ask Mom. Her father was a butcher," Dad continued, then turned to my mother, who was reading Agatha Christie in her easy chair near the fireplace. "Jane, tell Pete that the Polish use junk meat in their kielbasa."

"Not now, Spence. I'm at an exciting part of the book," my mother said, keeping her head down, pretending that she was so absorbed by Agatha that my father and his pontificating barely registered.

Yet I had noticed that it had been many minutes since she'd turned a page.

"Well, since she won't participate, I'll use her as an example, because, after all, your mother is a Polack," Dad said, returning his attention to me. His eyes were fierce. My mother's brush-off had made him angry, yet, as was his practice, he did not confront her directly. Instead, he took an extra-long draw on his Stroh's and began again. "You see, Pete, the krauts, the frogs, the commies, and those Zsa Zsa Gabor countries that surround Poland all make sausage, but they don't fart as much as the Polacks, your mother a case in point. Now I know it's not considered feminine—even though it doesn't bother me—when a woman farts out loud, but this is something that your mom does from habit. It's not her fault. After all, she never eats kielbasa these days. Hell, sometimes I think her entire diet is those little Gelusil pills. It's just her heritage, you see, all that Polish sausage her parents gave her as a kid somehow changed her system so that she can't stop passing gas."

He paused to fork a creamed herring from a jar my mother had placed on the coffee table in front of the couch. The Detroit Lions were playing the Chicago Bears on TV, and my mother had laid out her usual Sunday afternoon football game spread: herring slathered with sour cream, sliced salami, Ritz and Triscuit crackers, a crock of limburger cheese that smelled like fresh tires, anchovies curled around pimento centers, sardines in mustard, fried bologna with ketchup dip, and thumb-sized Vienna sausages she heated in the can before serving. Only my father could bear the limp silver herring and the limburger cheese, which repelled the rest of us. I fought my younger brother over the Vienna sausages, a battle that occasionally turned physical. To us, they were gourmet treats and worth wrestling for.

"At the same time," my father said, "the Anglo-Saxons, who are my people, rarely fart, perhaps because of our bland diet, perhaps because of our more illustrious history and the responsibilities that go with it. Not that the Poles are a lesser people in any way. After all, I married a Polack and a very beautiful one at that."

I didn't answer, certain that Dad wasn't awaiting a response and indeed would have been insulted had I done anything but accept his statement verbatim. Satisfied that I was silently digesting his wisdom, Dad sank deeply into the couch with a handful of Triscuits.

Bobby, who was sprawled on the floor, a protective arm around a paper plate containing three Vienna sausages, abruptly raised his head and said, "A car is coming."

Alarmed, Dad raised his index finger before his lips to quiet us, rocked back and forth on the sofa to gain momentum, and on the third try rose unsteadily to his feet. He shuffled to the living room window and pulled aside a shiny brown drape. "Someone's parking a white Thunderbird with a landau top in our driveway," he said, concerned.

"A landau top? Really?" my mother asked, snapping shut her book. "He must have the wrong house."

"Don't worry. It's Jackie, my friend," I interjected, brimming with the perverse satisfaction that his mere arrival was causing so much consternation.

My father was skeptical. "His parents allow him to drive their T-Bird?"

"It's Jackie's car. He owns it," I said breezily, packing up my *Complete Guide to Gambling.*

"He have proof?"

"Ask him." It was wonderful to see Dad grow increasingly agitated.

The doorbell rang. My father found a level surface to set his Stroh's and lurched out of the living room, the lord fully prepared to protect his three-bedroom, one-and-one-half-bath manor. Pulling on my jacket, I followed.

"What do you want here?" my father asked Jackie through the condensation-streaked glass of the storm door.

Dressed in work boots, blue jeans, and a ski jacket with lift tickets attached, Jackie looked my father up and down, and with a half-smile gently pushed his way inside. "A good table," he answered, then pulled out his gold monogrammed money clip and slipped a couple of singles into my father's right hand.

I was stunned into silence. I'd been taught to respect—no, revere—adults, especially my father. Yet clearly Jackie treated them all like he did his mother: with contempt and disdain.

We were out the door and spinning tires in the slush before my father could react. Turning down the radio, Jackie asked, "Why didn't you tell me your dad was a degenerate alcoholic?"

Embarrassed that Jackie had pegged my father so quickly, I snapped, "Beer drinkers can't become alcoholics."

"Where did you hear that one? Listen, he's a D.G. if I ever saw one."

"D.G.?"

"Degenerate. A loser who craves more of the same thing even when it's already wrecking his life—booze, gambling, broads, macaroni and cheese, whatever."

"Yeah, well, I guess my dad's a degenerate for Stroh's." Although I'd been defensive at first, I now found it curiously liberating to discover that Jackie saw my father as I did. "He's an asshole and a buffoon," I added, and when the landau top didn't collapse on my head, I felt positively thrilled.

Cackling, Jackie pressed the horn with the butt of his hand, which propelled me to the next level of joy. It was a triumph to get him to laugh, this guy with his stacks of party records. Redd Foxx,

Lenny Bruce, and Moms Mabley were his gold standard, so until Jackie quieted down, it was as if I had joined that elite league. Even if I had become a member on the merits of "asshole" and "buffoon."

Ignoring the stop sign, Jackie slid sideways around the icy corner, then righted the Thunderbird and nodded at my copy of the *Complete Guide to Gambling*. "So what have you learned from the world's foremost gambling authority?"

"John Scarne is an egomaniac, but I've read this book two times already and I'm going to do it again. It's incredible. I never knew there were so many ways to lose at gambling, but only one way to win in the long run. Which is to have the house advantage. In other words, gambling is a license to print money if you're the guy who takes the bets instead of making them." I'd been mesmerized from the first moment I'd started reading the book. I'd never been interested in gambling before, yet John Scarne, with his confident leer and oily combover, possessed just the right combination of knowledge, sleaze, and self-promotion to make the subject appealing.

Jackie pushed his glasses back up his nose. "You know, I've loaned that book to a lot of guys and you're the first one to realize that the whole seven hundred pages is about how gambling is a sucker game. In fact, I hate the word *gambling*. They should change it to *losing,* because that's what it's about."

Excited to be on Jackie's wavelength, I turned to page two of the first chapter, entitled "Gambling: America's Biggest Industry," and read aloud: "The $250 billion wagered at all forms of gambling includes betting both legal and illegal at all types of banking games such as craps, Blackjack, slot machines, Roulette, casino side games, carnival games, punchboards, and at racetracks, with race and sports bookies, in lotteries, bingo, baseball and football pools, Keno, raffles, numbers, and all other forms of gambling in which a professional operator or banker is involved.

"An analysis of the findings of my survey of organized gambling shows that the professional operators retain, on the average, fifteen cents of each dollar bet with them. This means that the price paid by 86 million Americans for the pleasure they received from organized forms of gambling totals $37½ billion. Women spent (or lost, if you want to look at it that way) $11¼ billion, men spent $26¼ billion."

Jackie responded, "Man, I love that fifteen cents on the dollar part. You understand it means that if we can seduce our fellow classmates into betting two thousand dollars per night at the casino, our take is a hundred and fifty dollars apiece? You ever make a hundred and fifty dollars a day?"

"Not in my entire career." My first job, at the age of thirteen, had been sweeping the parking lot at a Dairy Queen for fifty cents an hour. I worked two hours a day. Since then, my top pay had been the five bucks I earned shoveling snow the afternoon of a blizzard.

"How about the deck of cards I gave you? Did you figure it out?"

I pulled the warped and mottled Bee brand playing cards from my coat pocket. Chagrined, I said, "I spilled a bottle of Squirt on them. But I'll pay you what they're worth."

Jackie yawned, then answered with a shrug, "Ten bucks."

It struck me that Jackie's hesitant reaction meant that a similar deck of Bees probably cost much less than ten dollars. Nevertheless, I plunged ahead with my analysis. "These look like a normal pack of Bee No. 92 Club Special Playing Cards with a diamondback pattern. But on each card, one diamond is slightly larger than the others, corresponding to the card's face value. For example, this is a king," I said, after peering for a few moments at the back of a card. I turned it over and, indeed, it was a king. I felt quite proud of myself. I'd studied the Bees for many long, tiring hours until it seemed like the queens were winking at me.

Jackie knocked me down a peg. "You'll need to read the spots faster unless you want to get stabbed."

"I'll practice some more."

"Want a new deck of cards?"

"Good idea."

Jackie extracted a cellophane-wrapped pack from his breast pocket and threw it in my lap. "I'll add another ten bucks to your tab."

This was starting to get expensive. Feeling the financial pressure, I came up with a solution on the spot. "Remember that business card you gave me and then took back? The twenty dollar bill?" I asked.

"Maybe."

"Why don't you just apply the twenty bucks I owe you against that and call us even?"

A hint of surprise, then irritation, crossed Jackie's face. "Great idea," he said.

"Just makes sense." In truth, I'd seized upon the most opportune moment to call in my business card, and there was no way Jackie could argue with my logic.

We were now several miles out of town, traveling past wall-flower-plain farmhouses and empty, snow-covered fields. I seldom ventured this far north of Mineralton and was dismayed by the drab landscape. Then, to our left was a complex of sway-back barns, a handful of aging kiddie rides, and a few fake Old West storefronts. There was a ranch-style swinging gate, above which an arched sign read, "Welcome To Fun Village: The World's Only Theme Park Where The Theme Is Fun." It didn't seem a likely setting for a performing elephant until Jackie turned down a half-moon gravel road and I saw a trunk waving through a slot in a spacious, bright orange barn.

"And the dice?" Jackie asked as we pulled alongside the barn, the trunk simultaneously disappearing from view. "You learn how to throw them to come up the number you want?"

"I tried until my arm got numb," I answered, deeply discouraged that I hadn't aced Jackie's three-part exam. I'd improvised a craps layout on the upstairs bathroom floor. I'd sent the dice clattering across the cold tiles countless times and had experimented with a variety of grips. I'd even let my uncoordinated younger brother try his hand, hoping he'd bumble into the magic formula. Yet nothing had worked.

"I'll handle that one," Jackie said as he leapt from the T-Bird. I did the same and immediately sank to my ankles in dark brown mud covered with a thin crust of ice. Now I knew why Jackie had worn work boots. Struggling to his side of the car was like trudging through a vast, dipped Dairy Queen ice cream cone.

Humid, exotically pungent air poured out of a slightly open barn door. I felt the childish pull to rush inside, point, and squeal, "Look! An elephant!" Instead, I asked, "So I guess we're ready to open the casino in your basement?"

"Keep practicing. Get quicker on the cards first," Jackie replied, leading me around the barn, where a damp, cold wind rushed up a rounded brown slope. A hundred yards downhill, a frozen creek snaked through a grove of towering elms. Snow- and ice-encrusted trucks and unidentifiable machinery littered the slope as if they'd been destroyed and abandoned in battle. Near us were two empty corrals and a wooden circle surrounded by upended folding chairs. A painted plywood backdrop proclaimed in large orange letters, "Free Circus Here!" Below that in smaller script was, "Next Show Begins At___." The black hands of a weather-blistered fake wooden clock pointed at two o'clock.

"Hey, that's five minutes from now," I said, trying to make a joke of it.

Jackie struggled through the glop and angrily ripped the minute hand from the clock. "Sorry folks, the show has been canceled until further notice."

"You must be really pissed at your dad."

"No more than usual." He swept his arms around, taking in the dismal scene before him. "Actually, this is my twenty-eight-year-old brother's piece-of-shit empire. He bought it with money he made managing Party Time Shows and books corporate picnics here during the summer. Of course, most of the rides don't work, and the Free Circus has only three animals."

"Do his customers complain?"

"Sure, but there are so many corporations in Detroit it'll take years for Chip to burn through them all. And after that, maybe he can sell the property for a housing development. At least that's how Chip figures it."

We turned another corner and, at last, encountered a few workers shuffling between several low-slung, brilliant orange structures. Despite the temperature, some wore T-shirts or were shirtless beneath greasy bib overalls.

"How's that paternity suit coming, Charles?" Jackie said by way of greeting a man headed our way. Charles was a balding white man with a sleeveless tank top and an unfinished snake tattoo that ended abruptly halfway down his arm. His teeth were brown, and his bristling moustache was splotched with frozen snot. He seemed quite pleased that Jackie had noticed him.

"Hell, Jackie boy, we're getting married instead."

"I thought she was only sixteen."

"That's old news," Charles beamed. "I'm marrying her mom."

"Who's the best man? Mogen David?" Jackie asked, not breaking his stride. Frowning, he acknowledged several other employees in similarly sarcastic fashion as he led us down a footpath that ended at a long, white aluminum-clad house trailer. A few feet away from the trailer's bare wooden doorstep, a bearded man in smudged white coveralls was on his knees spreading gray paint on two tan Irish setters. Jackie squatted down and restrained the painter's brush hand. "What the hell are you doing to Babe and Ruth, LeRoy?" he said.

Startled, LeRoy replied, "Chip told a client we had a trained wolf act. I'm painting them up so's he can take a picture of them and mail it."

Jackie removed the brush from LeRoy's hand and dumped it in the paint bucket. "Keep your hands in your pockets until I talk to Chip."

"But Chip said he wanted 'em ready in five minutes."

"Do you have paint in your ears?"

Reluctantly, LeRoy worked his hands deep into his pockets.

The ease with which Jackie had dealt with Charles and LeRoy filled me with awe. Merely by assuming the authority, Jackie was making adults, albeit simpletons, dance to his tune. I wondered if I too had the guts to upend what I'd assumed was an inviolate pecking order, even when a higher order of grown-up was involved.

Jackie stood and made a comically grand gesture with his arm. "Pete, you have now reached the nerve center of Fun Village, where new ways to screw the public are developed every day. There are more pukes per square inch here than the toilet bowl at a fraternity party. Speaking of which, let me introduce you to my brother." Jackie unlatched the house trailer's door. Above the sill was a sign reading "God is ____Out____In."

"Simulated," a voice bellowed inside, followed by laughter and an enormous thud. "The whole scene was fucking simulated, I tell ya!"

I jumped back a foot. Jackie became visibly agitated, his usually pale skin now flushed and shiny. I was surprised to see him lose his composure. "Who the heck's that?" I asked as we stepped into a tiny anteroom.

"I call him the Chief Puke," Jackie replied, gathering himself.

We ducked through a beaded curtain into an office, where Chip Barron, a ruddy, muscular man, sat ramrod straight behind a cheap metal desk. "And I call your buddy here The Mistake," Chip said, eyeballing me and pointing at Jackie. "'Cause it had to be a mistake for Double-O to have sex a second time with Vera."

Chip had curly, swept-back blond hair, a lantern jaw, and a stiff handlebar moustache. He was half-hidden by smoke curling up from the newspaper movie section held between his forefinger and thumb. Chip's guest, a veined, puffy-faced obese man in a frayed orange ringmaster's uniform, was on the floor, laughing uncontrollably as he pointed at the flaming newspaper page. Fat strained the seams of his pants, and there were stiff, dark stains at the crotch. Standing behind Jackie, I could smell an acrid blend of stale urine, unwashed clothing, and body odor.

Chip turned his attention back to the fat man. "*La Dolce Vita,* my ass," Chip said, snuffing out the remaining shards of the movie section with a bookkeeping ledger. "I tell you, Dinkie, there wasn't a hard-on in the whole goddamn movie. I wasted seventy-five cents and two hours of my time based on a tip I got from one little jerk-off."

"Who's that?" Dinkie asked, wiping his cheek with the back of a hand.

"Him," Chip answered, locking eyes with Jackie and pointing his forefinger at him like it was the barrel of a gun.

I tensed, but Jackie remained cool, even with the implied threat. "Where's my fucking itinerary, Hopalong?" he asked Chip.

"I had Dinkie eat your fucking little itinerary, so if you want it, you'll have to pull it out of his ass."

"Stop bullshitting and give it to me."

The phone rang. "What?" Chip answered, barely concealing his irritation. He listened for a moment, then adopted the voice of someone talking to a young child. "Sure, honey, I remember the brand of diapers. I've got it written down right here," he said, grabbing his crotch. "By the way, what's for dinner? Sounds delicious. I'll be home at six sharp." He slammed down the phone.

Dinkie was now over a dull brown wastebasket, cleaning something from his mouth with psoriasis-red fingers. His face was purple and sweaty, and he still giggled occasionally. In equal measure, I had urges to bolt out the door and to pull up a chair in order to better witness the scene unfolding before me.

"Am I interrupting something?" a tremulous voice behind me said.

I turned to see LeRoy, the dog painter.

"I hope I'm not," LeRoy continued, walking up to Chip's desk. "But Chip, I need to know whether you want me to keep working on Babe and Ruth, 'cause Jackie said not to."

Chip bolted to his feet, causing the entire trailer to sway. "You know, LeRoy, you rub me the wrong way," he snarled, reaching across the gray desk, grabbing a handful of LeRoy's coveralls. "So you're fired, buttfuck. Turn in your paintbrush and split."

"Where you going to find anyone better than me?" LeRoy asked, trembling, his jaw bravely set.

"Dinkie would be an improvement. Get out."

LeRoy slammed the door behind him, shaking the fluorescent light fixtures. I snuck a glass ashtray into my pocket in case the violence spilled over onto me. That I even had such an impulse amazed me.

Exhaling, Chip dropped into his chair and flipped open his Rolodex. "Too much aggravation," he announced. "I need to get laid."

Chip then completely ignored us as he dialed a number and began to speak softly with a person I assumed to be a girlfriend on the other end of the line. I strained to understand what he said, mentally noting terms I would have to look up in the dictionary later.

In the meantime, Jackie initiated a purposefully loud conversation with Dinkie. "Is Wanda ready?"

"Sure, Jackie. The crew's putting the elephant in semitrailer number two now. Star the Wonder Horse is already there, and they've both been fed and watered." Dinkie rose to his feet in stages, supporting himself first by the wastebasket, followed by Chip's desk and a tall file cabinet. "I've got your itinerary, too, right here. Chip was just kidding before."

Jackie gave the sheet of paper a quick look. "Fine. Show us where the trailer is parked."

"Will do. I need a little air, anyway," Dinkie replied, wheezing. Hooking his thumb into his belt to keep his unzipped pants from flopping open, he headed out.

As we left, Chip put his hand over the phone and told Jackie, "You owe me for that bad steer about *La Dolce Vita*. So when you return from your little escapade, bring me seventy-five cents, understand?"

Pointedly ignoring Chip, Jackie folded a stick of Doublemint gum into his mouth. He flicked the wrapper onto the filthy, burnt-orange carpet and guided me ahead of him through the door. "If the devil has an asshole, it looks like Chip," he muttered under his breath.

Dinkie led the way to the semi, slipping on the muddy footpath every few steps. "Chip's good people and all that," he said to me breathlessly, "but sometimes I long for the good old days."

"When were those?"

"Years ago," Dinkie chuckled, leaning against the bright orange semi located at the far end of the half-moon gravel road upon which we'd arrived. "I was ringmaster for the Baker & Teasdale Circus, but I quit over creative differences. They stopped creating my paycheck."

I took my cue from Jackie and didn't react.

Jackie climbed into the driver's seat of the battered semi, every dent and ding covered with a layer of orange paint that had been obviously slopped on with a brush. The diesel engine was already warmed up and idling. "You ride shotgun," he told me as he adjusted the huge outside rearview mirror.

"We're going somewhere?"

Jackie peered down at me as if I were stupid. "To Cleveland and Akron. For three days with the Free Circus."

"Now? I don't even have my pajamas." My heart started beating faster as I contemplated my first-ever trip to Ohio.

"You get three hots, a cot, and ten dollars a day, courtesy of Chip and Fun Village."

"What'll I tell my parents?"

"I'll help you figure that out when we come back."

Jackie goosed the engine. Black smoke boiled from the vertical exhaust pipes on either side of the cab, the burnt petroleum smell overwhelming. The skin of the passenger door vibrated with bridled power. Fresh, wet mud on top of dried mud lined the wheel wells. Calculating, weighing pros and cons, I kicked a chunk of it off with my tennis shoes. I'd never sat in a semi, let alone one with an elephant in the trailer. And the chance to see Cleveland was an opportunity that might not come again soon.

I swung open the door and, arm muscles heaving, pulled myself into the cab, a sensation not unlike climbing hand-over-hand into the world's most magnificent tree house. Perched high above the road on a cracked vinyl seat, I had entered a self-contained capsule full of strange, fascinating buttons and knobs, half-folded maps, candy wrappers, girlie magazines, rolling Coke bottles, and crushed cigarettes.

"You damn sure you watered the animals?" Jackie asked Dinkie.

"Would I lie?" Dinkie replied. He was trying to catch his breath, one hand flat on the semi for balance.

Jackie threw the truck into gear and it bucked forward, the windshield lurching violently. We lumbered onto the paved road, and the ride smoothed as Jackie moved up through the gears. Soon we were on I-94 headed south, traveling at a rapid rate I assumed real truckers called "highballing." Relaxing in my seat, contemplating the roofs of cars as we passed them, I felt on top of the world. I asked Jackie, "What's Dinkie's position at Fun Village, anyway?"

"He's an assistant elephant trainer," Jackie said, then blasted the air horn to frighten the driver of a Ford Fairlane out of our way.

When Jackie's migraine blossomed and the flash of headlights nauseated him, I took over the wheel. His long, pained silences and intermittent moans didn't arouse much empathy, which I rarely experienced at that point in life unless the other person's travails were a carbon copy of mine. It would be two decades before I'd experience my own intense, vomit-level migraines.

At any rate, the act of driving a real, diesel-powered semi with ten forward gears and a thirty-five-foot-long trailer containing a horse, an elephant, and bales of hay stacked to the ceiling, was totally involving. Jackie had provided me with a fake Arkansas driver's license, a flimsy, photoless card with my name typed in at the bottom. This gave me confidence that I would not be arrested if I was pulled over, despite the reality that there was no way I would ever be mistaken for a true, grizzled trucker. My sole prior driving experience had been chainsaw engine-powered go-carts, which in no way prepared me for piloting the semi from the mile-high cab. After stalling twice as I pulled out of a rest stop, however, I was able to stay out of trouble as long as I didn't have to change gears or back up.

The huge black steering wheel was greasy from years of neglect, and my palms were soon creased by dark, sweaty lines. Exhilaration and terror battled for dominance. In alternating fantasies, I imagined myself being greeted at the next major truck stop by the huzzahs of my brother drivers or plowing absurdly off the road through a herd of stunned cows. Somewhere beyond Toledo, as Jackie dozed, I examined my reflection in the windshield and believed I looked much older and tougher. I wondered if I would see the same image the next time I saw myself in my mother's rounded vanity mirror.

Jackie told me he'd experienced his first headache at age six when Vera had forced him, kicking and screaming, into jodhpurs, tall black boots, a safari jacket and pith helmet. Double-O had then thrust an elephant hook into Jackie's hands and pushed him and Wanda the elephant into a makeshift circus ring on the Party Time Shows midway. When Jackie asked Double-O if Wanda was already trained, he'd replied, "That's what you're in there to find out. To help us decide whether to buy her."

The elephant hook was an axe-like tool with a solid brass coat hanger fitted onto the top instead of a blade. Raw pain spreading like molten lead across his temples, Jackie eyed the elephant hook and then the hole punched into Wanda's right ear. Rhythmically tossing her head from side to side, her ears flopping like gray blankets on a clothes line, Wanda seemed restless and unpredictable. A heckler, one of seven audience members, told Jackie to hurry up. Pressured on all sides, Jackie hooked the coat hanger into the hole and tugged, praying that Wanda didn't rear up and nail him into the earth with a massive foot. He was as surprised as his parents when Wanda obediently moved forward and continued to follow him around the ring. After several turns, Vera applauded loudly and told the crowd the free show had ended.

Later, his parents officially dubbed him The World's Youngest Elephant Trainer. Jackie grew to love the attention and Wanda, spending hours feeding and grooming her. He never taught her any new tricks; the sort of folks attracted to the Party Time Shows midway were easily pleased. Star the Wonder Horse was added to his act, and soon Jackie was paying his own way in the Barron family. If that hadn't happened, he told me, he would most likely have been abandoned in some small Michigan town with a note pinned to his lapel that read, "Goldbrick. Free to good home."

Jackie didn't know whether he'd been a mistake or not, yet he'd been born thirteen years after Chip and had spent his infancy in the ticket box with Vera, absorbing every sight and sound as she short-changed customers and engaged in a running monologue about idiots, marks, morons, thieves, retards, and fools. He learned to crawl on the midway, random carnies acting as reluctant babysitters when Vera tired of watching his every unprofitable move. His toys were the stuffed animals, novelty items, and gaudy electronic junk used to flash the joints and entice unwitting customers to play the rigged games. He cried when Double-O gave a huge Mickey Mouse doll to a cop who helped him out of a jam; for the first time, Jackie realized that the plush toys were not his to keep. They were prizes, Double-O consoled him, that folks actually believed they could win.

Jackie had attended grade school in Mineralton when he wasn't on the road, and, thanks to Vera's prodding of his teachers, was always provided with enough homework to fill in the gaps. Jackie earned A's when he was interested in the subject, C's when he was bored. His fifth grade teacher had proclaimed him "brilliant" and had recommended that Jackie skip a grade, but Vera had refused, claiming that she didn't want him to get a swelled head. Instead, she told Jackie that if he was so smart, he should be earning more money—and so she put him to work on the midway games when he wasn't conducting the Free Circus.

Chip resented Jackie because he was a surprise second heir, meaning that he'd have to split the Barron empire in half when Vera and Double-O dropped dead, which Chip had openly hoped for since he'd developed a taste for power and money in his early teens. Chip had toyed with Jackie throughout his youth. He gave Jackie billiard balls to play with when he was still in the crib, taught him to roll dice on the tray attached to his high chair, and introduced him to sex at the age of twelve in a Minnesota whorehouse.

Double-O had not been too thrilled with the presence of either son, once telling Jackie that children were "the downside of coitus." As Barron family legend had it, Double-O's father had been employed killing steers with a sledgehammer as they tentatively poked their heads into the slaughterhouse. Every night Dad lugged the tool home, cleaned it in a bucket of soapy water on the front porch, and stored it beside the door. When his wife objected, he'd drag her outside, point to the sledgehammer, and say, "That's how I put food on the table." At the age of fourteen, Double-O had fled his small-town Wisconsin home to join a traveling carnival. Double-O had barnstormed across the country for years before settling temporarily at a Coney Island–like amusement park midway between Detroit and Mineralton. It was there he met Vera, whose parents owned several food concessions, where one of her many tasks was to coquettishly cadge expired baked goods from grocers for resale by her parents.

Double-O and Vera married, or at least effected a merger of

mutual interests, and Double-O took over management of the food joints from Vera's ailing parents. He boosted the concessions to new heights of success with the introduction of "Double-O's 13-Inch Foot-Long," a hot dog that was actually a standard twelve-incher placed inside a shorter bun. No one ever complained because, as Double-O sagely noted, "How many people walk the midway with a ruler?"

Vera, who was apparently not close to her parents, had then secretly sold their concessions, leaving them ten cases of buns and a barrel of dehydrated onions with which to start anew. She and Double-O invested the cash in several traveling units, hit the road, and eventually placed 13-Inch Foot-Long stands on a half-dozen Midwestern carnivals. After a few years, the couple sold the business for a large profit to a naive Iowa grocer looking for a fun way to spend his retirement years. By the time he realized that the books had been cooked, Double-O and Vera were back in Michigan, pursuing their next dream. They purchased the assets of a bankrupt carnival, renamed it Party Time Shows, and over the years established a highly lucrative circuit of small Michigan towns. Party Time Shows' rides were nothing special and the food traditionally stale, not that Double-O and Vera cared. The couple's sole concern was the game booths that dominated the midway: Each game was fixed, and each was a money-making machine. The carnival deservedly earned its reputation as a "rackets show."

The entire operation revolved around the games, which were worked "strong" in order to maximize profits. To make that possible, Double-O paid off (or "patched") every police chief or county sheriff where Party Time Shows put down stakes. In return, the authorities would look the other way when their constituents lost. Leaving a trail of angry customers in their wake, Vera and Double-O became rich.

In addition to Party Time Shows, the couple now owned a ride manufacturing business, a piece of Chip's Fun Village, and plenty of real estate. Jackie estimated that his parents were multimillionaires, not counting the tens of thousands of dollars Vera had hidden around the house in order to avoid paying taxes and because she liked being surrounded on all sides by cash.

The truck kept slipping in and out of gear, and it wasn't until four in the morning that we arrived at the Parker Hotel in grimy, forbidding downtown Cleveland. The semi wouldn't fit into the hotel's underground parking lot. Angry and out of sorts, Jackie parked on the street and left the truck in idle so that the heating coils in each animal's stall would keep working. A bellman kept watch.

By the time we found our room, I was almost able to stop worrying about how much clothing to remove: Too much would be weird, and not enough would seem chicken. Jackie settled the matter by stripping to his underwear. I drowned out the grind of early-morning garbage trucks with a pillow over my head and the hum of my bed's Magic Fingers. I fell asleep on my last quarter.

We were awakened two hours later by a beaming, solicitous woman at the door. "Ith you boys ready for a wonderful tour?" she asked, smoothing Jackie's rumpled hair. It was Harriet of the husband-and-wife booking team Noyce & Noyce. Mrs. Noyce had false teeth that whistled, a wiry, silver-gray wig, and a ring on each finger representing the zodiac signs ("minus Pisces and Scorpio, the ones I don't like," she said). Floyd was a shy, taciturn farmer who had, Jackie told me, abandoned his first wife and four hundred acres upon encountering Harriet at a Kiwanis Club meeting because he'd discovered that "show business was in my blood." The Noyce & Noyce specialty was booking bump-and-grind shows for civic group get-togethers. The couple would be meeting us at each engagement to ensure it went smoothly.

The National Bank of Cleveland's employee family show was our first event at 10 o'clock. Jackie had been contracted to give elephant rides for an hour backstage, so he'd strapped a bright orange howdah onto Wanda's back, showed me how to make her stand up and kneel using the elephant hook, and then disappeared. With dots of sweat cooling my forehead, I led Wanda around in circles for the full sixty minutes. I persevered, even prospered: At the end, two small girls asked for my autograph.

Then the curtain rose, and the show went straight downhill when Wanda left a trail of steaming, melon-sized turds behind her as she roamed the stage during her act. Jackie, wearing a blue-sequined jacket, had prodded her into rearing up just before she went on, telling me that "elephants have weak butt muscles, so the shit usually just drops out." But Wanda hadn't unloaded, leading us to conclude that she was constipated. We found out differently.

"Get out there quick," Harriet ordered me. Floyd had just arrived with a garbage can and shovel. Until then, I'd been enjoying myself in the shadows, soaking up the show biz excitement. Now I shuffled into the spotlight for my stage debut. I received a standing ovation.

"Maybe we should keep that part in the act," Jackie said later as we wound through Akron. He was in a bad mood. Harriet's directions had been poor and we'd just unloaded the animals at the wrong high school, with only fifteen minutes to locate the correct one. In addition, Jackie had lost the key to Wanda's foot shackle, so now she'd have to perform with twenty feet of heavy chain wrapped around her leg.

The Harding High School Pageant was no more successful than the show in Cleveland that morning. Wanda's chain unraveled and caused considerable damage as it swept in wide arcs across the polished wood gymnasium floor. The unsuspecting audience applauded wildly, although the school's head custodian threatened to sue as we quickly exited the building.

"Let him try," Jackie whispered. "We're minors."

Our final performance took place sixty miles further east of Akron than Harriet had led us to believe, in a country club's tiny piano room. Small children swarmed over folding chairs packed so tight that Star and Wanda could barely turn around standing in place. Jackie had each of them do this a few times and called it a day.

"Let them sue us, too," Jackie shrugged.

Harriet and Floyd arrived in a dented 1959 Cadillac just as we were packing up the trailer for the last time. Floyd tensed as Harriet gave us each a big showbiz kiss on the cheek.

"Boyth, the three thowth were wonderful," she said, handing a cash-stuffed envelope to Jackie. When, with a skeptical frown, he deliberately counted the bills twice, Harriet added, "And here's a little something for you to spend as you please." She offered each of us a silver dollar.

"Harriet, you thuck," Jackie declared, recoiling from the coin like it was minted uranium. I took that as a cue and refused to accept mine.

"You'll never work in northweth Ohio again," Harriet shouted as we climbed into the semi. I laughed harder than Jackie's reply was worth, but there was something about the past two days that was making me giddy. Maybe it was how Jackie thumbed his nose at everyone, or maybe how I hadn't obsessed about phoning my parents or fretted about their reaction to my disappearance.

We were in high spirits on the return trip, mocking everyone and everything: Harriet and Floyd, the gymnasts who'd been forced to take the stage after I'd only partially removed Wanda's manure in Cleveland, the Akron party store owner who paid us five bucks when we bet him that we had an elephant in our trailer.

As we crossed into Michigan and it began to rain so heavily that the world beyond the windshield was no more than a shape-shifting abstract painting, Jackie, riding shotgun, turned to me and said, "You're on track, Pete. You catch on quick, you've got a good sense of humor, and you've got the right fucking attitude."

"What kind of fucking attitude is that?"

"You know the difference between being 'with it' and being like everybody else."

Actually, I had no idea what Jackie meant, and was too embarrassed to admit it. I assumed his reading of me was a good sign and was elated, though only in retrospect did I discover how perceptive he was. I was constitutionally suited to becoming part of an us-versus-them world—"us" being the smart folks, cons, and carnies; "them" being the fools, suckers, and marks, also known as everyone else on the face of the earth.

Jackie fell asleep, using his balled-up sequined jacket as a pillow, and didn't speak again until I bumped into Fun Village's desolate, windswept parking lot. "I think we're ready to make real money now," he yawned. "Let's open the casino."

CHAPTER FIVE

Honey, There's a Casino in the Basement

Even devout Mineralton High School sports fans may not recall that winter's basketball game against Dearborn, which the Magnificent Minerals surprisingly lost 62-50 when team captain and top scorer Buzz Fazio injured his ankle with ten minutes left and had to be helped off the court by his distraught teammates. But I do. Not that Buzz's pain was a searing reminder of my own career-ending football injury. The game was memorable because I was there to collect my first-ever gambling debt—from Buzz. The tall, oval-headed sports star had lost his entire bankroll at our basement casino the week before. He'd then borrowed more money from us, quickly lost it, and was now on a strict repayment plan, with the first installment due before this evening's Vegas Night, scheduled to start an hour or so after the game. Buzz needed to pay to avoid being banned at the door.

More moody and keyed up than usual, I arrived at halftime and positioned myself in a brightly lit hall where I could catch fleeting glimpses of the game while monitoring the locker room door. I did not intend to rough up Buzz. I hadn't slipped on brass knuckles, nor did I have a lead pipe concealed in the sleeve of the white trench coat I'd purchased during a shopping trip with Jackie to a Detroit men's store. In truth, I was worried that Buzz would beat the hell out of me. He was a half-foot taller and fifty pounds heavier, and he had broken his nose so many times he could snap it in and out of place like other people cracked their knuckles.

But Jackie had assigned me to pick up Buzz's payment, and I was going to come through. The spot I occupied in the hall allowed me to intercept Buzz as he exited—or, if necessary, sprint into the cold, dark parking lot in case he lunged at my head.

I didn't pay much attention to the game. Since the casino had opened, I'd grown increasingly removed from the excitements of school, although in no way did I hate my classmates or despise my teachers. As always, I had friends, never skipped class, and earned high grades. It's just that I had become as much a spectator of what went on in school as a participant. Having learned to manipulate people into gladly gambling away their money, it was hard not to feel somewhat distant, like a physician removing his hundredth spleen or a cop surreptitiously kneeing yet another recalcitrant suspect in the groin.

The bleachers on either side of the gym were packed with maybe eight hundred enthusiastic fans. MHS athletic events were important local activities, perhaps because there was little else to do, and both students and adults wore their best wool sweaters, overcoats, and new slacks. A few stern-faced men clomped around in black, snap-up galoshes—the weatherman had said heavy snow could be on the way. Underneath the too-bright lights that glinted off the polished gymnasium floor, everyone appeared well-scrubbed and immaculately clean. The scents of small-town fastidiousness were everywhere: Lavoris, Brylcreem, Sen-Sen, Mennen After Shave, pressed powder, and hair spray. It was as if anyone with bad breath or B.O. would be run out on a rail.

I, too, was clean, but somewhat out of sync in my white trench coat with blue-green iridescent sharkskin pants, plastic-soled pseudo-Italian shoes (I had been told they were real at the Detroit men's store), and a gray turtleneck sweater that was so hot my head was throbbing. For the first time in my life I was paying attention to what I wore, dressing now in a style I called "modified hip," which in reality was moderately ludicrous. Jackie complained that my new appearance was "calling attention to the joint," or making people too aware of my con-man aspirations, but I stood my ground. Though I never told him, I desperately needed the visual aid to help bolster my transformation into what I hoped was a racier me.

The final buzzer sounded and disappointed Minerals fans streamed past, already heatedly replaying the game. I made hurried small talk with my American history teacher, something about the relationship between Jeffersonian principles and a winning basketball team. A clutch of student council girls conspicuously skirted around me, only to begin whispering excitedly behind their hands. The morose, bespectacled guy who sat behind me in study hall shuffled past, averting his eyes. He'd lost big at blackjack twice, but I knew he'd be back as soon as he cashed his Dairy Queen paycheck.

The crowd had thinned to a group of children collecting plastic straws beneath the bleachers when the Magnificent Minerals, dressed in street clothes, began emerging from the locker room. Last to come out was Buzz Fazio, struggling on a pair of crutches, his letter jacket draped over his shoulders.

I approached him warily, fully ready to bolt. For all I knew Buzz could outrun me on crutches. "What happened to your ankle?" I asked. His foot and calf were mummified in a beige Ace bandage.

Incredibly, Buzz seemed just as worried about bumping into me, which took the edge off my own angst. Buzz swung toward me, the crutches making a dull thud and squeak. He surveyed either end of the empty hall and whispered, "Nothing."

Shocked, I pulled him behind the bleachers, where no one but the squealing kids could hear us. "Then why'd they carry you off the court?"

"I threw the game."

"For what?"

"I wanted to pay off my gambling debt."

"How's faking a sprained ankle do that?"

"So you and Jackie could win big betting against the Minerals."

"You dumb shit. Nobody bets on high school basketball. And even if they did, you'd have to tell us ahead of time that you're taking a fall."

"I thought you and Jackie would figure it out, because that's what players in debt to gamblers do."

"I appreciate the gesture. But you still owe us one hundred and seventy-five dollars."

"Can I give you five of that next Thursday? That's when I get my allowance." Buzz seemed near tears. Snot oozed out of his left nostril. He snorted it back up.

I marveled that the team captain was truly worried about how I would answer. I'd arrived terrified about his reaction, and now here he was, nervously awaiting mine. It was a moment to savor. I delayed my response until Buzz had to snort up again.

"Well, Buzz, I don't want to force you into the position where you have to beg your dad for an advance on your allowance so you can pay off a gambling debt. That would be humiliating. So Thursday's okay. Meet me in the cafeteria at noon with the money. Paper money. I don't want five dollars in change. But there's a catch—you're banned from the casino until you repay your debt."

"Pete, you're a real pal. The basketball team could use a guy like you if you were taller and weighed more," Buzz said, and squeaked away on his crutches. I felt a sense of accomplishment and wondered why. After all, I'd wasted an hour loitering in a hallway with nothing to show for it. Why should I feel good when Jackie would think I'd failed? I decided to cough up five bucks of my own, tell Jackie it belonged to Buzz, and replenish my own bankroll with the real payment on Thursday. That way I could pretend I'd succeeded, which was almost the case under the circumstances. This casino management stuff required thought. I flipped up the collar of my trench coat and headed home in a whirling snow squall.

Running a casino demanded intense forethought as well, something I'd realized two months before, on the eve of our inaugural Vegas Night. Jackie had handed me a thousand dollar bill. We were in the MHS cafeteria, and Mabel the kitchen worker had presented Jackie with a banana split as a surprise. We were sharing it, which upset her, thanks to her irrational belief that the more ice cream Jackie ate, the more likely one of her horses would win.

"That's Grover Cleveland, our twenty-second and twenty-fourth president, in case you're wondering," Jackie had told me.

"I feel like I'm going to get arrested as a teenager in possession of too much money."

"Grover is the cheese that will attract the mice. I have one of them, too. You and I are going to circulate around school, flash the money, and when a tip builds, talk about Vegas Night, and say, 'Some lucky stiff is going to walk away from the casino with a thousand dollar bill.'"

"What's a tip?"

"A crowd. Like the kind you get when you point at the top of a building and a bunch of people gather around and look up."

"We really going to give a thousand away?"

"No, this is just a come-on. The lucky stiffs who will leave with the money are us."

The grand opening was a rousing success. We draped a canvas over Jackie's pool table and used that as a surface for our dice game, blackjack, and poker. On the floor, bottles of store-brand soda pop floated in ice-filled buckets. Cartons of out-of-date cigarettes and bags of potato chips, popcorn, and pretzels left over from Party Time Shows' summer carnival season filled every other level surface. Nude volleyball magazines were scattered at random, and the pinball machine was turned on for a dash of color, although the steel balls were removed so no one could waste time playing it. All refreshments, due to be tossed out anyway, were free of charge. Beer and wine were too expensive to serve and would get us in trouble, Jackie said, so anyone who wanted booze had to discreetly bring their own bottle. Jackie claimed gambling put us in no legal danger, because the cop who patrolled Kibbee Flats at night was a good friend who believed any activity that kept teens off the street was a valuable community service. To keep Vera quiet, Jackie allowed her to charge a one-dollar "house entry" fee, which she was to split evenly with Double-O, although Jackie was certain she shorted him.

The casino opened at 10:00 P.M. and by 10:15, the basement was hot, stuffy, and noisy, packed with a hundred and fifty MHS students who were dressed as if this were an important social occasion, like the senior prom. Ricky Hancock wore a tuxedo, and several girls sported wrist corsages. Most significantly, no one seemed to be familiar with the fundamental aspects of gambling.

This would make our jobs much easier, Jackie whispered, as he evened up several packs of unsealed marked cards, because we could improvise rules as we went along. "The rules according to Barron & Fenton," he said, "instead of according to Hoyle."

To project a subliminal clue that this was a semi-sanctioned school event (subliminal being a hot concept at the time), I wore a red long-sleeved shirt and gray slacks, the Magnificent Minerals team colors. Jackie dressed unassumingly in a light blue pullover sweater and cords. We each had a white carpenter apron tied around the waist to hold our winnings and allow fast access to change. Standing next to Jackie at the pool table, I was so tense I began eating faintly rancid two-year-old Cheetos without hesitation. How would it be possible for us to cheat a hundred and fifty people without getting caught, even if they were our naive, trusting classmates? One savvy player in the bunch, and we'd be chased like twin Frankensteins through the twisted woods of Kibbee Flats.

Fortunately, my primary job was to act as bank: taking in cash, dispensing chips, and ultimately—as the night wore on and our success mounted—deciding on who should or shouldn't receive credit. Jackie didn't think my sleight-of-hand skills had been honed sufficiently, so he handled the marked cards and dice, which he'd learned to throw so that one die would come up the number he wanted. He achieved this by holding the die in the crook of his index finger with the desired number (let's say six) face up so that it would spin instead of tumble when he threw it. Ideally, the six would remain face up when it stopped. It was a technique that would be immediately spotted by seasoned players. In the entire history of our casino, however, no one ever caught on, a tribute to either Jackie's skill (and later, my own) or the clean-living cluelessness of our customers.

Our biggest moneymaker, though, was the Over and Under 7 dice layout I'd created with a black marker on a square yard of pale blue vinyl tablecloth. Inspired by my obsessive reading of the *Complete Guide to Gambling,* Over and Under 7 was a simple dice game that paid even money. If a customer bet a dollar on Over and the pair of dice totaled 8, he received his dollar plus another dollar in return. Ditto if he bet Under and the total was any number under 7. Since there were five numbers over 7 (8, 9, 10, 11, 12) and five under 7 (6, 5, 4, 3, 2), the odds would seem correct, at least to our teenage gamblers. But they weren't. Any true calculation of the odds needed to take into account that when a 7 was thrown, all Over or Under bets lost. This gave the house (Barron & Fenton) a six to five advantage either way, which in percentage terms is 16⅔ percent. Which meant that, over the long haul, our profit was $16.67 on every $100 that was bet. In comparison, the Las Vegas casinos earned about $5 of every $100 bet at the roulette wheel and $1.50 of every $100 bet at the craps table.

At two in the morning, when the last dejected gambler climbed the stairs to leave, Jackie and I untied our bulging carpenter aprons, emptied our back and front pockets, retrieved a heavy shopping bag we'd filled with cash and change, and emptied every cent onto the pool table. The volcanolike peak of paper money and coins obscured the entire Over and Under 7 layout.

Giant circles of sweat spreading out from my armpits, mouth sour, teeth furry, body reeking of cigarettes, spilled soda pop, and cologne, palms black from money, feet sore from hours of standing, and stomach churning from Cheetos and a six-pack of Coke, I found it hard to focus. When I closed my eyes momentarily, I felt as if I were still in motion, raking in cash, watching the many losers get all teary-eyed and the few winners jump with joy.

"Don't fall asleep yet, partner," Jackie said, dropping a shoe box filled with coin wrappers on the pool table.

"There must be a hundred bucks of pennies here alone," I protested.

"Just one of the perils of nickel-and-diming the public to death."

Moaning, I dragged an alluvial fan of change my way and began counting, the first of tens of thousands of coins I was to add up and wrap in the coming months and years. It became a ritual with Jackie and me, creating piles of forty or fifty coins (depending on their face value), then pinching open a flattened wrapper, inserting a finger, dribbling in the quarters, dimes, nickels, or pennies, and folding each end of the wrapper four times to secure the contents. Then starting over again. Quarters were my favorite: The wrapper was wider and the coins were heavier, which allowed them to drop flat into place on the tip of my inserted finger rather than stick at an awkward angle mid-wrapper and force me to start the whole process again. Customarily, I saved the quarters for last, as a treat. It was a relief when, much later, I graduated to high-stakes carnival games. Working with paper money only was as pointed a sign as any that I had risen in rank.

Jackie and I rolled coins and counted greenbacks through the night, and it's possible that our friendship peaked then. Much later our relationship deteriorated—fatally injured, once again, by money. But, in those early morning hours, cash and the shared triumph of accumulating it brought us together instead of pulling us apart.

"Remember Eddie Lubanski and that godawful counterfeit double-saw he tried passing on us?" Jackie, laughing, asked me at one point as he dug into a pile of quarters. "Saw," I'd learned, was carny talk for a ten dollar bill and "double-saw" was carny talk for a twenty.

I howled. "Did he really believe he could get away with that?" Lubanski had written the number 20 on a piece of onion paper and glued over the 1 on a dollar bill.

"I guess so," Jackie replied, "but he should've used better glue."

After replaying the incident a few more times, we returned to the rhythm of counting coins. The night continued like this: sporadic bursts of laughter, followed by the silent contentment of wrapping, until half the pool table was lined with neat Lincoln logs of change. Only then did we riffle through the paper money. The stunning grand total was $1,579.83.

Exhilarated, trembling, sick to my stomach, I offered, "Sure beats working as an usher at the Bijou Theater."

Jackie, who appeared much more collected, dragged a quarter from a scattering of leftover change. "Tell you what," he said, "flip you for who gets the coins in his cut."

I picked tails and arrived home with fifteen pounds of change straining the seams of my pockets. I later learned Jackie had purchased the double-headed quarter at a Detroit novelty store.

Using a new key I'd had cut, I slipped in the side door and creaked downstairs to the basement, where I had started sleeping the day I returned from Ohio. The basement was divided into finished and unfinished halves by a knotty-pine wall. The rear half was a combination washroom and workshop with a gray concrete floor, an oil furnace, and a cast-iron tank that held a couple hundred gallons of fuel oil. The entire room had the faint air of a refinery, especially in winter when the furnace cycled on, signaled by a dull thump that often woke me up on the other side of the wall.

The workshop was where my father would often vanish to practice his drumming on a plywood pad covered with a quarter-inch of rubber padding. He'd pound the same tattoo over and over, the beat growing sloppier as the alcohol set in, until finally stopping when his focus shifted exclusively to drink. No one was supposed to know that Dad guzzled beer as he played, yet I'd discovered hundreds of empty Stroh's cans hidden in a closet, behind his duck decoys, foul-weather gear, and rubber hip boots.

The finished section of the basement, where my parents held their rare parties, had a floor of brown and beige linoleum and a low, acoustic tile ceiling. The cinder-block walls were painted a festive pink, except for the knotty-pine divider, upon which was mounted a dartboard and a coconut with a carved face and seashell eyes that my mother had purchased in Hawaii. My fold-out bed and a few belongings were in a corner, alongside an ancient brown radio/record player the size and shape of a jukebox. Crawling across the unmade bed, I removed a grate from the bottom front of the radio, hid my $750-plus inside, replaced the grate, and collapsed onto the bed.

My parents had been understandably upset when I'd walked in the front door after my surprise Free Circus trip. Filthy, stinking of elephant dung and my own funk, I was ordered into the living room, where my mother and father sat on the couch. This was one of the few times I'd seen them together on the same piece of furniture. My father was sober. My mother had an ashtray in her lap and a glass of beer balanced on her knee. She looked pale and slightly disheveled, as though she hadn't pulled herself together with her usual care.

I stood directly before them, for the moment newly cocksure enough to muffle my familiar, burgeoning feelings of panic in their presence.

"You're very lucky," my father said, "I could have called the police, but I didn't want word to get around that a Fenton had run away from home."

"I was out of town on business."

Dad snorted and rocked back, forcing a little of Mom's beer to slosh over the edge of the glass. She deftly planted the glass in the bowl of the ashtray, where the beer drowned her lit cigarette with a sizzle. "Business?" my father asked.

"With Jackie Barron, you know, the Barron family that owns the carnival?"

"I do, unfortunately."

At that moment, I experienced a simpleminded epiphany: Even when he was sober, Spencer Fenton was a pompous fool and a weakling. But rather than say so to his face, I confronted him with what Jackie had revealed under the spell of his migraine: "Did you know that Oliver Oxford Barron ran an illegal casino in the attic of the Fenton Hotel—"

"That's a lie."

"—for an entire summer after he got off work at that old amusement park between here and Detroit?"

"Never heard of it."

"Only because your father never bothered to tell you. And from what I hear, he had a gambling operation in the attic for years. Maybe that's how he made all his money."

"Quiet," my mother snapped, almost dumping the ashtray and beer glass. "You have no idea how worried we've been," she said. "And now, the first thing you do is attack the Fenton Hotel. Go upstairs. Get away from us."

I shrugged and walked out of the room. That night I carried the *Complete Guide to Gambling* and an armload of clothes into the basement, unfolded the spare bed, and never again slept in my mother's room. Through the floorboards and the heat ducts, I listened to my parents argue for hours, bitterly denouncing each other as they grew even more drunk. The next morning, still wearing my stiff, stinking clothes, I went upstairs for breakfast—detouring into the living room, perversely drawn by the smell of stale beer, crushed cigarettes, and decomposing limburger cheese. There was a wide, dark circle on one sofa cushion where someone obviously had spilled a beer. Family photos, which my mother kept in a box in the bottom drawer of the dining room credenza, spilled across the coffee table and onto the floor. And curled in her favorite easy chair was Mom, passed out, breathing with a rasp through a half-open mouth, a well-thumbed

Agatha Christie paperback in her lap. As I tiptoed past her, her eyes fluttered open, and she stared at me without recognition. Stifling a scream, I hurried into the kitchen, filled a bowl to overflowing with Frosted Flakes, sat down, and started to cry.

When I strode back into the living room to apologize to Mom for upsetting her, she was already crawling upstairs, like a Slinky in reverse motion. I watched until she turned left in the direction of her room. Reconsidering—why should I be the one to beg forgiveness?—I rubbed away a tear, returned to the kitchen, poured milk over the Frosted Flakes, and lost myself re-reading John Scarne's thoughts on "The Mathematics and Science of Gambling" (Chapter 2).

My mother never again mentioned my long Ohio weekend or what transpired when I returned. As with my father's boorish behavior, she acted like it never happened. I continued to sleep on the spare bed in the basement, as if things had always been that way. That's when I realized my mother excelled at pretending: She had married into a Great American Family, and Spencer Fenton was an admirable husband and father.

But my dad refused to let up. After an extra-drunken couple of weeks (during which he'd arrive home late, then go straight to bed without eating), he returned to the dinner table, pointed a trembling finger at me, and said: "You think you're so smart, Pete? I could have been a millionaire if I had wanted to. Consider yourself lucky if one day you can say the same."

"And how would you have done it? Become a millionaire?"

"That's irrelevant."

"You're saying you could've become rich, but have no idea how?"

"Why waste time making all sorts of plans when I didn't want to become rich anyway?"

"Well, Dad, one day I hope I can follow in your footsteps and not become a millionaire, too."

"Fat chance. You're only half Fenton. The other half's Polack. You'll never be me, never."

"I'm going to hold you to that."

"You goddamn debater." With that, Dad stormed off.

After we had listened to him pound down the basement stairs and slam the door to the workroom, my mother said, "Pete, after causing all that trouble, the least you can do is finish Dad's dinner before it turns too cold to eat." Sighing, she also left the room. I took my father's meal and pushed my mother's plate smoothly across the vinyl tablecloth to my brother. He dove right into her onion rings.

And so began a new phase in my relationship with Dad. The kitchen nook became the scene of heated, nonsensical debate about everything from the history of badminton to whether chopsticks were better than forks. Eventually, everyone in the family began to take their meals elsewhere and alone.

But on this evening, returning from the basketball game against Dearborn, I was in a hurry to eat and run and hoped that I could avoid my father and our inevitable battle for rhetorical supremacy. Unfortunately, after I retrieved some money from behind the radio grate and called a cab to ferry me to Jackie's, Dad popped through the knotty-pine door that separated the workshop from my lair.

"Have you seen my other drumstick?" he asked, frantic. "I'm late for practice at Amvets." Dad was wearing his full dress uniform: gray slacks with pale green piping, a gray military-style blouse decorated with epaulets and large brass buttons, and a peaked gray-and-green flight cap with "Amvets Post #31" embroidered on either side. Agitated, he stopped to gnaw at the top of his lip, which was already red and swollen from his nervous chewing. When it came to Post 31, Dad had inherited my grandfather's desperate need to be punctual with regard to leisure activities. And I knew that he was preparing for the most important event of his year: the Amvets Drum and Bugle Corps National Finals, when Amvets posts from across the nation competed for the honor of being judged the top unit of the year. So, after recovering from the surprise of his visit, I responded with the rhetorical flourish, "Fuck you."

"Fuck you, too, buddy," he replied.

I rose to my feet. "Fuck you and your drums."

"Get the fuck out of my house," he hollered as I climbed the stairs.

"What the fuck does it look like I'm doing?" I answered, then walked outside and climbed into my waiting cab. Minutes later, as the cab tipped down the incline that marked the beginning of Kibbee Flats, I rolled down the window, removed Dad's missing drumstick from my sleeve, and tossed it into the gnarled woods— where I'd disposed of maybe half a dozen drumsticks before, just to fuck with his mind.

"Fucking with minds can get to be a habit," Jackie had informed me when, shortly after our return from Ohio, we'd gone on a shopping trip to downtown Detroit. It was a day when Jackie was full of advice. "To be cool, you've got to look cool," he'd added before burying his head in one of the dozens of *Racing Forms* beside him in the passenger seat of the Thunderbird. Jackie had purchased a mailorder horse-betting aid called Roy Talbot's Speed Handicapper and, in a dry run, was testing its accuracy in predicting the results of races that had already taken place. The Speed Handicapper cost $149.95, looked like a slide rule, and purportedly turned playing the horses into a science by crunching data to come up with a winner. I never quite figured out how it worked, and Jackie eventually smashed it to pieces after losing $780 at Detroit Race Course on a horse that the slide rule had indicated was a sure thing. But on this day, the Speed Handicapper was fresh out of the package and had Jackie's full attention as I cruised along at 110 MPH before slowing to 90 when I merged into the sparse traffic traveling from Mineralton to Detroit on I-94. Having succeeded in driving a semi at 55 MPH, I was a bit overconfident about my ability to handle a mere automobile at three-digit speeds, although, as I reached the Detroit city limits, traffic moved so fast that any number of drivers passed and gave me the finger as if I were blocking their way.

I quickly turned apprehensive. Detroit always seemed gray and overcast, even when it was sunny elsewhere, as it had been in Mineralton. Here, as the traffic grew heavy, the freeway became a narrow, grimy canyon littered with abandoned cars and twisted car parts. I slowed to 75 before braking to a complete, tire-smoking stop at the first traffic jam I'd ever encountered. Ahead of me, red brake lights pulsed on and off toward the still-distant downtown skyline. One mile and a half hour later, we passed a rusted Buick Electra parked on the narrow shoulder of the freeway, the hood up, "Just Married" whitewashed across the rear window. Traffic soon cleared, and a few minutes later Jackie put down the Speed Handicapper and directed me onto Woodward Boulevard, the main street of Detroit. Crowds of people—perhaps, I guessed, as many as the entire population of Mineralton during Farm-City Week—maneuvered around obstacles and each other on the broad sidewalk. Never-ending streams of shoppers spun through the revolving doors of Hudson's, the multistory department store that was the heart of the retail district. But what I found most riveting was a high, seemingly block-long billboard of a blonde in a bikini, kneeling and sucking her thumb.

"We'll get to that later," Jackie said. "First we need to buy you some clothes." He pointed at a parking spot in front of a nonde-script one-story building and I swooped in, barely beating a rotund man in an Imperial, who glared at me before screeching off.

"What kind of clothing store doesn't have a name?" I asked as I stepped to the sidewalk and stretched. There was no sign above the door, and the store's glass display windows were empty except for an unadorned male mannequin that had fallen onto its side.

"Among a select few, the place is known as Five-Finger Dis-count."

"As in shoplifted?"

"Don't say that inside."

At the locked front door, Jackie pressed a buzzer. Inside, a twitchy, middle-aged man in a black leather car coat gave us the once-over, and went back to reading *The Midnighter,* a newspaper with a cover story about a UFO alien crime spree. Perturbed, Jackie shouted, "Double-O Barron's son with guest," after which the man flushed with annoyance, folded the newspaper to mark his place, stepped to the front door, and flipped the deadbolt.

Five-Finger Discount was unlike any men's store I'd ever been in, but I hadn't visited many, so I decided to suspend judgment for the moment. A few customers, who avoided eye contact, were paw-ing through suits, overcoats, and wildly colored shirts hung from garment racks that filled the display floor at odd angles. Huge card-board boxes had been dumped randomly, usually with a corner ripped open to offer a glimpse of what they contained.

Awkward and unsure of myself, I whispered to Jackie, "Do you wait for somebody to help you?"

"Are you kidding? These guys wouldn't lift a finger if J. Paul Getty walked in the door."

Tentatively at first, I strolled through the garment racks, rolling them aside when I was finished, careful not to wheel them into my fellow customers. Nothing struck me—why would I want a gray pinstriped suit or wool sport coat?—until I spotted a trench coat, all white but for the metallic buttons and belt buckle. Transfixed, I pictured myself turning up the collar and floppy lapels as I strode through dangerous, garbage-filled alleys. It was the epitome of showboating style, and it fit perfectly, too. Enthused, I dove into the cardboard boxes, picking out two pairs of iridescent sharkskin pants (which I'd heard were increasingly popular), a silk shirt, and a handful of thin, see-through socks, like those worn by a dead body on the back cover of *The Midnighter*. Jackie didn't buy anything. As we headed for the cash register, which was atop a two-drawer file cabinet near the door, I asked him why.

"I like my people to be sharp. Myself, I prefer conservative."

I savored the prospect of becoming one of Jackie's "people," and wondered what the rest of "us" looked like.

We arrived at checkout only to be ignored by the salesman in the leather car coat, who was now sitting on the inside edge of a display window, girl-watching while he ate a sandwich.

"Can we get some service here?" Jackie called to him loudly.

Without looking up, the salesman answered, "Hey, relax. Sit down on a box or something for a few minutes. I'm busy with lunch."

"We're going to stroll with this shit if you don't get up."

"Fuck this goddamn retail crap." The man threw the remains of his sandwich onto a paper plate, wiped his hands on a scrap of cardboard, and strode to the cash register.

"How much?" Jackie asked.

The salesman gave my purchases the once-over. "How 'bout twenty bucks?"

"Fine," Jackie said, withdrawing a double-saw from his money clip.

Ignoring the cash register, the man pocketed the money. "What

labels you want?" he asked, pointing a finger at a wad of designer labels. "We got Christian Dior and some other French names I can't
even pronounce. Just grab a handful and get out of my sight."

Fuzzy about designers beyond Sears Roebuck, I cherry-picked
the Dior labels he mentioned. Then the salesman tossed everything
but the trench coat into a brown paper grocery bag and concluded
with the warning, "Don't tell anyone where you bought this."

On the sidewalk, I almost bumped into a beautiful woman in
high heels and a low-cut dress. She offered me an alluring smile,
which I was immediately convinced had to do with the trench coat.
Women like her would no doubt be even more impressed after I
sewed in the Christian Dior label.

"You haven't thanked me for treating you to the threads," Jackie
said as I tossed the bag of clothes into the Thunderbird's trunk.

"Get off it. You never paid me the thirty bucks I was supposed
to get for that job in Ohio. So minus the clothes, you still owe me
ten." This fact had long been gnawing at me, but the time to raise
the issue had always seemed wrong. A sexy female smile, I found,
could inspire me to strive for previously forbidden goals.

"That was Chip's responsibility, remember? I've been trying to
get your pay from him ever since."

I remained silent. If I really was one of Jackie's people now, he'd
come through.

Jackie, too, was quiet as he slammed the trunk shut. Finally, he
said, "Okay, okay, Mr. Persistent. I'll make good on the money, even
though it should be coming from Chip. In fact, I'll make it up to
you now," he said, leading me toward Cut Rate Luxury Shoes, several storefronts down the street. My spirits soared. It seemed I had
won Jackie's respect. I walked out of the shoe store in a pair of
burnt-orange imitation alligator-skin loafers that, as I said to Jackie,
looked real enough to bite.

Back on the street, several more women gave me the eye. And these weren't schoolgirls. These were snazzily dressed adult ladies who, I assumed, shared an appreciation for a sharp young man in a trench coat and alligator-like shoes. I dropped my usual guard and imagined what they would look like if I could see through their well-chosen clothes.

Jackie must have been reading my mind then, because he announced, "Enough of this shopping. It's time to relax and unwind."

Five minutes and two blocks later, we were standing beneath the brilliant marquee lights of the Duchess Burlesque Theatre. I felt like my bluff had been called. I'd been fantasizing about how women appeared beneath their clothes; now I was going to be confronted with their actual flesh.

A poster, far too small for the glass display case it occupied, advertised "2 Hot Movies! 10 Hot Girls! 1 Lousy Comedian!" A gray-haired, matronly woman waited impatiently for us at the ticket window, in the middle of which was taped a sign: "All Seats $1.50. Absolutely No One Under 21 Admitted."

"Follow me," Jackie advised. Nonchalant, he walked forward, shoved two dollars through the slot at the bottom of the window, and was given a torn ticket in return. I did the same and received my ticket. The matron neither looked at me nor gave me my 50 cents change. I decided not to quibble.

"It's the price we pay for being underage," Jackie cracked. I found it hard to laugh, certain that at any moment the bearded man playing solitaire behind the refreshment counter would call the cops or perform a citizen's arrest. Instead, he handed each of us a clammy, paper-wrapped hot dog and said, "There's a two-dollar food minimum each show."

Jackie flipped him a five, told him to keep the change, and pushed through swinging doors into the darkened auditorium. A night scene in a black-and-white film was playing, and we stumbled over a snoring, one-armed man before finding a couple of seats in the next-to-last row. As my eyes adjusted to the inky blackness, I saw that a full two-thirds of the audience was teens; the other one-third consisted of derelicts sleeping or carrying on heated conversations with themselves. A German shepherd roamed the aisles, apparently to keep us all under control. I ate my hot dog and, when I sensed Jackie was glancing at me, tried to act as if smoker films were nothing new.

The movie concerned a lonely plumber who was caught spying on women undressing to their girdles in the dingy apartment building across the street from his own. With the police on his trail, he escaped to Hell via a manhole cover, where he was greeted by Satan wearing a buttoned union suit with a pointed tail.

A second film was a stormy melodrama in which a wife tormented her crippled husband by staging orgies at his feet. Scenes of heavy petting were intercut with footage of giant waves crashing on rocks. In the final orgy, the actors never removed their industrial-strength underwear.

"Chip would've dynamited the screen," Jackie yawned. I had the opposite reaction: I could have gladly watched both movies again.

Instead, the house lights came on and the bearded concession manager, dragging a garden hose, announced that it was time for the 7:00 P.M. floor cleaning. As the audience moved to the right side of the theater, he began spraying water under the seats on the left.

Jackie and I exited, and he hailed a cab from the curb. "Tillis Show Bar," he told the cabbie, a snub-nosed man in a brown canvas jacket with his duck-hunting license still safety-pinned across the shoulders. Jackie turned to me and added, "You'll like this place. It's a bar where girls go to meet guys." Five minutes later, on a trash-strewn, dimly lit street, we arrived at our destination: the low-slung

Tillis Show Bar, with the phrase "Workingman's Palace" inlaid in tiles over the front door.

As we stepped out of the cab, a City of Detroit police cruiser was parked to our left, with two uniformed officers leaning against the front fender, talking animatedly to a man in a white, full-length apron. Yet when Jackie and I presented our IDs to a doorman, we were once again allowed inside without question, and the officers barely glanced our way.

The Tillis Show Bar had booths along one wall and a mahogany bar along the other, separated by a narrow, passenger-train-like aisle. Men squeezed past one another down the entire length of the room, spilling mixed drinks, ogling the idle women who sat with their backs to the bar. There was no show, only a jukebox playing scratchy records that often skipped repeatedly before coming to a welcome end.

Jackie and I took a booth and were joined immediately by two women in plain T-shirts and stiff black vinyl shorts. A waitress followed quickly, dropping four beers on the table and requesting twenty dollars, which Jackie paid. The girl seated on my side of the booth was dark-haired, bored, and introduced as Lucretia. Jackie's girl was a blonde who was already nibbling at his ear. He pushed her away momentarily, leaning across the table and whispering to Lucretia, who sighed, lit a Camel, stood up, and said to me, "C'mon."

Instinctively, I obeyed her. As I left the table, Jackie called out, "Be sure to get my money's worth."

I followed Lucretia, who never looked at me, across a side street and upstairs to a first-floor apartment, where she stripped naked and fell backwards on an unmade bed. Lucretia took a drag on the Camel and announced, "You have as long as it takes this cigarette to burn down."

In the spirit of Jackie's admonition, I asked, "Will you be smoking it or putting it in the ashtray?"

"Huh?"

"Well, the cigarette will burn longer in the ashtray than if you're puffing on it. So can I have my choice?"

"Doesn't matter to me, smart kid. This'll be over before you know it."

Lucretia, expert that she was, was correct. My first sexual experience ended while the cigarette still burned in a battered tin ashtray, the chattering cops across the street so distinct it was like they were in the room with us.

I returned alone to where Jackie and I had been sitting. The booth was already occupied by two other men and two other girls. Moments later, Jackie appeared and asked, "How did it go?"

I shrugged and, in an attempt to appear blasé, said, "Just okay." But on the ride back home in the Thunderbird, I was as buoyant as a helium balloon bouncing against the landau top.

Now, lounging in the rear of the cab that was carrying me from my parents' home to Kibbee Flats, I could barely recapture that floating sensation. For a moment I regretted not getting Lucretia's phone number and toyed with the idea of becoming a pimp, driving a maroon Cadillac—one girl in shorts riding shotgun, three more like her in the back seat. Then the cab stopped just short of the flimsy plywood-and-chicken-wire gate that marked the Barron property, and my grandiose sex fantasy was erased by the grim prospect that tonight's Vegas Night was already a bust. Typically, parked cars lined the narrow road that wound past Jackie's house, but this evening there were none, and that greatly unnerved me. The casino was the foundation upon which I had built everything: my friendship with Jackie, which led directly to money, the white trench coat, and even Lucretia.

I paid the cabbie and trotted into the garage; at least Jackie's Thunderbird was present. The kitchen door was unlocked, yet Vera, who usually sat here collecting money, was nowhere to be seen. I hurried downstairs, skirted the lines of drying clothes, and burst through the bamboo curtains that marked Jackie's side of the basement.

Jackie and Mandy were alone in the room. Jackie, wearing a gray sweat suit, baseball hat, and sunglasses, had pulled a chair up to the pool table and was poring over his handwritten financial ledger. Mandy stood nearby, full of nervous energy, rolling a cue stick back and forth across the felt. She was in a black strapless dress cut low across the front and back, like something she'd wear to a prom. Her lips and fingernails were deep red.

"Here's the five bucks I picked up from Buzz Fazio," I said, handing it to Jackie. "So where is everybody else?" I tried to avoid eye contact with Mandy while nevertheless examining her thoroughly. I still had a crush on her, despite my experience with Lucretia.

"I sent them all home," Jackie answered, closing the ledger. He removed his hat, his face and hair nearly washed out by the harsh light of the fixture that hovered over the pool table. From my point of view, he was little more than a pair of oval aviator shades. "I'm shutting Vegas Night down. With the money I've made from the casino, plus other cash, I'm buying my own carnival games. I'll be operating all the joints on Party Time's midway. I won't have to wear jodhpurs and shovel elephant shit anymore."

"We're 50-50 partners. Don't I get a vote?"

"You've done a good job, Pete. But the casino's here in my basement, and with the time I'm going to spend on the carnival joints, I won't be able to give it my full attention." Jackie paused a moment before speaking again. "However, I've been thinking about you. How would you feel about transferring our partnership to the

Party Time Shows circuit? This year's tour starts soon. I'll put you to work as a Hanky Pank agent with the goal of working you up to the top of the ladder on another game called the Flat Store. Sort of letting you earn while you learn. Of course, due to your inexperience, we'll have to adjust the 50-50 arrangement, but eventually we'll work our way back up to an even cut."

I was taken aback. After the countless "jackpots" (that is, wild stories) about Party Time Shows that Jackie had told me, I had been digging at him to give me a shot on the midway—in any capacity. But to offer me the chance to become a true carnival agent, well, it was like he'd finally recognized my potential for success at advanced deceit and treachery. Nonetheless, I decided it would be face-saving to answer, "Let me think about it."

"I hope you say 'yes,' because now that you know how to get money, get clothes, and get laid, you've got all it takes to be a top carnival agent. I put a lot of effort into you."

An annoying banging started upstairs. Jackie ignored it at first, then said, "More suckers. What am I gonna have to do, beat them off with a stave?" He stormed upstairs, leaving Mandy and me alone.

"You went all the way?" Mandy asked, blushing and tipping her head to the side. "You couldn't even look at me in English class."

"I've changed," I said, taking a step closer to her, near enough to see that she was sucking on something—a breath mint? A Life-Saver?

"For the better?"

I shrugged. "Want to cut cards?"

"Why?"

"A game. I draw high card, I get to kiss you."

"What if I do? Draw high card?"

"Winner's choice." Fully aware that Jackie had never told

Mandy about the marked diamondback cards, I shuffled a pack thoroughly and placed it face down on the felt. Keeping her eyes locked on mine, Mandy pulled an eight of hearts. In order to make the game appear close, I drew a nine of clubs. Then, putting the card as a keepsake in a trench coat pocket, I leaned forward toward Mandy. She met me halfway. Our lips touched. Her warmth and the smell of a cherry LifeSaver inspired me, and I pressed harder until our teeth clicked. Mandy responded, her mouth softening and opening. Then she turned aside, snapped open her little black handbag, and began reapplying her lipstick.

I stepped over to the record player and put on a Moms Mabley LP. Now, on top of having experienced sex, I'd achieved my first kiss.

The bamboo clattered. "That was Buzz Fazio," Jackie announced. "He brought this," he said, holding up a five dollar bill. "His first payment. Guess he forgot he already gave it to you."

"He deserves to pay twice just for being so dumb," I sputtered.

The three of us walked upstairs and piled into the Thunderbird. Jackie and Mandy were celebrating his purchase of ten carnival joints with a night in Detroit. I worried, after they dropped me off, whether Mandy would confess our kiss. That concern ended, however, when I lay back in bed, grabbed the *Complete Guide to Gambling,* and turned to the section titled "The Lowdown on Carnival Games."

CHAPTER SIX

Sleeping With Plush

1967

I blew up the balloon, knotted it expertly, and floated it basketball-style into a large cardboard box already brimming with hundreds of penny balloons. My cheeks and jaws ached; I wondered if I was coming down with the mumps. I already had a bad case of the flu, and each time a customer burst a balloon with a dart, I imagined my germs exploding toward them as payback for forcing me to inflate a replacement.

The first marks of the afternoon waddled toward my embarrassingly simple game, the Balloon Dart Toss. Lloyce and Jorge had won the Fattest Wife/Skinniest Husband contest that Party Time Shows had held the day before. Lloyce, a self-described housewife, had weighed in at 480 pounds. Her husband, Jorge, a shy Mexican farm worker, had tipped the scales at 125. They'd been awarded $250, and I thought it would help my mood to win some of it back.

Overnight, the temperature had plunged to thirty-five degrees, and a freak late April snow had dusted Pontiac, Michigan, a declining car town about fifteen miles north of Mineralton. I'd awakened on the plywood floor of the thirty-foot-long trailer that contained the Balloon Dart and another game called the Duck Pond, sweaty and shivering beneath a mound of gaudily colored stuffed snakes, teddy bears, giraffes, and turtles. The "plush" had served as my blanket, with a burning candle beside my head for extra warmth, or so I hoped. I'd been sleeping that way for over two weeks, since the carnival season had opened, resulting in the energy-sapping malaise that made me wish my mother was there to tuck an extra teddy bear under my chin. But my relations with my parents had declined so precipitously that I'd decided to live on the road and commute to school until I graduated in mid-June. After that, I'd remain with Party Time Shows for the summer, working to ensure that Jackie came through on his promise that, if I exhibited a talent for talking people like Lloyce out of their money, I'd move on to something better than inflating balloons and dodging darts.

My entry into the carnival had been delayed by a year. The prior summer, Chip had invoked a clause in Jackie's contract that required him to perform in the Free Circus for the entire season. Fortunately, when Jackie returned, our friendship took up where it had left off: We spent our senior year at MHS in the pursuit of cash, playing the stock market and the horses, despite our mutual abhorrence of gambling. With our casino permanently closed due to the increased scrutiny of school authorities, stocks and horses provided the only available action—and, like Jackie, I had grown fond of experiencing the jolt. We lost big; while this barely dented Jackie's huge bankroll, I was left nearly broke, which Jackie used to his advantage in assigning me to hustle five-year-old kids and their moms.

"I'll settle for ten bucks, Lloyce," I mumbled, kicking aside the stuffed animals to create standing room in front of the dartboard, "the price of a motel room."

Acknowledging a giggling pair of boys who recognized her

from the contest, Lloyce squished ankle-deep through hay and mud. The midway was located that week at the bottom of an empty, sloping lot off Wide Track Boulevard in the heart of downtown Pontiac. Rain and melting snow had settled there, and even several tons of hay had not sopped up all of the standing water. The mud reached mid-calf in spots; that, however, did little to dissuade the locals from descending upon the show. Such was the sad state of entertainment in Pontiac, where entire city blocks had been leveled for an urban renewal project that had fizzled before the rebuilding stage. It was in this undemanding environment that Lloyce had already achieved celebrity status: There were now more children trailing in her wake than there were "lot lice" staring at Channel 9's Bozo the Clown, who was refusing to exit his panel truck and parade through the slop.

"Say, pretty lady, where's your trophy?" I shouted at Lloyce over the roar of the mammoth orange generator supplying power to the carnival's games, rides, and food stands. The grimy, grease-oozing machine was mounted on an open flatbed trailer behind a semi-truck, thick black cables spreading from it, octopuslike, to all points of the midway. Several children's games like mine were located at this end of the lot, called the "doniker" because of the trio of Port-A-Johns stationed there. The reasoning, according to Jackie, was simple: Kids needed to go potty a lot, and en route they would badger Mommy into spending a few quarters on the games. The odor of the toilets mingled with the smoky tang of diesel fumes to create an overwhelming stench, the only potential advantage of which was, in the words of Talking Tony, a fellow carny, "You could crap in your shorts and no one would know."

"I want to pick up some ducks," Lloyce bawled insistently, banging a quarter on the plywood counter of the Duck Pond game a few steps to my left. Today she had fame and demanded immediate attention. Tomorrow she'd be back on her reinforced couch with only her silent husband and a bag of fried pork rinds.

"You have a customer, Tony," I hollered, my raspy voice quickly lost in the generator din. Talking Tony was a veteran agent whom Jackie had demoted for undisclosed reasons to the Duck Pond, which, like the Balloon Dart, was a child's game. Angry and humiliated, Talking Tony was seldom behind the counter, forcing me to cover for him, which I hated. At least the Balloon Dart had an arguable danger: I could be accidentally punctured by a poorly thrown dart. The typical Duck Pond mark was a three-year-old held up by Mommy, and all the harm one of those could cause was a wet burp on my wrist. Lloyce, though, could still have the better part of $250 on her person, so when Talking Tony didn't appear, I swallowed my pride and smiled.

"Be right with you, ma'am," I announced, climbing gingerly over the box of balloons into the Duck Pond. The two games were mounted side by side in the corrugated aluminum-clad trailer, built to Jackie's specifications that winter. Fluorescent tubing lit an interior "flashed" with plush stuffed animals dangling on hooks and stacked boxes of "slum," or cheap giveaways, like rubber worms, Chinese handcuffs, and plastic baseballs the size of a thumb. An unplugged GE portable TV rested on a bed of red velour stapled to a high shelf behind me.

The front end of the Duck Pond contained a stainless steel basin shaped like a horse race track, the back stretch of which was covered by a section of plywood to form a tunnel. A jet of water powered by a hydraulic pump pushed dozens of bobbing ducks endlessly around the circuit. Each pink duck had a number painted on the bottom that corresponded to a piece of flash. A customer who picked up duck #7, for instance, won a bubblegum cigar. If he selected duck #28, he'd win the grand prize, the GE TV.

"Do I still have to pay a quarter to play?" Lloyce whined. "I mean, shouldn't I get a discount, you know, because I won the contest, or something?"

On a day when all I wanted to do was be sick and sleep, her request especially irked me. It seemed like every mark wanted a special deal. Pretty girls because they were pretty girls, lawyers because they were lawyers, and Lloyce because she weighed 480 pounds. Only the girls lucked out with me. "A discount?" I countered. "If anything, I should be charging you more because you won that money yesterday."

"Why do I even bother to ask a favor from one of you lousy carnival people? Here, take your lousy quarter." Lloyce tossed it on the counter, screwing her mouth into a tiny pout. I placed it in the white carpenter's apron I had just tied over my black dungarees and red corduroy shirt. Lloyce's jaw was set tight. Her thin brown hair had been pulled into a bun the size of a clenched fist. She wore a daisy print muumuu under a lime green windbreaker and was leaning against the circulating pond, her overhanging flesh impeding the ducks' progress.

"Stand back a little, would you?" Exhausted and chilled, I was quickly growing impatient.

"Don't be telling me what to do."

"The ducks can't move around the pond."

"Show me the rule book that says they have to."

"Listen, if the ducks can't travel, you'll be able to pick the ones with the best prize-winning numbers again and again. I have a half-dozen people try the same scam every day, so back off."

"You listen, kid," Lloyce announced, standing erect and freeing the ducks to wobble and spin forward, "my cousin lives next door to a state cop, so don't start making false accusations." She drew two rolls of quarters from her jacket pocket. "I'm aiming at winning that

TV of yours and I've got more quarters here than you've got ducks in that pond. So if I don't win the GE, you're exposed as a cheater. And I get on the horn to my cousin."

"That's entirely your right, ma'am," I said. I ran my hand through my hair and smelled the Vitalis on my fingers, a nervous habit I was trying to shake. I had an incipient blond moustache and now wore my hair longer, sweeping it behind my ears (having decided, after a lengthy bout with a Gulf restroom mirror, that I looked too much like a pro golfer contemplating his club choice on a fairway at Pebble Beach). I was now in position to take Lloyce for a good piece of change; all I had to do was follow the simple rules of the scam Jackie had taught me.

First, while pretending to clear the pond of debris, I hid the #28 duck—the GE portable TV—within the tunnel the ducks passed through on their journey. That was the only prize worth more than a quarter, and I would not return it to the water until Lloyce ran out of cash. Next, I checked the lever that I could use to release up to three hundred additional ducks hidden in a chamber beneath the counter.

"Now, give me another quarter and you're ready to play," I told Lloyce.

"Fifty cents a duck? Who in heaven's name ever heard of a carnival charging fifty cents a duck?"

"You're correct. We usually charge a quarter, but this afternoon it's fifty cents. The boss is contributing the extra money to a good cause." Her bad attitude had inspired me to spontaneously double the price.

"Like a charity?"

"Maybe something better than that."

"What's better than charity?"

"I'm under orders not to say."

Suspicious, Lloyce slapped a second quarter into my hand. I dropped it into the carpenter's apron. Lloyce extracted a duck from the water.

"Number twelve," I announced loudly, so that the growing clot of adults and lot lice could hear. I presented Lloyce with the #12 prize, a Taiwanese paper bird whistle.

She glowered at me, harboring her quarters. Then she peeled two more from a roll and picked up a duck.

"Thirty-four," I said and handed Lloyce a one-inch-by-one-inch Confederate flag.

Over the next hour, the slum piled up before Lloyce. As she became more antagonistic, I tried my best to prod her into quitting, in order to ward off a final explosion of cop-calling anger. Yet she refused to give up her quest to win the TV until, $79.50 in the hole, she claimed to have run out of money. That was a worry. To say the least, it didn't look good for Lloyce to have picked up 159 ducks without winning the grand prize, particularly with a large tip of onlookers surrounding her and Jorge, who seemed only dimly aware of what Lloyce was up to. "Didn't you win $250 in the contest last night?" I asked, planning to cool her off with a teddy-bear consolation prize the very next time she picked up a duck. Maybe even throw in a plush purple snake.

"I'm broke. My husband lost big trying to win a set of dishes we needed. You know, if my cousin got his cop buddy to come here, I bet even he couldn't find a duck that wins the TV," Lloyce said accusingly, as a heavy shower began drumming on the aluminum awning over the Duck Pond, compressing the crowd of gawkers into an irritable, tightly packed square.

"The lady's probably right about things being fixed," a deep male voice called out. "I lost thirty dollars from some bastard carny down at the end of the lot." He was standing at the edge of the tip and rain was sheeting off his Caterpillar hat, rendering him unrecognizable.

"I got took for twenty bucks yesterday," yelled a woman in a T-shirt, shorts, and heavy winter coat. Several other members of the crowd loudly voiced their own complaints.

Reflexively, I brought my fingertips to my nose. Jackie had told me time and again that the Duck Pond was an easy game on which to break into the carnival business. I had believed that Lloyce would lose twenty or thirty times, swear at me, and leave. Instead, I had an angry, captive tip to contend with. The crowd was demanding justice, yet Jackie had made me promise never to give the GE away because he liked to watch it in his house trailer at night.

"See, I'm not the only one you people have robbed," the Cat hat guy said, waving his finger at me. Others in the crowd shouted agreement. The entire group closed in, its anger buffeting me. I couldn't believe that I had a potential riot on my hands, at the Duck Pond, a drooling *child's game*. Jackie had given me the chance to rise to the top ranks of carnival game agents, and I was blowing Little League.

A familiar voice startled me. It was Jackie, goddamit, arriving at my moment of weakness, wearing a yellow rain slicker complete with floppy seafarer's rain hat. Fat canvas money bags were crammed in either pocket, a few bills on the verge of spilling out. He pushed through the crowd, speaking loudly to the doubting man (or "knocker") in the Cat hat. "Mac, you're the kind of guy God would have to kiss on the cheek to turn into a believer. My man here is bonded for honesty. He teaches blind kids Braille in his spare time. He's one of the few Boy Scouts with more merit badges than pimples. Hey, just look at this angelic face." Jackie pinched my cheeks. I reddened, furious that Jackie had decided I needed his help.

"Who the holy hell you think you are, boy?" the knocker bellowed at Jackie. He forced his way to the front of the Duck Pond, planting himself beside Jackie.

Jackie stared at his accuser, his glasses slipping down his rain-splattered nose. He pushed them back up. "I happen to own all the games on this midway, my friend. You could pump gas all year and not make as much as I do in a week."

"I'm calling your bluff, punk," the knocker screamed. "And here's how I'm gonna do it. I'm buying every duck in that pond, and if there ain't one that wins the TV, I'm hauling you and your buddy in on a citizen's arrest."

Jackie whispered in my ear, "I hope you have #28 hidden where it's supposed to be."

"Of course," I answered, stifling the urge to peer inside the tunnel and make sure.

"Here's a damn hundred dollar bill," the knocker proclaimed, shoving it into my hand. "Now stand back 'cause I'm going to start turning over those ducks."

I looked at him closely for the first time. His face dripped water and his neck muscles were stretched taut, giving him the appearance of a snapping turtle about to bite. Despite that, I now recognized him. It was Buzz Fazio, former captain of the Magnificent Minerals basketball team, with a full beard, bib overalls, and bare torso covered with axle grease and Band-Aids. I'd seen little of Buzz since he'd paid off his gambling debt. I moved to warn Jackie, succeeding only in bumping him against the counter—where, pretending to balance himself, Jackie reached into the tunnel and returned the #28 duck to the water with a deft flick of the wrist.

"Don't worry," Jackie whispered to me again, "I know it's Buzz. I hired him yesterday to work on the rides."

With that hushed announcement, I quickly relaxed. I was struck by the crazy impulse to ask the crowd to applaud Jackie for the great job he was doing in bamboozling them. Instead, I watched in closemouthed admiration as Buzz turned over duck after duck, finally revealing #28 with a phony, joyous whoop.

"Hallelujah! We got a winner here!" Jackie cried, dancing a little jig. "TV, TV, TV—come on, everybody say it—TV, TV, TV." Jackie got a few kids to chant along as he presented the portable set to Buzz with a practiced flourish. Buzz splashed across the midway with the television atop his head as the sun momentarily cut through the thunderheads above.

Jackie nodded to me and we began dumping dozens of ducks back in the water—all but #28, which I returned to its spot inside the tunnel. With Buzz in the background, excitedly telling the curious where he had won, Lloyce considered for a moment, then raised her right foot and ordered Jorge to remove a twenty dollar bill from her plastic-soled blue moccasin.

"You have more TVs like that one?" she asked as I made change.

"I received a new shipment this morning. They're still in boxes out back, untouched by human hands." Sure.

While the rest of the once-unruly mob dispersed quietly, several more chastened hecklers stepped forward to press quarters on me. Whether it was wise for the fairgoers who had been threatening me to change their attitude toward the Duck Pond so abruptly, from unabashed fury to fighting one another to become the next big winner—simply because one scruffy guy had won a portable TV—was open to debate, but I found throughout my career as a carnival game agent that it wasn't productive to question the behavior of anyone who found strolling down a dung-strewn midway appealing. A more sensible approach was to shut up and keep taking the money.

Not that this made me feel better about the current state of my talent to manipulate others, because the angry crowd's sudden transformation was all Jackie's doing. "Now that's how you get yourself out of a rhubarb," Jackie said, frowning, as he departed. Despite my recently acquired ability to grow facial hair and the pride of a developing musculature, my emotions still rose and fell with the fluttering wind. Before the rhubarb, despite my illness, I'd felt like a con-man stud in tight pants. Now my jeans seemed baggy, and I wondered if I could talk my way out of a parking ticket. Jackie's tour de force had shattered that illusion.

I tried to console myself with the belief, instilled in me by Jackie, that on the midway my entire life could change at a moment's notice. I might win a G-note from the next mark or get laid by the next girl, right there in the Duck Pond. Even though neither of these events had yet happened to me, it was their possibility that was enticing. I'd been "with it" two short weeks, and was already under the spell of Party Time Shows: the sudden action, the Lloyces, the belligerent drunks, the runaway girls, and the overwhelming roar of the 600-horsepower generator pumping electricity to the battered orange rides, whirling, clanking, screeching, metal on metal. Then there were the smells: the stink of the diesel smoke billowing from the generator, the aroma of popcorn, cotton candy, fresh hay, oil, grease, sweat, beer, shit, and above all, the smell of money. It was like setting foot onto a junked-up, neon-lit planet, a tawdry, traveling Times Square where no one cared about who I was or where I came from because they assumed that any story I, a fellow carny, told was a lie. So why bother listening in the first place?

Every night in Jackie's silver Airstream trailer, he and I would count the proceeds from every one of his joints, emptying the canvas money bags onto the kitchen table, filling the room with the bitter odor of commerce. The count, as at the casino, was what the carnival was all about: dark pennies with Abe Lincoln nearly rubbed off, buffalo nickels, old dimes, nicked quarters, and worn-out singles, fives, and tens that had passed through tens of thousands of hands before arriving, for the time being, in ours. I loved every cent, even the silver-gray hue my palms took on after an evening's accounting. Money wasn't a confusing, polysyllabic word that, when used in conversation, raised the hackles of the metal-shop crowd. Everyone understood the concept of a buck.

I'd been running the Balloon Dart/Duck Pond trailer since the carnival season had started in a Sears parking lot in Warren, Michigan, commuting to school with Jackie in his Cadillac or on the Yamaha motorcycle I'd purchased when I was flush. As manager, I received twenty dollars a week, plus ten percent of whatever money I personally brought in, which had earned me a hundred and fifty dollars during our six-day stay in Warren and next to nothing in dismal Pontiac.

Still, there was always the chance. And at dusk, as I "sloughed," or closed the joints, a rough count showed that today my end of the take would be around thirty bucks, more than enough to pay for a warm, dry motel room. The surprisingly high gross was in large part due to the tip that Jackie had helped build—the quarters flew in for an hour or so after he walked away. Yet I remained pissed off enough at his meddling that I needed to let him know that I could have handled Lloyce without his intervention. Even though a part of me wasn't so sure.

I wrapped the heavy money bag in an old shirt, tucked it under my arm, shuttered and padlocked the sturdy aluminum awnings and door, and stepped onto the midway, alert for lurking strangers. As I hurried toward Jackie's Airstream, a purple Eldorado convertible shuddered to a stop near the darkened Ferris wheel, blocking my path. Simultaneously, a mudball fight erupted among a half-dozen off-duty ride operators, one errant missile splattering the Cadillac's buttoned-down, black cloth convertible top. Talking Tony, the tall, bony driver, with a streak of white in his otherwise jet black hair, wearing a short red leather jacket, purple double-knit pants, a ruffled red shirt and white vest, and purple patent leather shoes, switched off the engine and scrambled to his feet atop the worn leather seat. He stomped on the basso profundo horn with his foot, released it, and shouted, "Listen up, my little Ride Boys. Even the tiniest of teeny-tiny scratches on this Eldo costs five yards to repair. So unless you want a bill for five hundred dollars chasing your ass, you'd better go play in the mud some-fucking-where else."

"That refuge from a scrapyard must have twenty thousand dollars in damage already," one Ride Boy called out over his shoulder as the mud fight skittered off down the midway.

"Your goddamn momma it does," Talking Tony answered feebly, then smoothed his pants and slid back behind the wheel. The Ride Boy had obviously touched a sensitive nerve, because the Eldorado that Tony had recently purchased for a song was a very used vehicle. The driver's side of the car was sleek, immaculate, and impressive. But from tail fin to headlights, the entire passenger side was caved in—the chrome, door handles, and paint destroyed by a Peterbilt that had sideswiped the Eldo as it idled, double-parked, while the previous owner dashed into a Pontiac liquor store. Passengers now achieved entry and exit by climbing over the doors, taking care not to tear clothes or flesh on the jagged bodywork. The convertible top was jammed in the down position permanently, which was why Tony was now blotting the standing water on the dashboard with a Holiday Inn towel.

"How can you afford to stay at the Holiday Inn when you didn't work all afternoon?" I asked Tony.

"I'm frugal."

I had a better answer. I suspected that Talking Tony had started to "H.O.," or hold out money from Jackie. While I'd never met Tony before Jackie had inserted him beside me in the Duck Pond, he was indeed quite a talker, and one day he'd told me that we each should have been getting twenty-five percent of our daily take rather than the ten-percent cut Jackie offered. And when something insulting like that happened, Tony said, when your boss screwed you, as a general rule any carny who wasn't an ignorant fool simply held out his rightful percentage, the one that God had ordained when he'd written the chapter on carnies in the Holy Bible.

I kept mum despite Tony's slumping returns. If Tony wanted to steal, that was his business. I, on the other hand, would keep taking my ten-percent cut, even though it meant sleeping under stuffed toys some evenings. I had no problem removing money from marks: They were greedy squirrels trying to get something for nothing. But to H.O. money from Jackie was dishonest. I'd never cheated a friend in my life, except for most of the kids I'd known at MHS, but then, they, well—that's where my thinking on the matter typically shorted out.

"Where you heading?" Tony asked.

"The Airstream."

"I'll drive you. Hey, about today. No hard feelings, okay? I had an appointment to clean the Eldo at the car wash that ran a little long."

"You missed a good tip." Ultimately, his absence had earned me a motel room, so I no longer cared.

Tony gunned the car, and we splashed toward a gathering of house trailers ten yards behind the midway. Trailers were a carny status symbol. On Party Time Shows, few owned them other than the Barrons, and those who did advertised their status by wearing baseball hats with Fleetwood, Coachmen, or another manufacturer embroidered across the crown. It didn't matter that their trailers were often damaged goods, like Tony's Eldo, or in danger of being repossessed, which was one more reason to move from town to town every week. But only Jackie lived in an Airstream: the top of the heap, sleek and silver-bullet shaped, like a 1930s airliner. And it was paid for, in cash.

"I drive everywhere I can in this kind of weather," Tony said as we bounced over rutted turf. "No way am I gonna get these ninety-buck shoes muddy. You like 'em?"

"Sure do," I answered, and in truth, I did. I had acquired a growing taste for sharp apparel. I'd also found that Tony, like most carnies, had a fragile ego that could explode in scary directions when injured, so it was always wiser to play along. Despite Tony's incessant jabbering, I knew little about him—his real name, where he'd come from, what he'd done for a living before launching what carnies termed a "show business" career. Tony didn't hold a driver's license, not even the fake out-of-state type, so that former friends, acquaintances, and the law would have a harder time tracking him down. I'd accepted that Tony and other carnies were simply who they told you they were, and it was better to leave it at that. Though in Tony's case, I had an inkling of his true marital history, thanks to a forearm tattoo that read "I Love My X-Wife."

Tony pulled the Eldorado within a foot of Jackie's Airstream, shut off the engine, then climbed directly from the car to the trailer's grated front steps. "Got to watch the shoes," he explained.

I walked across the sodden leather seats to join him just as Jackie opened the riveted silver door. Dressed in red and blue striped pajamas, a royal blue terrycloth bathrobe, and leather slippers, he'd obviously been napping. "Let's get this over quick," he said, rubbing an eye, "I've got a girl supposed to be here in an hour." I tried to hide familiar feelings of longing and jealousy behind a knowing laugh. Losing my virginity across the street from the Tillis Show Bar hadn't given me Jackie's ease with real girls, the sort who could recite the symbols of the major chemical elements. It had damned me, however, with a vague sense of what I was missing. Jackie, meanwhile, enjoyed a wide assortment of female companions. He even continued to see Mandy, who remained the real girl I wanted more than any other, even though I was petrified about letting her know without a rock-solid, written-in-blood guarantee that I wouldn't be rejected. I wasn't worried about the impact this theoretical romance with Mandy would have on Jackie. One of Jackie's own aphorisms was, "Cheating is only meaningful when it involves money."

The Airstream, which was only two months old, was already littered with dirty clothes, half-finished TV dinners, money wrappers, and unopened mail. Drying clumps of hay and mud, interspersed with coins and crumpled-up paper money, marked the royal-blue shag rug. Jackie plopped down on one of the thin crimson cushions that flanked the small, fold-out dinette table, right behind a humming gray NCR adding machine. Now seventeen, Jackie had developed a slight paunch that he tried to keep in check by drinking orange juice for dinner. Slumping against a dozen plump money bags, one for every joint he owned on the midway, Jackie emptied a particularly well-stuffed bag onto the tiny table and said, yawning, "I'll take the coins, you take the bills," which was the opposite of what he proposed nearly every night. I wondered, probably much more than necessary, what the switch meant, why this time he was taking on the most tedious job.

Jackie had changed fundamentally since we'd gone on the road, and I was often unsure about where our friendship stood. I'd become resigned to Jackie's bullshit since well before our casino days—the twenty bucks here, thirty bucks there that he instinctively

tried to nick from me. I'd taken it as a form of rough male cama-
raderie, like when fraternity brothers bomb unsuspecting pledges
with urine-filled water balloons.

Yet Party Time Shows was Jackie's true work, not a high school
lark, and here I was starting to feel like just one of many employees.
Today, at the Duck Pond, Jackie had been relatively playful. More
typically, he walked the midway with a serious, even grim mien,
toting a yellow legal pad on which he took mysterious notes.

A few days before, when I'd asked him why, he'd said, "These
assholes—the agents like Talking Tony—think I'm too young to be
owning joints. Most of them haven't owned a dog they didn't con
from some kid, and they resent me, like I haven't earned my stripes
even though I've been in show business since I was six. They think I
don't deserve it. They're stealing me blind just on principle, if you
can believe that. So I try to scare them. Like making notes, pretending to count every buck that comes in. I'm usually just scribbling,
but what do they know? Believe me, Pete, these guys may be good
for a laugh, but they're pukes at heart, which is why I've got plans
for you. You're the only one who I know won't rob me."

Talking Tony approached the dinette. "Need another helping
hand?" he asked. Tony was always anxious to please Jackie, as if that
would blind him to his stealing.

A faint hint of amusement crept across Jackie's face, the vague
smile he had when regarding all but a few of his employees. "I
wouldn't want you to ruin your manicure," he replied.

I completed my count of the paper money. "Two hundred and
eighty-five in green stuff," I announced, neatening the bills into an
even pile.

"Who needs NCR with you around?" Jackie cracked.

"I can count fast. So what?"

"What's to get mad about?"

"Counting comes easy. I want to be recognized for pulling off hard shit. Like working my way out of that rhubarb this afternoon. I could've done it."

"I happened to be walking by, that's all," Jackie replied, a little taken aback. He was unaccustomed to my increasingly frequent harangues.

"Sure, and you just happened to bring Buzz along with you to shill."

Jackie threw up his hands. "Okay. All right. I saw a big tip at the Duck Pond and thought you might be getting into a little trouble."

"The only real trouble is that I'm still blowing up balloons and playing with ducks after two weeks on the job." I was surprised at how easily the angry words rolled off my tongue.

Jackie massaged the bridge of his nose. He'd been coming down with more migraines lately, particularly when marks weren't spending or he came within an arm's length of Chip. "Tony, could you go outside for a while and steal hubcaps or something?"

Talking Tony gave Jackie an elaborate salute, while slipping a roll of quarters from the table into his pocket. "How about I meet you duds—I mean dudes—at that lounge down Wide Track Boulevard when you're done?"

"We'll think about it," Jackie nodded, staring at Tony's pocket, breaking into his half-smile again.

Oblivious that Jackie had caught him, Tony stepped from the Airstream into the Eldo, humming the merry-go-round's theme music, a jangling nursery-rhyme melody that I had been trying, unsuccessfully, to get out of my head.

Jackie pushed aside the pile of coins before him and looked me in the eyes, which was unnerving because he did it so infrequently. "Listen, Pete. Most people don't get promoted after two screaming weeks on a new job. But I meant what I said. I want to build you up into a

Flat Store agent. First off, though, you need to work the Hanky Panks for a while, which you're doing. Next, you'll graduate to the Alibis and after you've got them down pat, it's the Flat Store, I promise."

I fidgeted in my seat, suddenly restless and itchy with doubt. I'd learned a lot about Flatties—the carnies who worked the Flat Store—by listening and watching. Flatties fascinated me. They wore golf hats and silk shirts, and they received pedicures. They could afford a house trailer or a room at the Sheraton. They worked inside a riveted, steel-clad trailer that could withstand a bazooka attack. A top Flattie could even eat a T-bone while working his mark for thousands of dollars. But those were arcane traits I hadn't developed studying for the SATs. I told Jackie so.

"Don't sell yourself short. You've got your own unique assets. You're smart. You can figure out trigonometry and memorize Shakespeare's sonnets. And you don't mind screwing anyone, even people you know. Given that, it's my theory that you can learn to work the Flat Store better than any kindergarten dropout who's been at it for twenty years. They all H.O. too much, anyway. You might win less from each mark, but at least you'll be handing me my fair share of the take. And you'll be the youngest Flattie in this nation's history, by far. How's that feel?"

"It wouldn't hurt to become the youngest at something." I knew a good part of Jackie's speech was pure bullshit, but I still found it reassuring, even inspiring.

Jackie walked to the refrigerator, removed a half-gallon of orange juice, and returned to the dinette table, where he poured two drinks in smudged glasses. "Best of all, Pete, you're not a puke," he added. "My parents are pukes. My brother is chief puke. And Talking Tony's a puke for H.O.ing on me."

"First, thanks for the compliment. But you know about Tony?" I was surprised.

"It wasn't hard to figure out. When you add it up, I've probably paid for the smooth half of his Eldorado." Jackie raised his glass in a toast. "To our friendship and continued business success."

Of course, I agreed. I slept soundly that night in my "Always $8" motel room, other than for a brief nightmare about a gang of sad-eyed teddy bears scratching in vain at the door. When I woke up to the faraway sound of the diesel generator, my fever had broken. I rolled over and drew aside the torn plastic shade, allowing an oblong of dazzling sunlight to warm my head. Spring was back with a vengeance. I dressed in a hurry; there was money to be made.

CHAPTER SEVEN

Stepping Off a Rackets Show

"This is a rackets show, High School. There's not nothing here that ain't illegal, phony, or fixed, and that's what I find so refreshing about Party Time Shows," Horserace Harry observed.

It was eleven in the morning, and Horserace and I were leaning on our elbows against the Swinger, an Alibi joint that Jackie had ordered Horserace to teach me only a few minutes before. Several weeks earlier, Jackie had transferred me out of the Hanky Pank trailer, but only in a lateral move to the Color Game, another simple joint where I earned a flat twenty-five dollars a day. I'd had to prod Jackie to get me schooled on the more challenging Swinger, where I could bring in serious money. Why Jackie was making it so hard on me to advance after his promise of rapid promotion, I didn't know, other than his competitive instinct had kicked in. Everything with Jackie was a test. As a result I was in a state of high emotional agitation, my digestive tract a bubbling cauldron of early morning popcorn, grilled sausage, excitement, and anger.

The Swinger was a lime green tent framed by sturdy two-by-fours painted the same color. Along the front of the joint, three wooden coat hangers were nailed down at yard-wide intervals on a chest-high plywood counter. A varnished bowling pin rested in the crux of each coat hanger. A croquet ball dangled from a chain above each pin. At the rear of the tent, four ascending shelves lined with black velour served as a backdrop, flashed with "Five-Minute Create Your Own Chrome Kits," teddy bears, "Amazing Waterless Steam Irons," and a vast selection of counterfeit watches carrying slightly misspelled brand names (Bolivia rather than Bulova, Temix instead of Timex), known as "blocks" by the trade.

There was purely a festive spirit in the parking lot of the brand new Kmart in Marble City, Michigan, where Party Time Shows had been hired to enhance the fun of the grand opening celebration. A rainbow of helium balloons bobbed over the store entrance, where a local newspaper columnist dressed as a clown offered children free snow cones and the high school cheerleading squad gave away miniature boxes of popcorn and free Cokes in tiny Dixie cups. A disk jockey doing a live remote interviewed thrilled Kmart shoppers as they entered the premises, after which the store manager presented each adult with a leaflet outlining his professional background and the Kmart retail philosophy.

"You see," Horserace continued, "in the old days every midway had sideshows with those goddamn freaks suckin' up money right and left. Yeah, all the rubes wanted to see the Fat Man or the Woman with Whiskers, or the fool with three noses or what have you. And those freaks raked in the dough, believe me. I once knew this broad who had an extra finger on each hand and drove a Lincoln Continental and had a winter home in Savannah, Georgia. Can you believe that? Getting rich just because she had twelve fingers, with the extra one only being some nub sticking out at the base of her pinkie finger? Some people may have felt sorry for the freaks when every state banned them for health reasons or good taste, or so on, but not me. My income went up by twenty percent the day that the state of Indiana, where I was at the time, sloughed the sideshows. I offered to buy the Continental from the six-fingered lady 'cause she probably couldn't afford it no more, but she gave me the finger and said 'F.U.,' and I guarantee the particular finger she gave me wasn't that little nub. I heard later the bank repossessed the car anyway, but that's show business, she should've known that. There are no guarantees, you hear what I'm sayin'?"

"How could I not? You're two feet away."

"That was what you high school seniors would call a rhetorical question."

"So keep talking." I was always ready to hear veteran carnies "cut up jackpots," or tell tales that may or may not have been true, based on the theory that absorbing their bull would help me become equally adept at shooting the shit. Because I was discovering that on the midway, career success was a function not of the veracity of what I said, but how believable I made it sound.

"Anyway, with the freaks gone, the question for carnival owners was which way to go to fill out the midway—more rides, which would win you more church dates and more legitimacy, but less money—or more games and more money, but bigger heat from marks, cops, and other authorities. So I got to hand it to Double-O and the boys that they pointed Party Time Shows down the path of true carnival purity, which is screwin' lots of people as fast as you can, then getting the hell out of town, with all them angry folks just nipping at your heels. Yes, this is a rackets show, High School. Spin yourself around in a circle; everything you see for the full 360 degrees is illegitimate, from the phony games like the Buckets to the ice-cold hot dogs to the rides that are more risky than steering a Roman candle into outer space. It's enough to make a petty criminal's heart go pitty-pat, not that you or I fit that category, right?"

"Is that another rhetorical question, or should I answer?"

"Up to you," Horserace shrugged, and took a final swig from the tall can of Colt .45 he'd hidden behind a giant stuffed Snoopy chained to an awning rod. Short, round, and brown, like a root-beer hard candy, Horserace was bald this week, after giving his toupee to Jackie as collateral against an advance in pay. Horserace was addicted to playing the horses, and it was possible to tell how he was faring by whether he was wearing his hair. His luck was usually bad, and he often peered into the distance with a pained expression, as if watching a sure-thing stakes winner pull up lame.

"Mind if I take a short break to find us more tall, cool ones?" he asked me. "There's a party store a little bit down the road from Kmart."

"When you come back, I'm getting my lesson, right?"

"Sure as shooting, High School," Horserace said, then hooked his arm around my neck and whispered conspiratorially. "Listen, don't tell Whitey or Phil this 'cause of the embarrassment angle, but I'm runnin' a little short today. Could you front me a double saw-buck? Pay you back the exact minute we count up tonight."

"Sorry, don't have it," I answered. I had just five bucks in my back pocket, which allowed me to answer honestly.

"Fine, fine. No hard feelings, I promise. Won't kick your ass, or nothin'. Just wanted to see if a socialite-type like you had the heart to help a brother in need."

"Wish I could've, sincerely." Not really. If I'd been awarded a dollar for every time a fellow carny had asked me for money, I would have had enough to give Horserace his twenty and much more. Carnies were nearly always "on," as ready to nick or ding their coworkers, pals, or even loved ones as they were midway marks. I'd become cautious to an extreme around them. Even during convivial moments like this one, I kept up my guard. Holding my own with my new friends was as intoxicating as extracting money from strangers.

As he left, morose, Horserace tossed the emptied Colt .45 over the broad plywood counter into the small, squared-off tent, where it landed on a pile of refuse consisting of soggy Kentucky Fried Chicken buckets, gnawed pork ribs, several cases' worth of empties, a broken bat, stiff pizza wedges, and a copy of *Billboard*. At the rear of the ten-foot-by-ten-foot joint, Philadelphia Phil and Whitey, the other Swinger agents, played a desultory game of poker. They were listening to a raspy car stereo speaker hooked up to a battered van parked behind the tent.

Whitey kept the air from becoming too fetid by raising a section of the canvas with his foot. His high cheekbones and sallow, sunken cheeks transformed his face into a skull, the waxen candle-type with a wick in the crown. Whitey's fine blond hair was combed into a pompadour disintegrating under its own weight. He believed without a doubt that Hitler was still alive, because "he had a plan, man, and anybody with a plan doesn't just die, even a pig turd like him." Whitey's own master plan consisted of hiding bottles of Boone's Farm wine in and around the midway so that in a personal or even national emergency, he would never die of thirst.

Coincidentally, Philadelphia Phil sported a black, Hitler-style haircut and moustache. He had no lower front teeth, a strong Brooklyn accent, and an unusual sense of humor, to wit: "You know why I call myself Philadelphia? Because I'm from Brooklyn—so to throw people a curve ball and put a smile on their face." Phil claimed to hold a graduate degree in pharmacy from NYU. Old, thick scars ran the entire length of every vein in his forearm; the end product, he said, "of a heavy schedule of homework in my youth."

The Swinger had the premier location among Alibi stores that week. It was the first "strong," or powerful moneymaker on the left-handed midway, the side of the lot where most marks entered and ran the gauntlet of games before escaping into the Kmart with what cash remained of their tight household budgets.

There were three types of carnival games: Hanky Panks, Alibis, and Flat Stores. Which one you worked, as Jackie had made clear, determined where you stood in the rigid hierarchy of the midway.

Hanky Pank agents occupied the lowest rung, with little more status than Ride Boys, the untouchables of carny society. Ride Boys put up, tore down, and operated the rides, working about a hundred hours a week for a salary of forty dollars, which they spent on tattoos, beer, and food, in that order. While the pay was abysmal, the typical Ride Boy considered his job a plum, a prime opportunity to meet the type of girl impressed by a man's ability to cause a carnival ride to turn in a circle or shake violently up and down. A classic, and surprisingly successful, Ride Boy wooing technique was to strap the girl of his dreams into the bucket seat of, say, the Octopus and—twisting the levers with expert precision to obtain the maximum herky-jerky effect—not let his love off the dizzying, nauseating ride for an hour or so, no matter how loud or long she begged to be released. Ride Boys sure knew how to pick 'em, because more often than not, after she overcame her pique by swatting him a few times on his bare, shivering shoulders, the targeted girl could be seen curled in the Ride Boy's voluminous flannel shirt. Her arms would stay wrapped around his waist until her irate mother came looking, after which the Ride Boy would disappear from the midway, having either eloped with his lady or been thrown in jail.

Typical Hanky Pank agents were somewhat more refined. They slept in trailers and trucks, or a Motel 6 room when money was good. A Hanky Pank was a simple kids' game, like the two I'd managed. Running the games required relatively little skill—essentially, if you could make change, stay sober, and work for twelve consecutive hours, you were secure in your job. Hanky Pank operators were usually rank beginners like me, or experienced agents who'd lost their nerve.

Talking Tony was just such a debased and fallen man. Tony had started the season with a hole (that is, a job) in one of the big money games, but Jackie, I'd found during one of our counting sessions, had become disgusted by his timidity. It turned out that Tony had never recovered from a beating he'd received the year before. A sore loser had blindsided him with a candy-coated apple thrown from a distance of less than six feet. The apple, its red glaze the consistency of a ceramic ashtray, had broken Tony's jaw, forcing him to spend the off-season in silence. He'd returned to the midway unable to look a mark squarely in the face. Oh, he still had a good call. The problem was he turned his back to the mark after obtaining the intended victim's attention, irrationally fearful that another apple was about to come sailing his way. More often than not, the puzzled mark would simply wander off.

A good call was an agent's bread and butter. Without one, he couldn't make a dime. The midway was a noisy, colorful place, with plentiful distractions, so the first challenge an agent faced was enticing the mark to look his way. This was the call. In its simplest form, as practiced on a Hanky Pank, the call was a wave of the hand and a shouted "Come on in, it's time to win" or "Break a balloon and pick a prize." That, however, was only the most basic approach. In more sophisticated hands, the call was a highly stylized endeavor, with endless variations depending on the situation and the agent's mood.

An agent eyeing good prospects, such as a factory worker on payday or a young couple in flashy clothes, might call, "Sorry for the bother, but have you been told about our introductory offer?"

or "Did the Boy Scout in the parking lot hand you your free pass?" Most marks would be intrigued enough to swing by for a chat.

When in a bad mood, the agent could use the call to express his hostility, yelling something like, "Hey you butt-ugly fuck, get over here now" or "C'mere and help settle a bet about how many dicks you sucked today." Riveted by a buxom woman, the agent might call, "Hey lady, can I suck your tits?" or "Bend over and let me look up your name and address." Of course, those calls would be made in a mumble, typically overwhelmed by the human and mechanical uproar of the midway. But they allowed the agent to vent and feel one up on the mark, who would often come over anyway, puzzled about what the frantic man inside the tent was gesticulating about.

The gestures that accompanied the call were also many and varied. Among them were the bread-and-butter beckoning wave of the full hand; the classy wave with all fingers closed except for the pinkie, which was fluttered; and the pissed-off bird with all fingers closed but for the middle.

In rare cases where the agent was ticked off, broke, frustrated, horny, pilled up, drunk, or in a hurry, there was no call, no finesse at all: The agent would simply grab a mark firmly by the belt buckle, drag him over, jerk his wallet out of his back pocket, remove a sheaf of cash, put the ball or whatever in his hand, and tell him, "Sorry for using force, but I haven't had a winner all day and I have a tingling sensation it's going to be you." As unlikely as it may sound, I was soon to see this approach work—with the agent keeping the money and the mark walking away, stunned yet fairly satisfied, a teddy bear dangling from one limp hand.

The second type of game, the Alibi, was ostensibly a game of skill. Therefore, the agent always had an alibi when the mark lost: He threw the ball too fast or slow, was nervous, or had his eye on a curvy blonde instead of the game. Not surprisingly, marks were usually men, for several reasons. Men generally carried more cash than women, and carnival games operated on a strict cash basis; agents also contended that leaving women out of the picture was chivalrous. More practically, if an agent beat a man, he knew who he was dealing with, size-wise, in the event a rhubarb ignited. If he took a five-foot-tall, hundred-pound female for a large piece of change, though, she might call her husband, boyfriend, or father for help, and her savior could top six feet, weigh two hundred pounds, and arrive toting a crowbar. Alibi agents had lots of scars, an occupational hazard in a business where the customer often had a bowling pin, baseball, or claw hammer in his hand after losing a couple hundred dollars or so. In addition to the Swinger, Alibi joints included the exotically named Cat Rack, Buckets, Flukey Ball, and Baskets.

The Flat Store was the joint in which every agent wanted a hole. That's where the money was. Working in a Flat Store was also less physically risky; Flatties didn't have to perform any real labor and were protected from angry marks by the sturdy, flat-roofed structure itself. Legend had it that a Flattie in Puerto Rico had won fifty thousand dollars from a single customer. And Flatties were cool, paying Ride Boys twenty bucks just to open their awnings. They considered themselves part of the entertainment business and subscribed to *Variety*.

I'd had my first up-close and personal encounter with a Flattie two days before in the empty Kmart parking lot, as Chip and Jackie "stepped off" the midway—positioning the joints, food stands, and rides in a deliberate fashion meant to maximize profit. It was a letdown, however. The Flattie, nicknamed the Ghost, simply exited a cab, paid the driver with a twenty, and turned away without waiting for change. The Ghost, Jackie had told me, was a big enough earner to afford a heroin habit. His skin was colorless, and his tailored silk suit now fit his body like he'd bought it off the rack at the Salvation Army. Philadelphia Phil's addiction hadn't bothered me so much, since it was in the distant past. But needles had always made me queasy, and the vision of the Ghost sticking a sharp steel point into his arm nearly made me retch on the spot. Thankfully, he dipped under the rope cordoning off the perimeter of the carnival lot and strolled without speaking past the three of us, nodding at Chip and Jackie while pointedly ignoring me.

"What's with the silent treatment from Mr. Prima Donna?" Chip complained to Jackie as the Ghost headed for the Kmart, tripping lightly once over a black power cable.

"He's saving his voice for the joint. Caught laryngitis last night."

"Fucking opera singer," Chip groused, then went back to stepping off the lot with Jackie.

The business of Party Time Shows was structured like that of most carnivals. Double-O, assisted by Chip, organized the route the show traveled and provided the rides, generator truck, Port-A-Johns, and other amenities. They also "patched," or paid off, the authorities in each town to ignore complaints about the games from sore losers. A well-patched cop would sooner run a "knocker" off the lot than cite Party Time Shows' personnel for stealing his heart medicine.

Space on the midway, in turn, was rented to the operators of the food stands and games. And since Jackie owned every joint this season, he'd demanded and won the right to step off the lot with Chip, a ritual that often ended with Chip threatening to double the nut and Jackie vowing to pay no rent at all. Double-O seldom left his top-secret basement workshop these days, preferring to let his boys continue their running battle, a struggle that he perceived as character building. In his sons' hands, Party Time Shows earned a mint, yet fleeced the public so baldly that even the best-patched city officials often regretted accepting their new color TV or seventeen-speed blender.

As it turned out, the midway lineup in Marble City was a classic example of the Chip and Jackie version of Party Time Shows. The white Balloon Dart/Duck Pond trailer was positioned at the most common midway entry point, promoting an image of innocent, childlike fun, marred only by Talking Tony's constant jive and the faint smell of sour wine hovering over his brother agent in the Balloon Dart.

The Swinger had "first call" among the Alibi stores, followed by the String Joint, a Hanky Pank traditionally operated by Whitey's girlfriend of the week, each of whom was given the moniker Eva Braun. To operate the game, Eva would grasp in her hand a hundred or so strings tied to a variety of prizes dangling a few feet behind her from the joint's rafters. The mark would pay a quarter, select a string, and win the corresponding prize. As might be expected, the strings leading to the more valuable prizes were shorter and harder to find in Eva's hand.

The Glass Pitch was one of three center joints that split the midway in half. Center joints were strictly percentage games, relying solely on favorable odds and a large volume of business to grind out a profit. At the Glass Pitch, a mark could win a beer mug, ashtray, or other glassware if the dime she lofted into the air settled upon it, which didn't happen too often. Regardless, no single item was worth a dime anyway.

The second center joint, the Digger, was a trailer lined with miniature construction cranes, each enclosed in a sizable glass-and-wood box along with mountains of "slum," or cheap prizes, and an attractive piece of flash like a wristwatch or bracelet. The objective was to manipulate the crane with a lever mounted on the exterior of the box so that it would scoop up one of the more valuable, and heavier, prizes. This, however, was impossible because of the way the jaws of the scoop had been tweaked.

The final center joint was the Color Game, which I currently ran. The Color Game featured a roulette-wheel–like device divided into thirteen brightly colored sections, onto which a selected mark threw a plastic waffle ball. The colors were repeated on wooden counters that surrounded the joint. Players placed twenty-five cent bets, and if the waffle ball settled on the color that they had chosen, they won two packs of cigarettes or a couple of candy bars. The cigarettes were off-brands that had seen better days, and the candy was stale.

Loudspeakers were used in the Glass Pitch and Color Game to hype the tip. Bryant Johnson had undergone a throat cancer operation and worked the Glass Pitch mike through the hole in his windpipe. I ran the Color Game microphone, endlessly repeating tired phrases like "Pick a color, win cancer sticks or candy" until I became unbearably restless and started reciting Redd Foxx jokes, Lenny Bruce routines—anything to avoid shouting, "We got a winner!" again. Surprisingly, riffing wildly didn't hurt the gross, and I learned that practically anything said with conviction would grab some fool's trust.

Back to the left side of the midway, where the String Joint was followed by the Nail Store: To win here, a mark needed to pound a finishing nail into a railroad tie. That's all. One swing was allowed, and the nail head had to end up flush with the surface. The "G," or gaff, was that some nails were altered so that they bent immediately under the force of the hammer. The gaffed nails were kept in a pocket of the white bib overalls worn by the joint's only agent, Frank Day, who'd switch them with the straight nails when necessary. Frank had frizzy brown hair and the fearful, recoiling posture of a man whose livelihood required handing a beefy, suspicious farmer a claw hammer to play a fixed game he was guaranteed to lose.

The adjoining Alibi store was the Cat Rack, a game that involved knocking a fur-fringed, two-foot-tall, sawdust-stuffed cat off a shelf with a baseball. Ellen Nortensen, the midway's sole female Alibi agent, employed calls on the order of "C'mon in. Knock off a little pussy, win a big prize." She wore red satin shorts and scissored one leg up onto the counter when working strong. Ellen was twenty-four and introduced herself as a former Harvard cheerleader, revealing only when you got to know her that she meant the high school in Harvard, Michigan. Ellen controlled the game with a hidden hydraulic lever that made it impossible to knock the cats off the shelf.

Chip and Jackie placed the Flat Store, the heavy, steel-clad trailer that was the crown jewel of the lineup, opposite the merry-go-round. Experience had proven that it was most often Dad (with his big, fat wallet) who accompanied the children to the "jenny." Poor Dad, nearly hypnotized by his endlessly circling, bobbing kids, would be anxious for a time-killing distraction. The Ghost, or someone like him, would beckon with a wisecrack and the promise of a non-transferable free game card fluttering in his manicured hand. Curious, Dad would approach the Flat Store. Ideally, he wouldn't return to the merry-go-round and his impatient kids until he was fifty, a hundred, or five hundred dollars poorer.

The Flat Store was forbidden territory to the lower order of carnies, which was why I hadn't been surprised when the Ghost avoided eye contact with me. Even touching the imposing trailer was frowned upon. Once a day a selected Ride Boy dusted the flash, a relatively impressive collection of color TVs, golf clubs, steak knife sets, and other expensive-looking items. The Ride Boy shined the agents' shoes, dry-cleaned their sport coats, made certain their steaks arrived warm from the Ponderosa, and that the onion rings were crisp. He mixed the agents' drinks and emptied the plastic cups the boys peed in when business was so brisk that they couldn't bear leaving the joint. Another young person, called the Outside Man, made certain that there were few spectators present when a ripe mark was getting fleeced. Flatties rewarded each of these young helpers handsomely and even spoke to them on occasion.

"Grab joints," or food stands, were scattered along the breadth of the midway. "Two-Fisted" Hank Malone, a former Golden Gloves bantamweight, owned the cotton candy wagon. Ramrod Hank held firm to his opinions that "honesty is the best policy" and that one should "always give a carny a helping hand." He was considered a snitch; anything said within his earshot would soon be reported to Double-O or Vera. Hank had recently begun managing the 13-Inch Foot-Long hot dog stand for them, where despite his expressed policy of honesty, he faithfully continued Vera's tradition of keeping a wiener until it was sold, whether that took a day or a week.

Margaret and "Dad" Foster, retired civil servants, ran a third grab joint based on a Double-O invention called the Smashed Sandwich. Double-O had happened on the idea for the joint after accidentally pressing a BLT in a waffle iron in his basement workshop. As a result, fairgoers could now buy Smashed Sandwiches in the shape of baseballs, thumbs, and butterflies, among others. Quality-wise, the sandwiches fell into the category of most carnival food. "Let me put it this way, Pete," Jackie had warned me early on, "if you just absolutely, completely, without a doubt, have no choice but to eat at a grab joint, pour extra relish on whatever you order and don't take a bite until you're locked inside a Port-A-John, because that garbage will have you shitting the moment you swallow." Like most carnies, I preferred the relative safety of McDonald's and

Kentucky Fried Chicken, or warmed-up Dinty Moore beef stew in a can.

Thrill rides capped the back or "barf" end of the midway with a whirling mélange of sputtering fluorescent lights, clanking gears, leaking oil, and nauseated, foul-mouthed teens. Blown-out speakers provided a different soundscape for each ride, the music selected by the resident Ride Boy, the result an arrhythmic din indistinguishable from the pounding, grinding noise of the rides.

Party Time Shows specialized in violent, lurching "barf" rides, the sort that kids dared each other to go on and left most of them with kinked necks, headaches, and brand-new clothes ruined by black streaks of grease. The Himalaya (which Buzz Fazio ran), Salt 'n' Pepper Shaker, Octopus, Squirrel Cage, and Tilt-A-Whirl were preferred by lot lice and Ride Boys alike for their exceptional severity. These rides made kids upchuck corn dogs, Jujubes, salted-in-the-shell peanuts, Hershey bars, Cokes, blue-tinted cotton candy, gin pilfered from parents, taffy, chili, 13-Inch Foot-Longs, and Smashed Sandwiches. Some Ride Boys augmented their meager incomes with the lost wallets and dropped coins of the disoriented, shell-shocked thrillseekers.

The right side of the lineup consisted of joints that weren't expected to earn much money even if the marks had significant "line" (or money) left when they made their way past. For example, the Flukey Ball, dubbed by some cynics the Bendover Store, was a physically grueling Alibi that required its agents to bend over hundreds of times daily to retrieve the baseballs that marks had attempted to toss into gaffed bushel baskets. Since most agents considered even modest physical activity beneath contempt, the Flukey Ball holes were filled by men too proud to accept Hanky Pank duty, yet too inept for the bigger money stores. Flip Claire, aka Chief Brown Eye, for example, was a hardcore Flukey Ball agent. A slight twenty-five-year-old from upstate Wisconsin, Flip claimed to have been hit by a truck when he was young, which was why his mouth had settled to the lower left of his nose. He made his call turned slightly away from the mark.

"See Live Reptiles" was Party Time Shows' sole remaining sideshow, an anachronism in an era of government crackdowns on freaks and animal oddities. Run by Mel Jewel, an aging crony of Double-O from the old days, See Live Reptiles passed muster with Michigan fish and wildlife inspectors because every reptile it featured was dead and had been since Mel had created the attraction thirty years before out of roadkill he'd pried off the pavement during his extensive worldwide travels. Although Mel usually had to close the joint early in the week of every engagement due to consumer complaints, he earned a modest living, with plenty of time off.

The "Guess Your Weight" game operated on the same principle as the Glass Pitch. The prizes were worth less than the fifty cents it cost to play, so even when the marks won, in effect they lost. Not surprisingly, the more frequently the agent guessed his customers' weight incorrectly, the longer the line to play the game grew, leading to a better payday for the incompetent weight-guesser. Of course, allowing everyone to win would make the gimmick too apparent, so in order to make the game seem legitimate, the savvy agent aimed to guess his marks' weight correctly on occasion.

A half-dozen "Committee Joints"—honest, straightforward games like the Milk Bottle Throw or Ring Toss, operated by local civic groups—completed the midway. Proceeds from these joints went to good causes. If Party Time Shows' agents had done their jobs properly, however, Committee members had no visitors other than irate townsfolk who'd just lost a significant part of their discretionary income to a gallery of gap-toothed bums.

"Where the hell's Horserace?" Philadelphia Phil asked me as he rushed to the railing that separated the interior of the tent from the midway. "He left fifteen minutes ago with my double-saw, and I have an itchy feeling he's gone for good."

"He went for beer."

"I know that, High School. But what I don't know is if he's ever comin' back. I heard he pulled this once last year in Toledo—borrowed five hundred dollars total from about everyone on the Big Tent Attractions midway and didn't show his face again." Phil made a show of scanning passersby in either direction, rubbing his hand on his unshaven chin. "And man, I could use a beer before getting to work. I find it loosens my tongue, primes the pump, so to speak." Then he glanced my way, making fleeting eye contact as he said, "Say, you don't have a double-saw I could borrow until I beat my first mark? Since you're Jackie's greatest pal, I'm sure you want all us agents to perform at our best so that he makes more money."

"I don't have twenty bucks."

Phil opened his mouth in what appeared to be feigned shock, his lack of lower teeth helping to form a dark, elongated oval. "You're telling me that Jackie's best buddy doesn't have twenty?"

"Right."

"How about five dollars? Tell you what—take the five bucks you're gonna loan me, go to the party store, buy Whitey and me a couple of six-packs, and keep the change. How's that sound?"

"I don't even have five bucks," I lied. I wasn't about to buckle under Philadelphia Phil's pressure or allow him to treat me like a mark.

"Wait a minute. You're like two peas in a pod with Jackie, and you don't even have five in your wallet?"

"That's the terrible truth." And it was. The five was in my back pocket.

"You're saying that a guy working the Color Game doesn't have any line to spare? That joint's a license to print money. You should be rollin' in it. Listen, pardon me for asking, I'm not trying to be smart or anything, but how much does Jackie pay you for working that Color Game?"

"Twenty-five dollars a day."

"Flat?"

"Yeah."

"Partner, the normal payout is ten percent of the gross. How much you bring in usually?"

Stunned, I told him I didn't remember; yet, of course, I did. The Color Game was grossing about fifteen hundred dollars a day. Ten percent of that was a hundred and fifty dollars, meaning that Jackie was shorting me a hundred and twenty-five daily, or almost enough to buy a good used Volkswagen Beetle in a little over a week, not that I wanted any form of transportation other than my Yamaha.

Phil twisted around and spoke with Whitey. "You hear that? Jackie's screwin' his best pal."

"Speaking of screwing," Whitey answered, opening the seal on a fresh deck of cards, "where's that five yards you owe me?"

"I paid you back Tuesday. You tellin' me you don't remember?"

"I have photographic, minute-by-minute memory of what happened Tuesday, and you handing me money isn't part of it."

The bickering of Philadelphia Phil and Whitey blended into the midway cacophony as I staggered back to the Color Game, where I crawled under the red and white canvas skirt that surrounded the joint. Fumbling, I plugged the microphone into the amplifier, turned on the power, and began my spiel by rote. My thoughts, though, were fixated on Jackie and his cheating me out of my due. I'd been giving him the benefit of the doubt. Now it was time for some sort of reckoning. Either that, or I'd have little choice but to crawl back to my parents—and then what?

By the way, Horserace Harry didn't return for three days, when he showed up bearing a brand-new hairpiece in a box, boasting that he wasn't going to pay back Jackie's loan because the collateral Jackie held, his old toupee, was now worthless to him.

CHAPTER EIGHT

My Cheatin' Heart

Not until two weeks later in Bay City, Michigan, was I able to confront Jackie about my pay. I was afraid that telling him I was unhappy would jeopardize the friendship that had become essential to me. Jackie was my enabler, the person through whom I was transforming myself from frustrated honor student to prospective Alibi agent. Clearly, Jackie had come along when I was insecure and needy, yet I'd flattered myself that he'd always considered me his equal, a quick study with whom he was creating a shady symbiotic partnership. I couldn't bear the thought that speaking my mind might end that. At the same time, I couldn't let him keep screwing me over, treating me as a lesser being than Talking Tony, Horserace Harry, and even Chief Brown Eye in the Bendover Store. So that night after closing up the Color Game, I planned to take my grievance to Jackie and let destiny take over from there.

On this point, in truth, I'd already hedged my bet. After endless bouts of self-flagellation over earning twenty-five bucks a day rather than ten percent of the gross, I'd started holding out my rightful share of the Color Game proceeds. I'd siphoned off about $1,250 thus far, hidden in a green stuffed snake, one of the few locations on the midway where Whitey wasn't concealing an emergency bottle of wine. Was I right or wrong to H.O. from Jackie? Either way, skimming the take signaled my true baptism on the midway. In taking that risk, I plugged myself into the alternating current of greed-fed euphoria and paranoia that was characteristic of every traveling carnival game operator. It was an unstable, addictive state that marked the rest of my stint with Party Time Shows.

Bay City was a gray, industrial splotch on Lake Huron in the crook of the Michigan thumb, the sort of northern Great Lakes community where winter always seemed one nasty storm away. Sagging plastic tarp was stapled over windows even now, in mid-July; taking it down wasn't worth the effort. Deer and duck hunting, ice fishing, and indoor shuffleboard bowling were the primary recreational and intellectual pursuits. Summer was a brief, mosquito-clogged respite when locals trudged from factories to the colored lights and bug foggers of the Party Time Shows midway.

"What's this one doing in there?" a vaguely familiar voice asked. I looked up to see Vera, pointing at me inside the Color Game, where I was trying to get the microphone to work. She had arrived at the front of the joint, arm in arm with Double-O and Jackie.

"Which one?" Jackie asked. I had help clearing quarters off the counters that day from Fred Fred, a five-foot, three-inch Ride Boy with a three-day growth of beard, dirt-stiffened blue jeans, a greasy T-shirt, and a dried-out flap of hair pulled across his balding head. I was feeling pretty cool in red jeans, red T-shirt, and a black leather wristband with a thin leather strip that extended the length of my index finger and was held in place by a snap. It was a style of wristband favored by tough guys, though I never discovered what was so menacing about the index-finger-length strip.

"The red one."

"You're talking about him like he's a towel. That's Pete, my high school buddy. He's been to the house."

"What's a high schooler doing in one of your joints?"

"He's a good agent. An up-and-comer."

Vera wore a blue housecoat over a yellow, daisy-print dress. A pink-and-white plastic flower, the rusted wire stem wrapped around a buttonhole, dangled from the coat's lapel, looking like something she'd plucked off a neglected grave marker. Spotting an object nestled in the sawdust at her feet, she bent from the waist to pick it up. "Look what I found! A nickel," she announced triumphantly, her face flushed from the exertion. "Probably more than your red-colored friend here will earn you all day, Jackie. Why don't you stick to hiring seasoned help, like that one," she said, nodding at Fred Fred.

"Not a good idea," Double-O announced. With his imposing, view-blocking stature, dressed in a white long-sleeved shirt and black trousers held up by red suspenders, he looked like a monument to the traveling, turn-of-the-century elixir salesman. "We need more people like little Red Pete here, high-school educated types. They're the future of the carnival business. Let me illustrate." He turned to Fred Fred. "Answer me this: How did Bay City get its name?"

"Trick question, right?" replied Fred Fred, who'd been pulling heavily on a pint of Kessler's. He dragged a bent cigarette from a crushed pack of Camels and used up two matches in a wobbly attempt to light it.

Fred Fred steadied himself in order to strike a third match. Double-O studied him for a moment. "Let me know when you're ready for a new challenge," he told him, then turned his hawklike gaze on me. "How about you? How did Bay City get its name?"

His piercing eyes shook me. For one weak moment, I worried

if this truly was a trick question. Cautious, I answered, "It's on a bay." Indeed, Saginaw Bay was clearly visible at the end of the midway.

"Aw, Mr. Double-O, that was unfair," Fred Fred protested, fighting to remain on his feet, his flap of hair now bent in the same direction as his still-unlit Camel. "I'm from Louisiana. They didn't teach Michigan junk in our school. How 'bout a second chance?"

Double-O watched him work at a fourth match and said, "Polish your smoking skills and get back to me."

Jackie interjected, "Now that we've settled the earthshaking question of where we are, why don't you slough the joint, Pete? Better yet, let Fred Fred do it as punishment for failing his geography quiz."

I didn't mind. Sloughing the joint was a lengthy pain that involved lowering the heavy awnings, then lacing them tightly to the wooden frame with nylon cords in order to prevent the weather and vandals from attacking the plush. Even worse was raising the tent at the beginning of each spot and tearing it down at the end. It was a bruising, tedious jigsaw puzzle that involved matching poorly identified lengths of tent frame, fastening them together by pounding nails through poorly aligned hinges, attaching the canvas top and bottom with even more nails bent around hundreds of eyeholes, then raising the several-hundred-pound contraption while praying it didn't collapse. Tearing down reversed the process, and both tasks took many frustrating and thumb-smashing hours.

"Don't panic, Jackie, but we're leaving you with your bosom buddies to stroll the midway," Vera announced. With Double-O trailing behind, she left the Color Game, scanning the sawdust as she went.

"What's she looking for?" I asked Jackie.

"More coins. Finding seventy-eight cents on the midway means more to her than the show having a ten-thousand-buck week. Hides it in the walls back home."

"Double-O, too?"

"He looks for discarded paper cups he can use again in the grab joints."

I untied my carpenter's apron, ordered Fred Fred to do the same, and gave both aprons and the money they contained to Jackie. He quickly stuffed them into an interior pocket of the tan, knee-length canvas coat he'd purchased simply because of the large number of pockets it featured. With most of them now filled with money bags or folded-up carpenter's aprons, Jackie was bloated and lumpy with cash.

"How about after I drop this bread off at the Airstream, we go looking for broads at the Blue Fin?" Jackie asked me.

"Worth a shot." The Blue Fin was a nearby bar where carnies gathered after the show to cut up jackpots and interact with the locals. And while I still did not drink, it would be a challenge to ingratiate myself with older women who did. Besides, going to the Blue Fin gave me a convenient excuse to put off confronting Jackie for an hour or two.

Even though I was far from a smooth-talking seducer, I'd had considerable success meeting girls on the carnival, for the most surprising of reasons: In the small towns and outlying districts of Michigan, where a disabled tractor was entertainment and Detroit was an exotic destination, carnies were celebrities. Not to every female, for sure. But enough girls found our lifestyle glamorous, exciting, and sufficiently Hollywood that romantic success with them was far from the typically stressful struggle faced by rural Lotharios. Romance, to be fair, consisted largely of anonymous groping in wheat fields and tall grass with girls I usually never saw again. But after a while, I got over the hurt that my love partners didn't want to go steady, or even have a second date. Like me, they were experimenting, trying out tongue-kissing and breast-holding for the first time so that they'd be less awkward when the boys at school (who would not be leaving town, *ever*) shyly attempted to do the same.

Sometimes a girl, starstruck by my status as the man on the microphone, would hang out at the Color Game. We'd flirt, she'd try to wheedle a free teddy bear, and after the show or on my break, we'd walk into the woods holding hands. On other occasions, I'd loiter near the Himalaya, hoping to parlay my celebrity into a date.

The Himalaya was the loudest, fastest, shiniest ride on the midway; for the week of the carnival, it was usually the hippest teen hotspot in town. The made-in-Germany ride was expensive, at $100,000 new, though Chip had obtained Party Time's Himalaya for much less at a bankruptcy sale.

The Himalaya provided its thrills thusly: Eighteen gondolas raced over an undulating circular table tilted at a thirty-degree angle. That was only the beginning. Eight thousand sequenced, multicolored marquee lights flashed in waves across a painted wood-and-steel canopy suspended above the ride, throwing off enough heat to melt snow in April and cotton candy in summer. Each gondola and the crowded entrance ramps were festooned with scenes of dancing, singing Bavarians. Canopy-high mirrors offered a dazzling backdrop, reflecting a blur of screaming kids, swooshing lights, and charging gondolas.

But the core of the Himalaya's success, what made it so arresting, was the sequined booth high atop the angled walkway surrounding the gondolas. Inside was a reasonable facsimile of a radio station disk jockey booth, complete with turntables and microphone for the jock. Half a dozen huge Jensen speakers playing Top 40 hits completed the system, so that riders on the Himalaya were surrounded by a wall of sound they could practically lean against. The Himalaya was absolutely the coolest place a young someone could be, especially if he or she lived in deep rural Michigan, where the alternatives on the radio were either the local evangelist or static.

On this Himalaya, the playlist was controlled by Buzz Fazio, who'd finally found his true calling after failing as a high school basketball star. Running the ride offered him a status far above the generic Ride Boy. Buzz and his three-man crew spent eighteen hours a day on the Himalaya, polishing, adjusting, fine-tuning it so that it always shone like a jewel. It was his territory, and he guarded it jealously.

Night and day, teens mobbed the ride. The boys wore home-made cutoff jeans that exposed the pockets, drag race T-shirts or leather vests over bare torsos, and headgear obviously selected after hours of study before a mirror: berets, Stetsons, Australian bush hats, and floppy leather "hillbilly" fedoras. Cigarettes and rum poured into Coke cans were standard accoutrements, hastily tossed aside when a cop or Kiwanis Club member strolled by—and just as quickly retrieved when the authority figure left. Most boys grew accustomed to smokes and booze polluted by pebbles and sawdust.

The girls wore tight shorts and billowing blue nylon jackets with their first names stenciled across the shoulders. They had tiny decals on their enameled fingernails and carried cigarettes rarely smoked, just swirled around to emphasize a point and tapped occasionally to remove the drooping ash. Many went barefoot, their ankles blackened with dust, the lucky ones inspiring gallant boys to carry them, squealing happily, to the Himalaya's gondolas. The girls came in all shapes and sizes and, as I learned, could possess charms as enticing as the women of nude volleyball magazines. Not that a perfect figure mattered much. My standards were different: Any girl who seemed remotely interested in me became the object of my desire.

The Blue Fin was a true corner bar, with large picture windows overlooking the streets on two sides. While the sidewalk was empty, the square, smoky Blue Fin was jammed with revelers, their loud whoops and the throb of a jukebox clearly audible when Jackie and I arrived below the bar's broken neon sign. Jackie had dumped his cash-filled coat at the Airstream and was now in khaki pants and a striped, short-sleeved shirt, under which he'd slipped a bottle of Arrow peppermint schnapps, his most recent headache remedy. I'd thrown on a black leather car coat with the hope that it would make me look legal.

Affecting a scowl, I led the way through the swinging doors, covered with stuffed black vinyl cinched down with fake brass buttons.

"Stop right there, chump," a bearded doorman growled. He must have weighed three hundred pounds.

"I–I've got my ID right here," I stammered, fumbling for my Arkansas driver's license.

"Lighten up, Bobby," Jackie intervened, "he's with the show."

"Sorry about that, Jackie," Bobby, the doorman, smiled. "Go in. Have fun, guys."

Relieved, I shoved my fists into my pockets and strutted inside.

The long, walnut bar was filled with carnies, including Bobby Joe and Billy Whipper, two roughneck Alibi agents from Alabama whom Jackie had invited to join the show a few days before. Slapping backs and hollering, they appeared to be cutting up jackpots with locals lured by the excitement. A few silent regulars, looking like they'd been there forever, sat hunched on their bar stools, downing beers while half-listening to the voices beside them. The institutional green walls, dirty from years of neglect, were dented here and there with half-circles left by flying beer cans and pool cues. The square, black tables were bolted to the floor. In my early

youth I would have been sickened by the atmosphere, which reminded me of the hours I'd lost in bars watching my father grow
pants-wetting drunk while I tried to swat flies with my hands. In
the alternate universe of Party Time Shows, however, what had
filled me with sorrow was now dangerously electric and alluring.

"Most of the chicks in here have beehive hairdos older than us.
But there's a couple of live ones there in the corner," Jackie observed, nodding toward a gathering of tables.

"I thought you were still with Mandy."

"First of all, she isn't here. Second of all, she isn't here. Third,
she's changed."

"How's that?"

"She was accepted at U of M. She's into that going-to-college
crap. You know, buying clothes, choosing majors and minors, and
that sort of thing."

"I didn't know she was interested in college."

"Me either. But that's the way it goes," he said, pushing through
the crowd.

I was both startled and intrigued by Mandy's sudden turn. A
few days before, I'd also received a letter of acceptance from the
University of Michigan. My interest in college was limited; I'd only
applied at my mother's insistence and had not decided whether I'd
even attend. Yet with Mandy headed for Ann Arbor in the fall—
well, maybe it was worth dropping by her home next time I was in
Mineralton, especially now that it appeared the relationship between her and Jackie was rocky.

Unfortunately, Dinkie Barnes buttonholed us halfway across
the room. "Boys, boys, you got to help me," he wailed. "My wife's
leaving me. She's packing her bags right now." Dinkie's orange ringmaster's uniform was unbuttoned down to the waist, and his wrin-
kled shirttail was like a jagged, knee-length skirt.

I hesitated to speak. Everyone on the show knew that Leni, Dinkie's German mail-order bride, had been set on leaving him since she'd arrived a few weeks before. She and the Ride Boy with whom she'd hooked up were planning to open a potato pancake stand on Buckeye State Midways in Ohio.

Jackie tried to console him by saying, "Dinkie, about the only person on this show who didn't screw Leni is you."

"I was working up to it, Jackie."

"Better start saving air mail stamps again, Dinkie. Leni's history."

"If it's any comfort to you, Dinkie," I interjected, "I never had sex with her." That was true. Plus, I didn't like seeing him humiliated, even though Star the Wonder Horse had kicked over my Yamaha while under Dinkie's supervision.

Dinkie placed his hands on my shoulders. "Pete, you're all right."

"Think nothing of it," I answered, shrinking away. As usual, his palms smelled like crabgrass and elephant manure.

"As for you, Jackie," Dinkie waggled a fat finger at him, then stopped and managed a weak smile. "Oh, Jackie, how can I get mad at you and your jokes." He slapped Jackie's shoulder with the rump of his hand, then turned back to me. "I remember Jackie as a tyke, no taller than a donkey's knee." His smile disappeared. "Now he's taller than a horse's ass and full of twice as much shit."

"Dinkie," Jackie responded, acting unperturbed, "I'm not letting even you faze me tonight. Go find your wife, if you want. Just don't do anything to embarrass Party Time Shows."

Dinkie dismissed Jackie with a wave of his hand and made his way toward the vinyl-covered swinging doors.

"Should we follow him?" I asked.

"No. He's too pathetic to do any harm."

Now there was nothing between us and our quarry, two women

in their mid-twenties sitting stone-faced and silent at a table. One played with a swizzle stick, while the other twisted a napkin. Fear of failure transformed me into a sociologist: I decided that they were blue-collar girls looking for guys with the pink slip to their Peterbilts, not me. But Jackie forged ahead, and I obediently followed.

"Hi girls, mind if we wait here for the bus?" he asked brightly.

The napkin twister, husky and square-jawed in a blue windbreaker, eyed him with deep suspicion.

Jackie was already sliding into one of the table's two empty chairs. "You going to blow a kiss or strangle me, dear?" he asked, winking.

Napkin-twister chuckled without humor. "Strangle, I think. You're a man, and all men are garbage."

Swizzle-stick intervened. "Don't mind Terri. Her boyfriend totaled her car last night robbing a party store." This one was pleasingly thin, with bleached-blonde hair and a blue windbreaker just like Terri's, except for the name Anna silk-screened across the shoulders. Jackie scraped his chair closer to her, leaving me to sit beside Terri.

"Gee, that's too bad, Terri," Jackie murmured, leaning across the table. "Is your magnificent boyfriend in jail?"

"No, goddamn him. He's hiding in our attic with five cases of 7 Crown. He keeps bugging me to come up and party with him, but there's no way I'm gonna party with that man with all that dust and those rats."

"Our attic does not have rats," Anna said vehemently. "You—"

"Ladies, ladies," Jackie interrupted, "let's call a truce and sip schnapps." He removed the bottle from the back of his pants and placed it firmly on the table.

Anna studied the label. "Arrow, my favorite," she enthused, unscrewing the cap and taking one ladylike sip after another.

"I told you these were live ones," Jackie whispered to me. He downed a slug of schnapps and offered Terri a drink.

"I never share bottles with strangers," Terri sniffed, and drained her whiskey sour through a straw. A bar napkin hugged the glass. The table was littered with six or seven similarly empty glasses, each surrounded by a wet napkin with the stem of a ravished maraschino cherry sagging inside. Disintegrating Kleenex and soggy beer nuts followed the erratic trail of a spilled beer. All this gave me heart. It was common knowledge that women put out more when they were drunk. On top of that, Terri was verging on fat and it was also known that the heavier the woman, the easier she was.

"How old are you?" I asked her. There was a thick line separating my grandiose dreams of conquest and my talent for seductive small talk.

Terri paused, as if deciding whether I was worth a response. "Twenty-two," she finally replied with a frown.

Keep talking, I told myself. Any subject.

"I turned twenty-two yesterday myself, and—"

I was interrupted by a Deep South drawl.

"That's my fiancé you're toyin' with there, High School." It was Bobby Joe Whipper, carrying a tray laden with a couple dozen mixed drinks.

"Prepare to die, motherfucker," another guy growled from behind as four stubby fingers dug into my windpipe. I gagged and reflexively pulled away, coughing.

"Hey, just joking, High School," Bobby Joe chuckled, cracking a wide smile. "The lady and I just met, although the way she and I are gettin' along, wedding bells might not be far away."

"Yeah, only funnin' with you, pal," Billy Whipper added, cuffing the back of my neck. Turning to the locals at a nearby table, he asked, "Mind if I borrow this chair?" He took it before anyone could answer, then sat in it backwards, rubbing what remained of the fingers on his right hand. "You got a tough neck there, partner. Should've warned me before I got hurt." He winked, apparently joking again, although given my limited exposure to the Whipper brothers, it was not easy to tell.

The Whipper brothers were the first carnies I was afraid of physically. Their mercurial nature and steamroller aggression made even casual conversation with them feel like an unnecessary risk. A sense of menace exuded from the Whippers like week-old sweat. Around them, I was on constant alert—aware that an improper response might result in a punch in the face or, worse, dismissive laughter that would strip away my fragile carny façade the way a tornado peeled off trailer-home siding. But the sense of jeopardy that consumed me in the Whippers' presence was part of their appeal; each time they didn't pummel me into pulp, I felt as if I'd passed yet one more test.

I'd first met the Whippers in Jackie's Airstream, where they were drinking and grousing after driving nonstop from their mother's home in Screw's Trailer Park, Mobile, Alabama, to Bay City. As the evening wore on, Billy revealed that the fingers on his right hand, except for his thumb, had been severed at the first knuckle by a lumber mill's band saw. He subsequently claimed they'd been chopped off in a meat cleaver accident. Regardless, he used the thick, hairy stubs as a tool of painful intimidation, grinding the bony ends into my neck to emphasize any important point.

Billy's hazel eyes were chromelike in their impenetrability; they revealed no inner life, thought, or feeling, offering zero chance to connect with the person inside, not that anyone but a forensic psychologist would have had that desire. He had dark brown hair parted on the side and tough, leathery skin cured by years of working in the sun and partying at night. Only thirty-six, Billy appeared ten years older. He was short, thick, and so well-muscled that it was hard to believe his exercise regimen consisted of drinking and fighting. Perhaps as a result of his years as an Alibi agent, he talked in a low, conspiratorial growl only inches from my face, as if daring me to pull away. It took great willpower not to. That he'd served time behind bars was a given, though probably in county jails rather than state or federal prisons.

While he possessed his older brother's threatening aspect, Bobby Joe leavened it with an energetic charisma. Blond, with a strong, hooked nose and the same chrome-hubcap eyes, Bobby Joe had a roguish, dimpled smile enhanced by a long, deep scar curving from the right corner of his mouth to a point far up his temple.

According to Jackie, Bobby Joe was a genius with women. He adored them. He lived off them during the off-season, but their money was just the icing on the cake. Every so often, he'd have something new to show for his talent—a car signed over to him, or a bank account opened in his name for one thousand dollars. Jackie said that Bobby Joe had once shacked up for the winter with a nurse in Mobile who gave him her Goodyear credit card on permanent loan. Periodically, Bobby Joe would buy new tires in Mobile, drive over to Biloxi, sell them, and pocket the cash. The nurse didn't mind, or so went Bobby Joe's story. Women were mesmerized by him and couldn't shake off his spell until they'd given him their love, money, and whatever else they sensed he needed.

Soon after I met him, I watched Bobby Joe in action for several days. His greatest success was with ordinary housewives. They came to the carnival in the afternoon with their children trailing behind them. I don't know what he said, but an hour or so later, I'd see Mom emerging from a tent, carrying a stuffed Snoopy in one hand, brushing her hair back with the other. Bobby Joe soon followed, grinning and adjusting his pants.

This was why the Whipper brothers' arrival at our table was so unwelcome to me. I'd already been choked by Billy. Thanks to Bobby Joe, my chances with Terri were dimming; she was already giddy with pleasure at what he was whispering in her ear. On top of that, Jackie was hanging on Bobby Joe's every word—cackling too heartily, I thought, at his idle remarks.

"What you drinkin' there, Jackie's buddy?" Bobby Joe asked me as he shoved the tray of drinks through the debris of wet napkins. "Take your pick. I got gin and Squirt, 7&7, and rum and Coke for those who like soda pop with their alcohol, plus J.D. on the rocks and Crown Royal straight for people serious about their liquor. Me, I gotta be honest, I go for the soda pop stuff, 'cause it reminds me of being a child again."

"I don't drink." Despite my other lapses, I still held a firm line against alcohol.

"You got a medical condition?"

"It's some sort of principled stand," Jackie interjected, seeming to enjoy my discomfort.

Bobby Joe's eyes narrowed. "Then you must be John Law."

"Are you joking?" I couldn't tell if he was.

"No. You cop types can't smoke Mary Jane on duty. Maybe in your precinct the same goes for demon alcohol."

"I'm only seventeen. I can't vote, let alone wear a badge."

Bobby Joe broke into a wide grin. "I know that. Just teasin' around again. It's a Whipper bad habit."

"No problem."

Bobby Joe lost the smile. "Then drink up. I'm serious now."

Whether he was really serious didn't matter just then. I was rattled and anxious to change the subject. So, for the first time, I knowingly took an alcoholic drink in my hand, held it to my lips, and allowed gin (and my favorite soda pop, Squirt) to sluice down my throat. The experience was not at all what I had imagined it would be. I didn't lose my senses; I didn't act like a baby and need someone to wipe the dribbles from my chin. I didn't, in other words, react like my father and regress to an infantile state. All I felt was a rhythmic, burning sensation as the liquid descended to my stomach, from which point the warmth radiated to my furthest extremities.

But the next swallow didn't have the same atomic effect, nor did the many sips, swallows, and chugs that followed. Nevertheless, I continued drinking throughout the night, if for no other reason than to prove to Bobby Joe that I could. Eventually, the Blue Fin began to revolve at an angle, as if it was a giant Tilt-A-Whirl, and I wanted nothing more than to lie back and enjoy the blur of color and sound. Instead, I was forced to watch Terri squirm on Bobby Joe's lap, her arms enveloping him like she was holding on for dear life.

Jackie was similarly involved with Anna, and my spirits started to plummet. Billy had wandered away from the table, leaving me isolated between two grasping couples. Horny and humiliated were not what I'd expected to feel after I'd swaggered through the swinging doors, successfully passing as twenty-one.

I was saved from further ignominy by Piss Willy, a Ride Boy with the build of Hercules and the face of Barney Fife. Always eager to spread bad news, he arrived at our table and announced breathlessly, "Dinkie was trying to stop Leni from leavin' the show, and she ran over him with her car."

"Is it still drivable?" Jackie asked.

"Bumper's only bent. Dinkie's layin' under it in the mud."

"Fuck," Jackie groused, flushed and dreamy from making out with Anna.

"Need the Whipper brothers to help?" Bobby Joe inquired, at the same time shaking his head no.

"Stay here and make sure the ice doesn't melt in those drinks," Jackie answered, and motioned for me to accompany him.

A short while after my third or fourth drink, my every movement had acquired a momentum of its own. Now, nodding yes to Jackie turned into a near-headlong collapse. The floor of the Tilt-A-Whirl fell away beneath me, and I barely kept from sliding under the table.

"Want another round first?" Jackie asked, smirking. Scraping back his chair, he almost lost his balance, supremely plastered himself.

It was an ugly journey, but Jackie and I found our way back to the Party Time Shows lot, where a bog near the house trailers was helter-skelter with shouting carnies, bouncing headlights, and car horns. Above it all was the sound of a rusted-out Mercury, engine revving wildly, bald tires whirling as Leni threw the powerful car into a fishtailing tantrum that only dug it further into the muck. The driver's side door was open, swinging madly. As a headlight illuminated her momentarily, I could see that Leni's face was blotchy and dripping, and her fine, freshly permed black hair had wilted completely. Abruptly, Leni got off the accelerator. Smoke and steam rose from the idling Mercury. I caught a flash of orange underneath a rear wheel well—the color of Dinkie's uniform. Then Leni stomped on the gas again; the rear wheels spun sideways and tore across the immobile orange mass. There was a squeal and a cluster of sickening crunches. The Mercury shot a hundred feet forward to the curb of a paved city street, where the engine sputtered once and died, resisting Leni's brief attempt to restart it.

For the first time in my experience, there was silence on a carnival lot. Not one wisecrack. Then, after several aching moments, a woman began sobbing. Dad Foster, owner of the Smashed Sandwich, fell to his knees and retched. I forced down my own welling stomach, biting my lip until it hurt. I looked at Jackie. His hands were shaking.

Ellen Nortensen, the Cat Rack agent, was the first to speak. "That's it. I'm going back to stripping," she spat, turned around, and left.

Slowly, I became aware of a bustling at the rear of the crowd. Then, his face dark with fury, Chip broke into view, wearing a Stetson and polished cowboy boots that he tried to shake clean after each step in the muck. Surveying the row of stricken, aghast faces, he queried, "What is this? Some sick sort of love-in?"

Horserace Harry stepped forward. "Uh—boss, Dinkie's wife ran over him twice with her car. That's him face down there in the mud," he said, pointing at the barely visible orange lump.

"I told him to order an Okinawan," Chip mused aloud. Grimacing, he resumed his careful walk to the accident scene, cursing once when he stepped into a pothole and mud curled over the top of his boot. After traveling about thirty yards, he paused, hitched up his custom-made pants, and squatted beside the soggy orange form. Sighing deeply, Chip rubbed his unshaven face. Then he turned to the crowd and shouted, "Why is it always me who has to put out the fires?"

With a massive effort, Chip unstuck the orange mass, wrapped it in a blanket that had spilled out of the Mercury, bundled it in his arms, and approached us. Wary about viewing a dead body, especially that of a fat man who had been squashed twice by a car, I fought the urge to flee.

"I had no idea Chip was so strong," observed Mel Jewel, the See Live Reptiles owner, who had elbowed his way in for a closer look.

Chip arrived, breathing heavily, the uneven mud line on his pants up to his knee. "Catch," he said to Jackie, and unfurled the blanket, his orange burden tumbling into Jackie's arms.

Dad Foster screamed. Bending forward, Mel Jewel noted, "See, I could've told you it was too light to be Dinkie. Practiced eye," he added, tapping his brow.

As more people crowded in, there were titters, then guffaws. I was both relieved and amused. Only Jackie remained somber.

"It's a spoofer," Chip shouted in his face, spittle flying. He plucked the huge orange stuffed toy from Jackie's arms and held it up above his head for all to see. What once had been an oversized dog was now a mass of torn velour and exploded foam stuffing. A single plastic eye dangled on the cheek by a thread. "It's a piece of plush that's been sitting on the back shelf of the Duck Pond. I think it's supposed to be that dog from that kiddie cartoon, you know—what's-its-name," he added.

I recognized the stuffed animal as one of the many I'd used to blanket me on the frigid spring nights.

"Party's over, kids. Go home. The German dame's no killer, even though you can understand why she'd try. Clear the area, people. Big travel day tomorrow," Chip announced, clapping his hands as if he was shooing away a pack of stray dogs.

After a few minutes only Jackie and I were left, the immediate area darkening fitfully as the cars that had been lighting the scene drove away and carnies returned to their house trailers, the Blue Fin, or sleeping bags beneath semitrailers. Jackie was sitting cross-legged on a flattened patch of grass now, his head in his hands. I hadn't seen him so morose since we'd taken the Free Circus to Cleveland.

"Why couldn't I have been born into a family of chemistry professors?" he mumbled into his chest. At least that's what I thought he said, though his voice was so muffled it was hard to be sure.

"Your migraine getting worse? Maybe the peppermint schnapps isn't working any more," I responded.

"All schnapps does is give me a different headache that covers up the migraine. My only real remedy is to get out of this racket."

"You mean Party Time Shows?" I was stunned at the thought.

"You're just a visitor here. I've had to put up with jazz like this nearly every day of my life. I grew up with liars, scumbags, and con men. And that's only my family," Jackie sighed melodramatically. "I never had a close friend I could trust until you."

Jackie's phony sentimentality infuriated me. "Now who's the liar?"

"Hey, calm down. Trust is a relative thing. Relative to other people, I trust you. I don't trust my parents or Chip. How could I after this?" he said, parting his hair at the crown.

"I can't see anything."

"Feel it."

I did. There was a centipede-like scar across his head.

"That's seventeen stitches. Chip put me on the Swinger when I was ten, and taught me a rough con called the Georgia Gig Shot. I pulled it on a biker who beat me in the head with a motorcycle chain."

"Fine, you've got a scar. But, as far as I'm concerned, becoming an agent is the best thing that's ever happened to me. I feel great when I'm working a mark, putting one over on him. Even a ten-year-old kid." And at that moment, I understood why. Whether or not my family history played any part, I was constitutionally suited to being an asshole carny.

"I'm so, so happy for you. Not many people find their life's niche in the Balloon Store. Talking Tony and the gang will be flattered when I break them the wonderful news about High School Pete. Me—I'm getting out of the business."

"That's your second lie in sixty seconds."

"Thanks for keeping track."

"You're welcome."

"But I'm serious. I applied to Wharton School of Business. It's in Pennsylvania. It's prestigious, which is good. Because after graduating I can earn my degree and go to work for one of the big Wall Street firms. I never pushed for top grades. But my SATs were high, and my work experience will impress them. I mean, how many seventeen-year-olds make $125,000 on their summer jobs?"

The Tilt-A-Whirl I'd been flying on all night screeched to a stomach-churning stop. "You're pulling down that much, while I'm forced to sleep under teddy bears because I'm not getting a fair cut of my take?"

"Who told you that?" Jackie exploded, rising to his feet.

"A lot of people."

Suddenly we were nose to nose—although to accomplish this, Jackie had to severely tilt down his head. I returned his unblinking gaze. Neither one of us were barroom brawlers, but I sensed our conflict could descend to a physical level, a violation of the venerable carny tenet that the best way to avoid a fistfight was to keep talking, and fast. And if that failed, run for the hills.

Jackie must have felt similarly, because he stepped back, relaxed a tick, and adopted a conciliatory manner. "Look, I understand how you feel," he said, throwing up his hands helplessly. "It's just that I'm in debt big time to Double-O for the joints, so I'm asking you to wait for your cut. I'll pay the rest of your share as a bonus—a lump sum at the end of the season. How about that?"

"Let me think," I answered, though I'd already acted on a more reliable employee compensation plan.

"Hey, the beauty of doing it this way," Jackie added quickly, as if he was worried about closing the sale, "is that you won't piss the money away as soon as you earn it. Consider it as an enforced savings account. Believe me, when the season is over and I'm handing you a grocery bag full of cash, you'll kiss my feet."

"Sounds like a good idea," I replied, not meaning it.

"Shake hands, my man," Jackie said, smiling. I did.

I honestly couldn't say I believed Jackie would come through with the bonus. On the other hand, I couldn't guarantee he'd stiff me. Given that, I had concluded that my best option was to continue stealing from my best friend, who had long been stealing from me. "Glad we ironed this out," I lied.

"Me too," Jackie replied, probably lying as well. "Let's keep focused on the future. We've been best buddies for years."

"Still friends, huh?"

"Of course," Jackie answered, apparently surprised by the doubtful tone of my voice.

"My feelings entirely," I responded.

"Tremendous," Jackie added. "I'd buy you another drink to cement things, but I think the Squirt would start seeping through your eyeballs." He yawned. "Well, since it looks like we're not getting laid tonight, I'm hitting the sack."

My head needed clearing, and I decided a spin on my Yamaha would do the trick. "I'm going for a ride," I answered, fumbling for my keys.

"Don't take off with the Hell's Angels."

"Can't. I'm not wearing their colors," I replied, turning up the collar on my black leather car coat. Jackie left, and I was soon atop my motorcycle, dead set on turning all 90 cc's of the Yamaha into a bullet streaking through the Michigan thumb. I inserted the key and pressed the starter button, the engine shrieking to life like a supercharged sewing machine. The Yamaha was definitely not a deep-throated Harley, but there weren't any big, hairy guys around to snicker. I popped the clutch and leapt forward, only to brake just as suddenly to a dead stop and shut off the engine.

Half a football field away, bathed in a tall wedge of yellow light cast by the Airstream's partially opened door, was Bobby Joe Whipper, a bottle in each hand. A giggling Anna clutched his waist, while

Terri rode on his shoulders. Jackie came out of the trailer to greet them, took a slug from one of the bottles, and moved aside so they could enter. Then the door slammed shut, and all that was left was the muffled sound of good cheer.

I was overcome by the strange desire to visit my parents and sleep in my own bed for a change, just one night before returning to the show. Mineralton was a hundred miles away, but I was confident that I could snooze, shower, and be back on the midway in plenty of time for the noon call. I restarted the engine and, after a sluggish start, hustled the Yamaha off the lot and onto the adjoining asphalt road.

A few minutes later, I was headed south on an arrow-straight road through flat Michigan farmland. The humid air wetted my chin. I wound the Yamaha to its limits, the speedometer bouncing wildly between 70 and 80 MPH. The night smelled of newly turned earth, young leaves, and limp, wet crabgrass. I felt a lulling sense of relief. I'd taken control of my own fate with my decision to H.O. It was a matter of fairness. Whether that fate was a fat bankroll or a centipede-like scar, skimming the take was the only way I felt I could retain my standing with Jackie, not to mention my self-esteem.

Without warning, the engine banged once loudly and seized. I began slowing dramatically in the now-silent night. At 35 MPH, I hit a slick patch that made me lose control, shoot off the road, and go flying into a large plot of snap beans, the Yamaha and I following separate trajectories. I touched soft earth, caught my foot on a furrow, and tumbled.

The world was drained of color when I came to in the predawn twilight. At first, I remained still, reluctant to move and discover that I'd been broken. The sky grew brighter; a distant cow mooed. At last, I stood up. Nothing bled or protruded through a jagged hole in my pants. Limber as a career wino, I'd flown, crashed, and cartwheeled without major injury. Alcohol had its good side.

I left behind my broken and bent Yamaha; as the day passed, scavengers would pick it apart. They could have it. Two hours later, I was back at the carnival lot, where Dinkie Barnes was cadging donations toward a new mail-order bride. I gave the poor man a five and started to walk away—then returned, took back the five, and handed Dinkie a twenty instead. With my new business plan, I could afford to be generous.

CHAPTER NINE

Vera's Treasure

It was Vera who rescued me from Jackie when he discovered I'd H.O.'d $1,253 and seemed ready to slap my head with the fat end of a bowling pin.

In honor of becoming an Alibi agent, I'd outfitted myself in what I thought was appropriate style: blue sharkskin pants, white satin shirt with western-style fringe, and black silk briefs in the event a female admirer was starstruck enough to relax with me amongst the Queen Anne's lace swaying behind the midway.

Before purchasing the swinging briefs I'd never worn anything but standard white cotton Jockey shorts, the sort my mother didn't replace until the labels were faded. So I didn't know that silk became slippery when wet and would cause the sweat-soaked bankroll concealed in my underwear to slither into the sawdust while Jackie was schooling me on the Swinger.

And this was where Vera came in, albeit indirectly, when New Clarion Assistant Sheriff Billy Welu approached us with a grim mien—and only the right side of his handlebar moustache stiffened by wax, as if he'd been forced to suddenly abort his grooming.

Sheriff Welu sighed. "Jackie, I have terrible news. I received a call from Double-O and hurried over here as fast as I could. Your mother had some sort of attack and well, she passed away. She's gone."

For a moment, all was quiet. Jackie flipped the bowling pin onto the Swinger's painted plywood counter, where it rolled several times in a half-circle before stopping. I relaxed my white-knuckle grip on the croquet ball, secure for the moment that I wouldn't need it for self-defense.

A variety of expressions crossed Jackie's face, as if he was sampling the welter of potential responses to his mother's sudden death. Then, apparently having selected the most practical, he asked Assistant Sheriff Welu, "Does Chip know?"

"Funny, that's what Chip asked about you," Welu replied.

"How long ago you tell him?"

"'Bout ten minutes. Jumped into that big Imperial of his and laid a patch twenty foot long."

Curiously alarmed, Jackie turned to me and said, "Find the Whipper brothers and meet me at the Cadillac. We're making an emergency trip to Mineralton."

"Isn't this something you want to do on your own?"

"I need every good hand I can get," Jackie answered cryptically. He broke into a jog, one of the few times I'd seen him move at greater than deliberate speed.

I scooped my bankroll out of the sawdust, whispering, "Bless you, Vera."

I found the Whippers in a rare relaxed mood. Bobby Joe sat hunched on the grated steps of the Airstream as Billy kneeled in the grass, dabbing with a long, thin paintbrush at a framed canvas balanced on his knees. It wasn't unusual to see them here. Jackie had become enamored of them from the first time he'd seen Bobby Joe drag a mark into the Buckets by the nuts when he didn't answer his call. And so intimidated was the mark by Bobby Joe—and Billy lurking about, kneading his stubs—that he emptied his wallet (save for a buck) as Bobby Joe ordered, lost all $173 playing the game, and never uttered a peep, never called the cops, and was never again seen on the midway. "Now that's what I call playing the joint strong," Jackie had said admiringly to every chastened agent within listening range. Since then, the Whippers had become Jackie's pet rattlesnakes, weapons he used to intimidate the public and employees alike.

The brothers invariably made me nervous, and it was a relief to find them at ease: Bobby Joe peeling apart a blade of crabgrass, Billy filling out what I now saw was a paint-by-numbers version of a charming Norman Rockwell scene.

"What do you do?" Billy asked by way of a greeting.

"When?"

"In the off-season."

"Well, I've been going to school."

"Where's the angle in that?"

"You can graduate. Go to college."

"And what does that win you?"

"A diploma. A job."

"In other words, nothing. Listen, you naive son of a bitch. Forget that good-citizen bull. You got to get yourself an off-season trade so you can keep living this life year 'round, like we do."

"Otherwise, it's no shoes, November," Bobby Joe, balling up the blade of crabgrass, interjected.

"What's that mean? Never heard that one."

"Aw, he's just talking about this old carny, No Shoes Red, who usually wound up broke and barefoot before Christmas," Billy explained. "He was an Alibi agent, a good one, but he didn't have no decent off-season plan, so he usually spent the winter at the Salvation Army or a nuthouse."

Bobby Joe smiled, "That ol' boy was pretty good at acting insane. Got him three hots and a cot, so he was satisfied. Problem was, he got too good and after a while, the insane act was all he could do."

Billy added, "But I imagine that's not how you'd like to spend your winters, is it, High School Pete? With your refined sensibilities."

"Yeah. Straightjackets aren't my style," I answered. I was concerned, perhaps too late, that this was heading somewhere I didn't want it to go.

"Tell you what, then," Bobby said, setting his paintbrush aside. "Pay me five hundred bucks, and I'll teach you how to work this painting scam. I guarantee you'll never spend a day in an insane asylum just to put food on your plate. You can make up to a thousand dollars apiece on these artworks if you can convince folks they were done by the real Norman Rockwell. And all you got to do to create them is match the right color paint with the number. I go south every fall with a trunkload in the car, and before I reach Georgia, I'm sold out and got enough cash to spend the rest of the winter at the Fontainebleau in Miami Beach."

I grew even more tense. Now that I'd made the mistake of letting Bobby get this far, he wasn't likely to stop until I handed over five hundred bucks, willingly or not. Fortunately, I had a hole card to play—the truth. "Listen, guys, I hate to interrupt this highly educational lesson, but Jackie's mother has died. He's hot for you to meet him in the parking lot now."

The Whipper brothers' aspect suddenly changed, from hyenas stalking their prey to insincere clergymen affecting sorrow and concern. I'd hit their sweet spot: Jackie was their current gravy train, and next to nurturing him, all other grifts paled. For the time being, I was five hundred bucks to the good.

"How's he taking it?" Bobby Joe asked, frowning.

"Not too bad." That seemed to relieve him of the need to mourn. He lost the frown.

"You know," Bobby Joe continued, "when our momma died, it was an emotional experience. Every one of her johns showed up to pay their respects. Damn funeral procession musta been two miles long." He winked. "Just kidding. She's not dead yet."

Jackie's bright blue Eldorado was waiting with the top down behind a row of Port-A-Johns, the giant 462-cubic-inch engine rattling their fiberglass doors. Fiddling with the rearview mirror, Jackie greeted us as I took the shotgun seat and the Whippers climbed into the back. "Sheriff Welu filled me in on the details of Vera's death," he said, motoring carefully out of the dusty, makeshift parking lot. "Apparently she had a heart attack as she was berating the paperboy for throwing the *Daily Herald* into a mud puddle. It was the Wednesday edition with Kroger double coupons."

Bobby Joe leaned over the seats. "Sorry to hear that, buddy."

"She would've wanted it that way," Jackie said, "although I'm sure she would have preferred to drop dead after she cashed in the coupons." I thought I could detect the vague outline of heartfelt emotion breaking through Jackie's cynical veil. I changed my opinion when he added, "Two really important things to keep in mind about Vera: She loved money, and she hated banks. So she used our house as a sort of safety deposit box. There are thousands—maybe tens of thousands of dollars—in coins hidden around the place, and Chip has a ten-minute start on us to claim as much of it as he can. I'm offering you guys ten percent of what you can dig up before he gets it."

"I'm not trying to be smart," I said to Jackie, "but isn't this a ghoulish way to make money?"

"It's all a matter of perspective. I knew Vera as well as any decent son should, and this is how she wanted to distribute her assets: first come, first served, with a lot of fighting between her loved ones."

Jackie's explanation was sufficient to quell the uneasiness I had about our mission. I was seventeen, and the death of Vera was a remote abstraction, especially if it was cool with Jackie.

New Clarion was about a fifty-mile drive northeast of Kibbee Flats, beginning on a two-lane road that curved through empty marshlands before entering a fast stretch along the shores of Lake St. Clair. The road's soft shoulders were littered here and there with families on fishing outings. Children raced across the road with bamboo poles, while jalopies stopped suddenly and without warning so that the occupants could shoot the bull with friends.

After impatiently working his way through the human hazards, Jackie pulled over suddenly, put the car in park, leaned out the door, and retched twice. Pale, he sat upright and said one word: "Migraine." Out of the corner of my eye, I saw Bobby Joe elbow his brother and smirk. I remained silent, wondering if there was more happening inside Jackie than even he knew. Jackie then floored the Eldorado, reaching 105 MPH on more than one occasion. An hour later, he pulled into the Barrons' front drive, braking to a halt next to Chip's empty Chrysler Imperial, still ticking from the heat.

"Look anywhere," Jackie told us as we scrambled out of the car. "Up the chimney, in the toilet, under the washing machine."

"I feel like a six-year-old on an Easter egg hunt," Bobby Joe hollered, leading the charge. The door connecting the garage to the kitchen was locked. Without waiting for Jackie to produce a key, Bobby Joe rammed the door once with his shoulder, tried again, then stepped back and kicked at the deadbolt, shattering the frame. He stumbled inside, falling over Chip, who had been trying to block the door with a wheelbarrow overflowing with small change.

Quarters, dimes, nickels, and pennies flooded the floor, engulfing the legs of the kitchen table.

"I put up with Vera twice as many years as you. I deserve 100 percent of the money," Chip raged at Jackie.

"Percentage-wise you're not even right," Jackie replied, seemingly unperturbed. "Break it down mathematically, Chip. Putting up with the shrew twice as long as me would only earn you a 67 percent–33 percent split, rounded off." Turning to me, he said, "Check that old couch in her sewing room. She kept a money box beneath it."

Chip righted and began refilling the wheelbarrow. I dashed down a hallway and turned left into a windowless room containing a chair, an electric sewing machine, and a sagging brown couch covered with rolls of tickets and carnival posters. Grabbing it by the right corner, I tried to pull the couch away from the wall. It wouldn't budge.

Jackie entered. "Use this," he said, offering me a red plastic letter opener, "Property of Bell Hardware" written in marker on the blade.

"For what?"

"Cutting the cushions," he answered, sweeping posters and ticket rolls onto the floor.

I followed instructions and ripped open the cushions, the armrests, the seat backs. All discharged a small sea of change.

"Now you know why she learned to sew," Jackie said.

Billy called from a distance: "Two suitcases full of dimes, here."

"A bowling bag filled with silver dollars," Bobby Joe said, dragging it into the sewing room.

Our run on Vera's makeshift private bank continued for the next sixty minutes, moving from the main floor to the attic and down to the cool, humid basement. At the periphery of Jackie's lair, Jackie and I ran into Chip, who was leaning on a sledgehammer alongside the knotty-pine-paneled room that had been padlocked on previous visits. Today, the padlock was missing.

"Don't bust it up," Jackie called out. "That's Double-O's sanctuary."

"All the more reason why it's probably hiding cash up the wazoo. Vera didn't think we'd touch it," Chip asserted.

Jackie's retort was obscured by a vague hissing noise, followed by Double-O's booming, amplified voice: "Attention, ladies and gentlemen. This is Oliver Oxford Barron with an emergency warning: If you are cowardly, pregnant, or mentally unstable, please do not enter this exhibit. Because those who venture inside will be eyewitness to a horrible scientific tragedy. Shockingly, a sweet, kind, pure American mother, much like your own, will be transformed into—pardon my French—a butt-ugly vicious gorilla, her porcelain smooth skin slowly turning leather-like, hairy, and repulsive-smelling. Admission is free, but donations will be accepted by the two large gentlemen guarding the exits so that the frightened don't trample each other upon leaving. The show is about to begin. Would the emotionally fragile please stand aside so that the brave and courageous may enter?" After a few additional moments of the hissing sound, the announcement began again. I followed Jackie as he stepped carefully inside the workshop.

Groping in the darkness, I happened on a light string and pulled. A bare, swinging bulb popped on, illuminating Double-O, dressed in a dark blue suit, black tie, and leather house slippers. He was immobile on a padded bar stool, curled over a reel-to-reel tape machine. Decades of memorabilia scaled the walls: a news release trumpeting Party Time Shows as winner of the "Pulitzer Prize for Family Entertainment"; an Army surplus air raid siren once used to startle the crowds; "Free Inch" passes that entitled the bearer to an extra-long hot dog; campaign buttons supporting a wide array of law enforcement officials; shaved dice in a box; a faked proclamation presenting Double-O with the key to New York City; and several photos of a youthful, voluptuous Vera posing in a bathing suit between the trick mirrors that transformed her image from fresh-faced housewife to simian beast.

Jackie draped his arm over Double-O's shoulder and asked, "Is this for real, Dad? I didn't know you and Mom ever had a Woman-into-Gorilla joint."

Double-O shut down the tape machine, reached up, and squeezed Jackie's hand. "That little lady was all I lived for, son. She had the yokels tearing through the canvas trying to escape that gorilla. Your mother scared the hell out of everyone. Except me. I'm the only nut she never cracked, and that's probably why she kept me around."

"That's a love story straight out of Shakespeare," Jackie said.

In slow, arthritic increments, Double-O slid off the bar stool, bent over, and began fiddling with a two-foot-by-two-foot panel set into the wall. "This is probably what you and Chip were looking for," he said, allowing the panel to drop to the floor. Simultaneously, thousands of pennies sluiced out of the square hole, filling the workshop with their bitter, copper smell.

As the pennies continued to cascade, Jackie observed, "You know, with those in the walls, this room could've withstood a nuclear bomb."

"Take all of them away," Double-O said to Jackie and Chip, who had abandoned the sledgehammer and silently entered the room. "The coins were always meant to be yours. Your mother collected them for years as a parting gift for her boys."

"She could have at least put them in rollers," Chip said, impatiently eyeing his watch.

And that was the end of the coin hunt.

★　　★　　★

"Funerals remind me of church, and I hated church," I complained. "My mother made me go in itchy wool pants." I was pacing just beyond the clutch of mourners around Vera's grave, my only concession to formality a loosened red tie beneath my leather car coat. Then, agitated in the extreme, I threw the neckwear to the ground.

Bobby Joe Whipper quickly retrieved the tie, cinching it to a recently planted maple sapling. He was wearing a white T-shirt and black slacks, the same outfit he'd had on when we'd fled the midway three days before—although I knew for a fact that it, along with Billy's threads, had that morning been cleaned at the Easy Monday laundromat next to the Crossroads Tavern. He and Billy had held court at the bar in their underwear until the giddy female laundry attendant hurried over with their clothes neatly folded and gushed to Bobby Joe, "Oh, for you, darlin', no charge."

"What a frigging bore," Billy said, pulling at the waistband of his stiff, freshly washed jeans. He popped a Stroh's, drank half of it, wiped his mouth with his forearm, paused, jiggled the can to ascertain how much remained, swore, and consumed the remainder.

"Where's Jackie, anyway?" I fretted. "If we're here on time, why isn't he?"

"He'll come around," Billy assured me. "Folks always show up for their momma's funeral."

Suspecting that something else was afoot, I wondered if Jackie would. It had taken two days to haul away the coins and have them counted and rolled by a team of moonlighting bank tellers. Fortunately, the entire process had been peaceful. At Double-O's insistence, Chip and Jackie had agreed to a 50-50 split of the $78,000 we'd gathered. With uncharacteristic largess, Jackie had kept his promise to give each Whipper brother and me a ten percent share of his $39,000 cut, or $3,900 apiece. In paper money, no less. My concern was that we had yet to receive it, and I was suspicious that Jackie's absence from Vera's funeral was part of some greater nefarious plan.

The three dozen mourners, most of them unsuspecting middle-class acquaintances who'd only known Vera as a sadly neglected, wheelchair-bound housewife, stood stiffly as Reverend Earl Anthony, an Episcopalian minister, intoned a final few words.

"I can't stick around here any longer," I told the Whippers, then strode away, fists balled in my pockets. The grass was parched and crumbled under my feet. These were the waning days of July, and the only shade in this new part of Elm Grove Cemetery was provided by frail maple saplings tied to stakes here and there. I walked aimlessly, full of fire, pausing only to cuff the gone-to-seed dandelions unlucky enough to cross my path.

A cicada called out, haltingly at first, then with a long, soaring whir as I plunged into the stately gloom where the established families of Mineralton were interred beneath massive old elms. The trees blocked the smoky disk of the sun completely. Thick moss marked the massive, weather-stained gravestones, along with an erratic latticework of silverfish trails and the rings of oil cans left by someone who'd found the cemetery a convenient place to change five quarts and a filter.

My parents had often told me that this was where the better people were buried—the Jacobys, the Frinkmeisters, the Harewoods, the Fentons; considering my family's recent track record, I wasn't quite sure we belonged. Nevertheless, the hushed, earthy spot usually comforted me, as when I had accompanied my father to the exclusive Mineral Club, with its oiled oaks, leather-backed swivel chairs, humidors, and crystal jar filled with the mud in which Teddy Roosevelt had bathed.

The memory of that stirred emotions I'd been keeping in check. I began to wrestle with the idea of visiting my parents. I hadn't been home in weeks, other than to crawl through a basement window in the middle of the night to retrieve personal items.

Before I knew it, I was at the foot of my father's incomplete headstone, with the year of his death to be chiseled in at a future date. To the right was my mother's similarly unfinished marker, along with the long-occupied graves of my father's parents, all overwhelmed by a pillar of granite etched in descending letters: FENTON. Beneath this row was an empty space, the length and breadth of which I had never truly digested before. It was about eight feet by eight feet, or enough room for my brothers, me, and no one else—no wives or children. I was taken aback. My father had never touched me that I could recall. Yet he had determined that after death, I would lie alongside him, or, more accurately, directly beneath his desiccated feet.

Shuddering, I closed my eyes, only to be assaulted by a vision of my father in his tilted, rotting casket, his skin shriveled, leaving him with a dash-it-all, Dr. Sardonicus grin. Cartoon skeletons in Amvets caps surrounded Pop, drunkenly whistling the "Colonel Bogey March" while a hooting bartender spritzed them all with the contents of a bottomless seltzer bottle. Then, in my vision, the ground gave way beneath me and I fell into my father's grave, earth pouring down from above, peat and stone filling my nostrils. My father welcomed me with an ecstatic bear hug and exclaimed to his pals, "Well, look who finally showed up. Boys, next round's on me."

A blaring car horn rescued me from further imaginings. It was Jackie in his Eldorado, the top down, the Whipper brothers in the back, preoccupied with counting cash. I dropped any thought of going home; if my fantasies were that harrowing, I wasn't ready to confront my parents in the flesh.

"Hop in," Jackie said, beckoning me to the front passenger seat. He was wearing a blue sport coat over an orange Party Time Shows T-shirt.

"You missed the party," I replied, still shaken by my vision. In the distance, Vera's service was breaking up, mourners hurrying out of the intense sun to their cars.

"Things went slowly at the bank," Jackie explained, drawing an oversized, dun-colored envelope from inside his sport coat. "Here's your end."

I took a quick peek at the thick packet of bills. With no disrespect to Vera, it was a thrilling sight. "Where you headed now?" I asked, folding the envelope into a rear pocket.

"Back to New Clarion. We'll hold an observation for her on the lot. Probably be the first wake where pink cotton candy is served."

"Can you drop me off downtown? I'm buying a new motorcycle. I'll see you on the midway tonight."

"Have it your way," Jackie said, studying me, as though he suspected there was more to my plan.

And he was correct. An hour after he let me out at Van Motorcycles, I was speeding toward Mandy's house, as I had arranged in a phone call, on my new Triumph 650, a powerful bike that put the Yamaha 90 to shame. As a cover, I'd told Mandy I wanted her thoughts on the University of Michigan's freshman program. My real goal, of course, was to ignite a romance that we would continue on campus. Jackie still claimed they were dating, although I hadn't seen them together in weeks.

Mandy had retained a hold on my imagination since I'd stared at her helplessly, day after day, in junior high English class. She was the flirtatious and desirable girl of my dreams. Sleeping under the plush on chilly spring nights, I'd seen us as the first couple on the moon, bouncing weightlessly, wearing nothing but helmets. I'd fantasized about playing scratch golf with her at Pebble Beach, in the nude. To me, at seventeen, such dreams were romantic.

Mandy lived with her parents, Ken and Marion Ladewig, in a stylish house perched on the high side of the Williams River, about a quarter mile from where my grandparents had lived. The four-acre lot sloped down to the river, where it was an easy swim across to Kibbee Flats, if the swimmer didn't mind doing the crawl in slow-moving industrial waste.

I'd met her parents a couple of times. Mr. Ladewig had a curly gray pompadour and satisfied paunch, typically snugged under a cashmere sweater vest. He was a successful architect with three controversial attributes: He hadn't grown up in Mineralton, he worked in Detroit, and the house he'd designed for the family was low, rakish, and modern. Mrs. Ladewig was a wiry chain-smoker who had once been observed in her airy kitchen drying the same plate for a half hour before the housekeeper had led her to bed. She was a Mineralton native, however, best remembered as a two-time MHS homecoming queen.

Mandy held her hands to her ears until I shut down the rumbling Triumph, locked in the kickstand, and walked to where she was perched on the inlaid brick front steps. The first sign that something was different was her manner of dress: mature, almost beyond collegiate. She wore a button-down blue shirt, a black skirt, and black flats. Pearl earrings and a simple pearl necklace were her only accessories. Her thick hair was pulled back with a length of yarn into a very short ponytail.

"Listen, Pete," she blurted. "Sorry for misleading you over the phone, but I'm not attending U of M."

"But Jackie said you were accepted."

"I told him that so he wouldn't know where I really was going."

"You broke up?"

"Haven't gone out for months."

"Funny. Jackie never let on."

"There's probably a reason for that."

I wondered if Jackie's reason was to delay my seeing Mandy. Not that she had contacted me. I tried to hide my disappointment, although my stomach was sinking. "So, what school are you going to, then?"

Mandy considered for a moment. "Promise not to let Jackie know?"

"On my honor as a carny."

"Marygrove College."

"You mean where the nuns lock you up at 9:00 P.M.?"

"It's not that bad."

Trying to salvage something out of the encounter, I asked, "Maybe I can visit you sometime? Take you for a motorcycle ride, although you'd have to remove your habit. Wouldn't want it to get snarled up in the chain."

Thoughtfully, Mandy replied, "Pete, I really liked you in the old days when we stared at each other every English class. I thought you were sweet. But now . . . honestly, one Jackie a lifetime is enough."

"Problem solved. I'm not him."

"I don't know you well enough to say." Mandy stood up, adding, "Here, let me give you something to remember me by." She removed the six-inch length of red yarn that held her shiny hair in place, allowing her dark locks to fall and frame her face the way they had in junior high school.

I reluctantly accepted the yarn. "Can I kiss you at least?" I asked. "Maybe then you'll reconsider."

Mandy smiled indulgently. "Let's just hug."

I moved forward and, for the first time, drew the warm curve of Mandy's body into mine. I took a long moment to smell the hint of shampoo in her hair, the Dial soap on her skin. I pulled back and we locked eyes one last time, both of us breaking into grins.

I can say today that hugging Mandy was a greater thrill than anything I'd experienced in the dark behind the midway. As I fired up the Triumph, though, I was loath to admit it.

As for Jackie, he never again mentioned the wad of cash that had dropped from my pant leg like an errant turd. But that didn't necessarily mean he'd forgotten it.

CHAPTER TEN

My Georgia Gig Shot

In Pigeon, Michigan, the Whipper brothers presented me with the gift of the Georgia Gig Shot. It was the week after Vera's funeral, and Party Time Shows had put down stakes in this earnest farming community where the midway became lifeless after sunset, when apparently the entire population went to bed.

The first day in Pigeon, I was given a refresher course on the basics of the Swinger. The next day I worked my first marks, netting $185, gaining a good deal of confidence that quickly disappeared in the face of the Whippers' relentless needling that I had not worked the joint strong enough. I hadn't pulled a mark in by the belt or lapel—and to the Whippers, this was a sign of weakness. Indeed, they did such an effective job of belittling me that, in order to salvage my pride, the next morning as we raised the Swinger's awnings I foolishly asked Bobby Joe to school me on the infamous Gig Shot.

Bobby Joe's eyes brightened. He finished securing an awning in place and said, "Glad you've seen the light, High School. You'll never regret learning this move, because it's the only way to earn big money on the Swinger."

"Tell him about Larry Larry," Billy added, as he took a few cursory passes over the flash with a tattered feather duster.

"Good old Larry Larry," Bobby Joe reminisced. "He was this Swinger agent from Macon, Georgia, who dreamed up the Georgia Gig Shot. They should have called it the Larry Larry Gig Shot in his honor, sort of like they did with Einstein's theory of relativity, but that's another story. Anyway, Larry Larry beat a mark with his new method for fourteen thousand dollars back in 1955. The mark was this Korean War veteran who had just cashed some kind of back paycheck, not that Larry Larry was unpatriotic, mind you—he was a decorated vet himself—but war is war, peace is peace, and everybody's got to make a living, right?"

"So what's the G?" I asked, anxious to see if the gaff was within my ability to pull off well.

Bobby Joe took one of the bowling pins off the counter and placed it upright on the ground between us. "Larry Larry just stood the pin up like this and bet Mr. Korean War the whole fourteen grand that he couldn't kick it over with his foot. The mark, thinking Larry Larry was a simpleton ripe for taking advantage of, agreed to the bet and, after Larry Larry matched his fourteen grand, kicked the bowling pin over like this." Bobby Joe gave the pin one swift, straight kick, toppling it so that it fell backwards away from him. "Mr. Korean War hollered for joy and reached for the twenty-eight thousand bucks, but Larry Larry restrained him, as well he should have. Then Double L looked the mark straight in the eye and, I swear this was with a tear trailing down his cheek, told him, 'I'm sorry because you're a fellow veteran, but you lost, sir. You forgot the cardinal rule of the Swinger.' Then he reminded Mr. Korean War that the object of the game was 'miss it going, hit it coming.' The mark should have kicked the bowling pin over with the heel of his boot so that it fell toward—not away from him. After a tiny, but bitter, scuffle, Larry Larry kept the entire twenty-eight grand and the Georgia Gig Shot was born. Simple as pecan pie, wouldn't you say?"

"One quick question. How do you keep from getting killed by the mark?"

"A few agents have gotten cut and bruised along the way, but no deaths yet, as far as I heard. 'Course, I don't know who's keeping track."

Billy killed a sixteen-ounce 7-11 black coffee and said, "Guess that's too strong a way to work a joint for you, hey High School? Scary enough to make you pee in your pants?"

Both Whippers were now grinning and searching my face, I supposed, for some sign of fear.

"No, I'm still game. And as far as me peeing goes, you'll never know because I'm wearing diapers," I answered, wondering if I might actually need a pair when I found my Gig Shot mark. Then I assumed my hole at the Swinger alongside Bobby Joe and Billy and waited for willing customers to amble past. But there was truly no good opportunity to pull the Georgia Gig Shot over the next three hours. It was often a battle to drag a buck or two from the tight-fisted marks of Pigeon, so much so that the Whippers decided to pack it up for a while.

"These damn two-bit dirt farmers are so cheap they probably spread their own crap on the crops to save money on store-bought manure," Billy spat, transferring the few bills he'd earned from a cigar box on the counter of the Swinger to his breast pocket. "The only reason people like them have sex is to spit out more cheap labor. A smart man could make more money betting on a mule in the Kentucky Derby."

"Well, this might make me a dumb ass, but I'm going to stand here sweating until I Gig somebody out of a lot of cash," I responded.

It was a long wait, the good citizens of Pigeon perhaps deciding that they couldn't hold off until sundown to crawl into bed. Other than for a few carnies, the midway slowly lost all signs of human life. A loud argument broke out among the Ride Boys about whether the Salt 'n' Pepper Shaker was harder to operate than the Squirrel Cage. Across the street from the midway, an elderly woman spent forty-five futile minutes attempting to back out of an unpaved drugstore parking lot. Finally, a teenage boy who had just finished painting a shed alongside the drugstore guided her onto the street with hand signals. At dusk, three hours later, I paid Fuzzy, a Ride Boy, three bucks to run over and place his hand on the shed. Fuzzy returned, his palm unmarked. I had actually spent the afternoon watching paint dry.

I was ready to go looking for the Whipper brothers, who I assumed were off with Jackie, when a bulky deliveryman in a Coke hat, plaid shirt, Bermudas, and work boots bumped into me without apology. His hairless thighs were the size of my waist, and his wiry red hair was unyielding in the evening breeze. A dangerous guy, yet he possessed a beating heart, which made him a potential mark.

It had been so long since I'd spoken aloud, I choked a bit before making my call. "Hey, partner, step into my office here and let me show you the prizes you can win for your wife or your girlfriend—whichever one's not mad at you today. The name of the game is the Swinger, otherwise known as Aerial Bowling. All you need to win is knock over this bowling pin," I said, pointing to the pin standing behind me on the plywood counter.

Coke Man released his hand cart, laden with empty, clinking glass bottles of Coke, making sure it remained upright on the undulating turf of the midway. Then he leaned across me and slapped the bowling pin down with the meaty butt of his hand. "Give me the table radio over there in the corner and hustle. I'm on a tight schedule."

"Sorry," I refused, pressing forward until I stood belly to belly with Coke Man. I sensed I'd have to brazen my way through this in order to survive, let alone pull the Georgia Gig Shot. "Hands don't count. You've got to push this chained-up croquet ball so that it misses the bowling pin traveling forward and knocks it down on the way back. Here, take a free practice try." I shouldered Coke Man into the plywood counter, ground the varnished croquet ball into his hand, and wrapped my finger around the rear of the bowling pin so that when I slid it into the crux of the nailed-down wood coat hanger, it was imperceptibly off center. This, in accordance with a basic principle of physics, would allow the croquet ball to miss the bowling pin on its swing forward and knock it over on its swing back. In other words, I had arranged the pin so that Coke Man's practice throw would be a win, hopefully planting the idea in his head that he would also win when he paid, which of course wouldn't happen because of my subsequent manipulation of the pin.

Coke Man pushed the croquet ball hard, almost jerking the chain from its moorings. The ball swung back and knocked the bowling pin into his thick chest.

"Now hand over the goddamn radio," Coke Man ordered.

"Sorry, but like I said, that was a free practice try. My boss here tape-records every sales pitch for accuracy. Want to hear a play-back?"

Horserace Harry, who had wandered over to watch me work, patted his coat pocket as if it held a tape machine.

"Okay, smart fuck," Coke Man said, reaching for his wallet, "how much does it cost to play?"

"Two bucks. And you could win that two hundred dollar AM-FM unit," I answered, remembering that Jackie had purchased it for $9.95 at a Detroit pawnshop.

"Here's your two dollars. Put the radio next to me on the

counter and stand a few feet away when I swing the ball. I got to be careful about you pulling some scam."

"I'll stand back, but I'll keep the radio with me in case you try to run off with it."

"Thanks for the trust."

I reset the bowling pin dead center in the crux of the coat hanger. There was now no way that Coke Man could win. He closed his eyes as if to concentrate, then opened them and pushed the ball hard again. When the ball swung back toward us, it missed the bowling pin by a wide margin.

"This thing has got to be fixed," Coke Man exploded. He up-ended the bowling pin and began searching for a gaff.

I snatched the pin from him and rammed it back on the counter in the losing position. "You threw the ball too hard, that's all, muscles," I snapped. "Try treating it with a little finesse this time, like it's an intimate body part on your woman."

"She's filed for divorce."

"Sorry for bringing that up. I'm just ticked off because I want you to win. Makes for good advertising. In fact, would you make me one promise?"

"Like what?"

"When you win the radio, would you walk around the down-town area and tell everyone you got it here? As you can see, I need the business." Other than for a few lot lice, the midway remained devoid of marks.

"I'll see." Coke Man handed me another two bucks.

But it was time to raise the ante. Coke Man was already hot, and I sensed the longer he hung around, the angrier and more physical he'd get. So, improvising, I replied, "Sorry. Costs you a fin to play this time."

"What are you trying to pull here?"

"I run a business, not a charity. You're experienced now. My risk is greater. So I have to charge more."

"Only if you throw in another prize." It looked like Coke Man had concluded that the best way to punish me was by winning—and the quicker the better. For the first time since we'd begun our relationship, our interests coincided.

"Sounds fair. How about this $175 watch?" I asked, pointing out a snazzy, gold-sprayed Bolivia block worth $1.50.

Coke Man grunted, which I took for a "yes." He gave me three additional singles.

"Throw this one easy. I'm rooting for you." I reset the bowling pin in the losing position.

A rapid $150 later, I said gravely, "I hope to heaven you haven't run out of money to play with."

Stunned, like a boxer who'd just endured a surprise series of punches, Coke Man answered, "And why's that?"

"Because I'm about to make you the sole recipient of today's special offer. I'm allowed to give this gift to but one person a day. Most of them kiss my feet, they're so happy. But that's not a requirement, so don't worry." There was a sudden spray of goose pimples across my skin. If ever I was to attempt the Georgia Gig Shot, it was now. "Here's how it goes," I said as I extracted two wads of bills from deep inside my red Levis. One, wrapped multiple times with a rubber band, contained $750; the other was Coke Man's $150. "This is what you've invested so far." I slipped the $150 under the 7-11 coffee cup Billy had left behind.

Next, I unwrapped the $750, fanned it out, and placed it under the coffee cup as well. "To that I'm going to add this seven hundred and fifty dollars, for nine hundred total bucks. And because I'm generous, I'll bet this whole stake against the cash you have left—whatever the amount. To win it all, you simply have to knock the bowling pin over with your foot." I snugged the bowling pin upright into a level patch of earth. Sweat dribbled down my spine and into my pants. Soggy, my red T-shirt clung to my chest. I couldn't believe I was actually pulling a Gig Shot.

"No shit?" Coke Man hacked up a thick stream of spittle and snot, barely missing my shoes.

"Yeah, no shit." I jabbed my fingers into my mark's rib cage. "I've put my hard-earned money at risk. Let's see you do the same." I knew I had irritated Coke Man to the point where a red-blooded rustic like him had but two alternatives: Tear me to ribbons, or play.

Coke Man pulled out his khaki-colored cloth wallet and quickly counted the contents. "Let's make it quick, 'cause I'm late making deliveries already. This is two hundred and eighty-five bucks."

"Wow. I didn't know there was big money in soda pop. Maybe I should quit this job and join you," I said, as I placed his stake beneath the 7-11 cup along with the rest of the pot. "Now you get this whole kitty—one thousand, one hundred and eighty-five dollars—when you win. Just kick the pin over with your foot. And that's why this deal is called Today's Super Special. I think the boss is crazy to do it, but then, who am I to question? He's contributed more money to charity than the federal government." Adopting a grim mien, I stepped back and folded my arms to watch. Shaking his head, Horserace Harry began quickly walking away.

Coke Man tapped the bowling pin with the toe of his much-maligned work boot. It toppled to the ground, rolling slightly. He reached for the kitty with his rough, case-of-Coke-carrying hands.

"What the hell you doing?" I shouted, springing between Coke Man and the money. The moment of Gig Shot truth had arrived.

"I won."

"You lost."

"Bullshit."

"Let me remind you, sir, that the object of the game is to 'miss it going, hit it coming.' You kicked the pin down with your toe so that it fell away from you. You should've knocked it over with your heel so that the pin fell toward you. You lost." I scooped up the kitty, roughly shoving it into a back pocket. The Coke Man turned to grab an empty bottle from his hand cart.

I could almost feel the adrenaline crackle through my veins. My fight-or-flight response was kicking in, confronting me with a simple but quite significant decision: Did I stay to fight a furious guy fifty pounds heavier than me, not counting the Coke bottle? Or did I flee and risk losing the respect of my peers, while avoiding a vicious blow from a swinging Coke bottle?

I took a step toward Coke Man, hip-faked to the left, and sprinted right. He lunged at me and tripped over a cart wheel, sending cases of empty bottles crashing. I slipped between the Swinger and the adjacent Flukey Ball tent, then embarked on a bit of broken-field running that would have made my great-uncle, the football All-American, proud: high-stepping over tent ropes, cutting between moving cars, dashing around arriving marks, and finally breaking into an open pea field.

Catching my breath, I scanned the distant carnival lot for any sign of Coke Man. I didn't spot anything but his red delivery truck, so I walked slowly to the men's room of a nearby Mobil station, where I removed my shirt, doused myself with water, organized my money, and otherwise stayed out of sight while flipping back and forth between joy and panic.

A couple of hours later, the Coke truck gone, I carefully made my way back to the carnival, now closed for the night, and knocked lightly on the door of the Airstream.

"Hey, I had ten people trying to find you," Jackie said, allowing me in. "Business was so slow a bunch of us drove to Saginaw Bay and went swimming." He was sunburned and wore a bathing suit under a thick terrycloth robe. "And now I'm celebrating because I received a letter from Wharton. I was accepted without patching the admissions department."

"Congratulations."

"I've also got good news for you. This great agent named the Fireman is coming here to manage the Flat Store for me. He's agreed to test you as a Flattie."

My excitement was leavened, when, after I gave Jackie his half of the take (minus the two hundred dollars I'd H.O.'d), he revealed that he'd okayed the Whippers' plan to teach me the Georgia Gig Shot. My mood improved as word filtered in that the Whippers, after borrowing a hundred dollars each from a couple dozen brother carnies, had left the show in search of other adventures. And without so much as a "Good-bye" or a "Get screwed" to Jackie.

CHAPTER ELEVEN

The Con Man and the College Prep Student

"What a great moment," Jimmy "The Fireman" Hite's shapely wife, Cat, said as I stepped into their brand-new thirty-two-foot Coachmen trailer home. We were in Bellevue, a small town on the St. Clair River between Lake Huron and Lake St. Clair. "Here in one room at the same time—a man of the world and a future college student."

I sat down opposite the Fireman at the fold-out kitchen table while Cat fawned over me, pouring a tall, strong 7&7. A small portable TV blared in the background while a toy French poodle tore at a rubber bone between my feet.

"So Jackie wants me to make a Flattie out of you, hey?" Jimmy asked. His voice was a mixture of New Orleans drawl and the throaty rasp of a spaced-out jazz musician. Dressed in a blindingly white cotton-knit shirt and pressed, pale yellow seersucker pants, the Fireman chewed a golf tee like a toothpick. Around forty, deeply tanned and handsome, with attractive lifelines around his eyes and prematurely white, razor-cut hair, the Fireman was the quintessential Flat Store agent. He was a cunning, yet seemingly cultured man of leisure, which was why Jackie had hired him to manage the Flat Store for an extra taste of the action. The Fireman remained silent for nearly a minute as he sized me up by the make of my watch, the cut of my clothes, my hair. Although I'd dressed up in a pullover, gray dress pants, white shoes, and black sunglasses, I felt like an undershirt-wearing rube. "I forgot your name already," Jimmy finally said.

"Peter Fenton. The other agents call me High School Pete."

He rolled my real name around in his mouth. "Veddy British," he said, seeming to be lost in thought for a moment. "Probably the best thing you got going for you. But you say you're headed for college?"

"University of Michigan."

"Then it's time we got you a new nickname." He paused. "How's Joe College sound?"

"I really don't care what anyone calls me."

"How about Joe Prick, then?"

"I'll pass."

The Fireman fell silent again. Cat and I nervously sipped on our 7&7s and made small talk. Actually, she talked and I listened. Cat was a cute bleached-blonde in her late twenties, dressed in an expensive-looking pantsuit. Her real name was Gina. "Cat" was the nickname Jimmy had given her because she'd been the reigning Catfish Queen at the Seventeenth Annual Catfish Festival in Blacksburg, Mississippi, when they'd met a decade before. Back then, Blacksburg's most noteworthy event took place during the festival, when an Evinrude outboard engine was awarded to the person who correctly guessed how many catfish would be killed after a stick of dynamite was tossed into a swamp. So, two weeks after Jimmy's traveling carnival left town for West Memphis, Arkansas, Gina ran away to join him, and they'd been together ever since. It was a good life, she said, because Jimmy was such a talented Flattie—so hot, in fact, that he had come to be called the Fireman.

Jimmy revived and launched into a long-winded jackpot about a pyromaniac he had worked with on a Texas carnival. "You see, this guy's name was Smoky," Jimmy said. "Did I tell you he was on Texas State Shows? Anyway, Smoky was such a fucked-up pyromaniac—pardon my French, because I know you Joe College types frown on vulgarity—that he had three round-the-clock security guards whose only job was to make sure he didn't put the match to another building and wind up back in prison. Anyway—he—uh—did I tell you that his moniker was Smoky or Hazy or something? He was a helluva earner, had to be to pay back all those security guards. But to get back to my point . . ." The Fireman's slurred syllables burbled into a murmur, and his jazz trumpeter's voice finally sputtered to the end of its set. After a minute or two, it was clear he was asleep, his chin rolling on his chest.

"This is so embarrassing," Cat said, her face flushing. She shook Jimmy gently by the shoulder. "Honey, the boy here wants you to teach him his job."

The Fireman opened his eyes as if nothing had happened. "Yeah," he mumbled, then bolted up from the table, walked into the kitchen, and unplugged the TV.

"Hey, hon, I was listening to that," Cat protested.

"Your soap operas can wait for a change. Joe College here and I have got to have a serious discussion. Freshen the kid's drink and bring me a glass of Coke with a couple inches of shaved ice on the bottom."

"Say pretty please."

"You'll have to settle for plain 'please.'"

"Thank you."

"She's on a manners kick," the Fireman told me. Cat filled his beverage requests and returned with three glasses on a cork-bottomed tray.

The Fireman drank half of the Coke before asking me, "What makes you think you have what it takes to be a Flattie?"

"I did pretty well in the Swinger. Pulled off a Georgia Gig Shot."

Mention of the Swinger seemed to incense Jimmy. He finished off his Coke. "Listen, in order to prosper as a Flattie, you'll need to forget everything you've learned about being an agent so far. All that Alibi nonsense. All of it. I don't care if you hypnotize yourself, hit your head on the pavement, or hire a doctor to perform a lobotomy on the appropriate part of your brain. Forget it all—the rough stuff, the Georgia Gig Shot, the Alabama Shuffle, the California Caper, or whatever other goofball crud Billy Joe or Bubba Joe and his stubby-finger brother showed you. Those two are gone. History."

"I hear they're in Florida."

"Probably selling old ladies do-it-yourself enema kits."

"Jimmy, please. You're in mixed company," Cat interrupted.

The Fireman continued unabated. "That Alibi crowd is an insult to us folks who use the power of the mind, not the bicep, to earn a decent living for our families. But you know the real difference between an Alibi agent and a Flattie, the one that sets us apart?"

"I give up," I answered.

"Class. Fuckin'-A class," the Fireman said with a hint of a smile. "And by the way," he added, "no profanity in the joint. I just used a sprinkling of it now to make a point, with apologies to Cat and you, if you're the sensitive type. You're not, are you?"

"Don't think so."

"Then start becoming sensitive, right now. That's right. Sensitivity is important when you're a Flattie. You'll need to be sensitive to your mark's every thought, like you can see into his mind. Because it's classy marks who play the Flat Store. These are people who don't want to get their fingers dirty playing lowlife Alibi games with lowlife agents in smelly T-shirts. And these kind of marks are a devious lot. That's right. Beneath their bland exteriors, they're as greedy as a stickup man in a liquor store. But they're smart. And that makes them dangerous. There isn't a classy mark out there who wouldn't steal the Abe Lincolns from their best friend's penny loafers if they could do it in a gentle, sneaky way that didn't involve a knife or hitting their buddy over the head." Jimmy swished around the shaved ice that remained in his glass. "You heard of armed robbery?"

I nodded.

"That's not the classy people's way. They practice *dis*-arming robbery; you know, the sort of crime people do wearing a sport coat or maybe a golf shirt, which is why you'll need to dress the same. Blend in. Wear nice clothes in the Flat Store—tailored shirts, something silk, maybe wear a golf hat or lean a bag of clubs behind you in the corner like you just walked off the links. And whatever you do, remember this: Classy marks think you're stupid, otherwise they wouldn't be wasting time at your half-assed carnival game. It excites them to believe they can take advantage of us."

The Fireman stopped and bent over to play with the poodle. Cat cleared her throat and asked me, "Don't you think Jimmy would make a good Cadillac salesman? He received an offer once from a dealer in Baton Rouge."

"And most of all, Joe College," Jimmy said loudly, ignoring Cat, "you'll need to learn how to riff like me."

"How's that?"

"I've been talking for ten minutes and don't remember a word I said. I made it all up on the spot and if you paid me to repeat it, I wouldn't make it beyond word one. What's important about that? Only this: You can say and do anything you want in the Flat Store. Just keep saying and doing it faster than the mark can think."

I let that sink in.

The Fireman stood up, walked into the kitchen, and plugged the small portable TV back in. "I'm going to get a whipping if I don't let Cat get back to her soaps," he told me. "Now haul yourself over to the Howard Johnson's restaurant and get acquainted with the Ghost and Flopper. You'll be working alongside them if they give their approval. I'll look you up tomorrow and tell you the verdict."

I deposited my empty glass in the sink, said my good-byes, and left for the next phase of what was shaping up to be a multipart job interview.

The Ghost spooned the chocolate froth into his mouth, savored it tentatively, then made a face and spit it into his white cloth napkin. Folding up and tossing the napkin onto the brown Formica tabletop, he complained to our teenage waiter, "This doesn't have double malt."

"Yes it does," the waiter answered, gazing out the window. He was riveted by an all-white Chevy Impala that was revving up in the Howard Johnson's parking lot.

The Ghost clapped his hands inches from the teenager's face in order to get his attention. "I specifically ordered a chocolate malt with double malt, and this doesn't have it." Close up, the Ghost was truly wraithlike, with pale, translucent skin, fine blond hair, and a fluid way of moving, as if he'd been deboned with a razor-sharp fillet knife.

"Okay, you win. I'll take it back to the kitchen," the waiter replied, lifting the tall malted glass while whispering under his breath, "Shithead."

"Do that. And bring the manager along when you come back. I have a suggestion for him."

"The kid insulted you," Flopper observed without rancor as the boy left. He was as substantial as the Ghost was ethereal, with curly blond hair, a dark brown silk suit, light brown silk shirt, and matching amber pinkie rings. His ruddy face had a mole on the right cheek that looked like a tear.

"Not really. I am a shithead," the Ghost replied, eliciting a chuckle from Flopper, who then went back to dipping his fried clams, one by one, into a pool of ketchup he'd made on the edge of his plate. I was sitting with them in a robin's-egg blue, upholstered booth at the rear of the bustling Howard Johnson's. I nervously fondled a Coke while Flopper and Ghost worked on their fried clams, which had arrived at the same time I did.

"Sorry for ignoring you, pal, but the clams suck when they're cold," the Ghost told me, forking a single fried clam and then a French fry, a method of eating that he'd employed from the start. It was an honor of sorts to be directly addressed by the Ghost, having been pointedly ignored every other time our paths had crossed. The same held true for the Flopper, who also avoided any carny beneath the Flat Store level. Yet I knew that my current elevation in status would come crashing down abruptly if I did not measure up to their standards. And I did not precisely know what those were.

Swallowing, Flopper turned to me. "My friend's whole double-malt situation here and how he took care of it," he said, gesturing at the Ghost, "shows that in order to receive what you deserve, you've got to demand it in no uncertain terms. No matter how little what you deserve is."

"Nobody's giving anything away," Ghost affirmed. "But somebody can always make you the exception."

Flopper abruptly changed the subject, asking me, "Who do I remind you of?" Without waiting for my answer, he said, "I'll tell you—Reverend Billy Graham. Matter of fact, I'm so much like him I can walk down the street carrying a collection plate and have it filled up before I reach the end of the block."

"Sorry, but I'm not following your—"

"Say something loud enough and long enough, and you'll have believers. The paying kind, too. Same holds true working a joint. To earn money, you need to turn marks into believers. Get them holding onto your every word like Billy Graham does at a White House prayer breakfast."

"Boy, can that guy build a tip," the Ghost mused.

The Howard Johnson's manager, balding and fortyish, arrived, the teen waiter following sullenly in his wake. "Here's your malted, with double malt. Sorry for the inconvenience, sir," the manager apologized, sliding the remixed malted in front of the Ghost.

The Ghost nodded, officiously unwrapped the new straw he'd been provided, and took a sip. After a moment's consideration, he announced, "Excellent double malt. Best I've ever had. In fact, it's so good I think you should make them for the entire house."

"Really?" the manager asked, smiling broadly. "There must be twenty people in here."

"All the better. And here's a little something for your trouble," the Ghost replied, reaching into the inside pocket of his tailored, charcoal gray sport coat. "A free game pass to my carnival booth. It's the one with all the big prizes."

"You didn't have to."

"Nevertheless, I did. So hurry back to the kitchen and start making those malts. I can't wait to see all the delighted faces." The Ghost waved an arm grandly, taking in the spacious, brightly lit room.

Barely containing his glee, the manager left, pulling the waiter along.

"I think you've made him the happiest Howard Johnson's manager in Michigan," an amused Flopper told Ghost.

"For the time being, at least," Ghost chuckled, and began working on his malt.

Ten minutes later, as the manager began distributing the malts among his surprised customers, Ghost and Flopper stood abruptly and strode toward the exit. I scrambled to follow.

"Hold on. Say, fellas, that's $47.50 for the malts," the alarmed manager announced, trotting over.

"What are you talking about?" the Ghost asked, appearing genuinely puzzled.

"The malts you bought for the house."

"I think there's been some sort of mistake. I'll let my partner here straighten it out," the Ghost said, nodding at me.

All at once, I knew the true purpose of my get-acquainted meeting with Flopper and Ghost: It was a test of my ability to worm my way out of an unforeseen tight spot. In order for us to walk away without paying for twenty malts, I now had to turn the increasingly furious Howard Johnson's manager into a believer or, at the minimum, sow in him the seeds of reasonable doubt.

I swallowed hard and took the plunge. "Raymond," I said, tapping his name tag, "let me ask you what I think is a fair question: Why should *we* pay for *your* generosity?" The puzzled expression on Raymond's face gave my confidence a boost.

"Your friend here bought malteds for the house."

"Let me remind you of what he actually said. And that was, 'I think *you* should make malts for the house.' My friend did not shout out, 'Hey gang, the malts are on *me.*' He's a responsible father with a wife and four kids. He doesn't go around blowing money like that."

"So then who's going to pay?"

"You are. But I'm going to reward your grand gesture. It may surprise you to learn that the three of us are traveling philanthropists out to identify America's do-gooders, and with this selfless act, you qualify for our grand prize. Could I have your full name for my entry list?" We were bunched at the cash register. I picked up a pen and notepad and waited for Raymond to offer his last name.

"I don't know what sort of contest you're talking about—but, okay, my name is Raymond Chester."

I pretended to write that down and stuffed the pen and paper in a shirt pocket. Then, feeling pretty good about my performance thus far, I told Raymond, "Now all I need is twenty bucks, and you're entered for an all-expenses-paid trip to fabulous New York City."

Raymond started to pull out his wallet, then seemed to have second thoughts and said, "Just get out of here, would you?"

"Have it your way. But I'll have to remove your name from consideration," I said as Ghost, Flopper, and I made our way through the double front doors.

Outside, in the parking lot, I waited for the congratulations to begin. After all, I had talked us out of a $47.50 bill. Instead, the Ghost frowned and admonished, "Twenty dollars is a little steep to ask for an entry fee. I would've told him ten. He might have been good for that."

In an offhand manner, Flopper added, "By the way, we're going up to the Flat Store. How about meeting us there in an hour, unless you have something better to do."

"To work the joint?" My handling of Raymond had impressed them, obviously.

"Not yet."

"Just how many more tests do I have to pass?"

"One. We want to see how you do as our new Outside Man."

The Ghost peered down at me from his perch inside the imposing, steel-clad Flat Store, his face passive and imperial. He finished cleaning his hands with a perfumed towelette and handed me a brown paper lunch bag.

"What's this?" I asked, looking inside.

"Tools of your new trade."

The bag contained straight pins, carpet tacks, a pack of Camels, and a stink bomb. I had a sinking feeling about how I was supposed to utilize them.

"Your job as Outside Man will be to keep a tip from building as we work our marks," Ghost said. "At the other joints, an agent wants a big crowd. But here, all Flopper and I need is one good nitwit each to notch a lucrative day. So we don't want any gawkers hanging around to knock the joint. That's where you come in. Use this stuff to keep the rubberneckers away and, if none of it works, improvise."

"We'll signal when we need you," Flopper added, looking over my shoulder at a few approaching marks.

Stashing the contents of the paper bag into various pockets, I wandered over to the merry-go-round, in its customary position a short distance from the Flat Store. A dozen kids were screaming above the taped calliope music, while their attending fathers carefully observed a voluptuous woman in tight capri pants scoop her child out of a baby stroller. The men were perfect Flat Store material: relatively affluent and bored, eager for a game of high-stakes action to help ease the strain of parental duty. While maybe winning several big prizes to impress the wife after she worked her way through the long line at the ladies' room.

It was late afternoon, and business at the Flat Store was slow. The sun emerged from behind a cloud bank. I shaded my eyes while the rest of me sizzled. Like a method actor, I worked myself into a utilitarian anger to draw on when I was directed to push the public around. To do this, all I had to do was imagine Jackie, waiting in his air-conditioned Airstream for word that I had failed as an Outside Man. At last, around five o'clock, a tip began to build at the Flat Store, and the Ghost beckoned me with a waggle of his pinkie finger. Feeling suitably mean and hostile to proceed without it, I stashed my bag of tricks behind a trash bin and bulled my way forward.

The Ghost had an engrossed player bellied up to the counter below him. I went to work with a vengeance. "Excuse me, pal," I said, elbowing aside an elderly farmer, spilling his nearly full box of caramel corn.

Shaken, he stuttered, "Th-that's fifteen cents you owe me, young man."

"Got a receipt?"

"Of course not."

"I'll trust you," I replied, giving him a quarter. "Now go home to your sheep. Your kind's not wanted here." When he didn't move, I crowded him again. With startled, rabbit eyes, he staged a face-saving retreat. I trembled involuntarily at committing such a violation of middle-class norms. Dummies, I forced myself to remember, all marks are dummies, who'd stare in drop-jawed fascination at a spinning hubcap if admission were free. Marks were drawn to the midway by cheap thrills and danger. I was just giving them what they came for.

My spirit quickly replenished, I went back to work, stepping on the peeling, sunburned toes of a vacationer in sandals. I coughed on two teenagers and muttered obscenities behind a picture-perfect family of five. I got into a shoving match with a shirtless, muscle-bound trucker until his wife saved my skin by pulling him away. Despite the narrow escape from a beating, I swelled with pride of craft: I had succeeded in driving away every stinking loiterer with obnoxiousness and bare hands alone. Let that be a lesson to every Outside Man who required thumbtacks and other crutches!

Pumped up, I retreated to the merry-go-round, while maintaining a vigilant eye for another tip to form. Fifteen minutes later, the Ghost beckoned me as his crestfallen mark shuffled off, arms wrapped around a consolation-prize teddy bear.

"Lose yourself for an hour," the Ghost ordered in a low voice as he tidied up a stack of tens and twenties with the prim efficiency of a bank teller.

"Best Outside Man we've had in days," Flopper said to me admiringly. "You're a real scumbag—and I mean that in a good way. With a *Billboard* and a dime, you can get a job anytime, anywhere. You've got security."

"You ever do it?" I asked.

"What?"

"Outside Man."

"And risk getting hurt?"

"Just wanted to know," I said, turning away. With conflicted emotions, I retreated to the Scenic Lounge, where I ordered a boilermaker at the bar using my fake Alabama ID. I felt proud because I'd performed a job even a hardcore carny like the Flopper was reluctant to do. Stupid for the same reason.

I spotted Jackie at a window table, impatiently tapping a swizzle stick. He wore a blue sport coat and gray slacks over a lemon yellow shirt. The spiral notebook he used as an informal ledger was under his left elbow. "Hey, Outside Man. I've been looking for you," he called out.

I took the chair opposite him, moving aside a wicker basket laden with plastic-wrapped saltine crackers and garlic sticks. "That was some hazing you put me through. I nearly got myself turned inside out by a Mack truck driver," I said, placing my hand atop Jackie's in order to stop him from compulsively rapping the swizzle stick. The end nearest me was frayed badly, as if it had been chewed on. Despite his typical calm, I sensed that Jackie had been concerned about how I'd react when we met. This was heartening. I had become substantial enough that Jackie needed to reckon with me.

Jackie withdrew his hand and flicked the swizzle stick onto the peeling, sun-faded windowsill. "Young men have endured more just to join a fraternity. Do you know that some have actually died?" When I didn't answer, he loudly ordered a rum and Coke, after which he said to me, "Listen, it was all toward a good cause. Flopper and Ghost will respect you more now that you've been put to the test."

I was about to tell him to fuck himself when a soft, warm hand pinched me hard on the nape of my neck. I realized that it was a friendly gesture when the Fireman said to me, incredulously, "Joe College, you should be drinking champagne on this momentous occasion. And without putting up a dime."

The Fireman called for a bottle of bubbly, but the lounge didn't stock it, so he asked for three Champales instead. Then he unbuttoned his black silk sport coat, twirled around a chair and sat in it backwards with his chin on the back seat and his dark brown eyes level with mine. Still, although we were a mere foot or two apart, the Fireman avoided direct eye contact, focusing instead, it seemed, on my right cheekbone.

"What's to celebrate?"

"Didn't Jackie tell you?"

"Not unless he's using ESP."

"You're going to be the youngest Flattie in America. Soon as we finish our Champales, I'm starting you on an intense schooling program that'll reduce ten pounds of fat from your head and add twenty pounds of muscle to your wallet. In return, all I ask is that you start exercising after class, because the ladies are gonna be chasing you from now on instead of the other way around. And I don't want you to run out of breath and get screwed to death, 'cause Jackie and I are making a big investment in you."

I spent my entire two-week training period thankful I hadn't said "fuck you" to Jackie, including the time we drove to Five-Finger Discount together, laughing and cutting up jackpots. I purchased three sport coats—one of sharkskin, two of silk—and three matching pairs of tailored pants. I considered, and decided against, an ascot.

CHAPTER TWELVE

The Rise and Fall of Two Flat Store Marks

It was 7:00 P.M., starting time for Flatties. Party Time Shows had been open since 11:00 A.M., but not the Flat Store. No, the Ghost, Flopper, and I had been lolling about our rooms at the Timbers Motel, sipping 7&7s, the Ghost and Flopper emerging occasionally to conduct important business like placing bets over a pay phone, wincing at the bright daylight that glanced off the dial. I'd spent the afternoon removing my new clothes from the flimsy Hot Sam's boxes, laying them out on the bedspread, making sure to avoid the stains left by the cold Kentucky Fried Chicken wings I'd consumed for breakfast.

Now, though, it was nearing time to work, and I tensed up. For the next five hours I'd be confined to the Flat Store, working mark after mark, never leaving the place because the Fireman couldn't bear the thought that one of his agents would miss a customer, miss making some money for him and Jackie.

I stripped to my red silk briefs, swatting one of the mosquitoes that had slipped through a wide tear in the screen, along with a few horseflies that had sensed the chicken. I dressed quickly and walked into the bathroom, where I admired my new salmon pink sport coat and gray silk shirt in the mirror. Then I stepped onto the toilet seat and checked out my gray pants and white patent leather shoes. The Fireman could no longer claim that, even though I was only seventeen, I didn't look the part of a Flat Store agent. At least, that's what I thought.

I hooked my smoked, black aviator sunglasses over my breast pocket, spotted one of the horseflies landing on the mirror, and in one swift move slapped it dead with a wet hand towel I'd left dripping over the sink. Good omen. Maybe this would be my night to land the fifty-thousand-dollar mark of wishful thinking and Flat Store legend.

The midway, a combination of beach sand, tufts of crabgrass, smooth rocks, and pebbles, was just beginning to fill for the evening: barefoot, barely teenage girls picking their paths carefully, leaping and squealing when a pebble caught the soles of their feet the wrong way; boys in drying bathing suits and souvenir T-shirts, trailing conspicuously behind them, tossing pebbles at each other, bolting suddenly and cursing; all followed by their parents, gamely plowing strollers through the sand.

Oscoda, Michigan, was a resort town near the northeastern tip of the Lower Peninsula, where families from Detroit took cabins that overlooked Lake Huron. They swam and fished for perch during the day, and at night they hid in their cabins or in taverns from the thick clouds of mosquitoes and mayflies. This evening, it seemed that everyone was making their way to Party Time Shows, praying perhaps that the black fog of diesel exhaust, the noisy rides, the heat, and the lights combined to keep the maddening insects at bay.

The Flat Store, a steel-plated, twenty-foot-long trailer painted bright Party Time Shows orange, was being opened by a Ride Boy I knew only as Squirmy. With a broomstick, he struggled to raise the heavy steel awnings horizontally above each of the three agent holes. According to tradition, it was undignified for a Flattie to perform physical labor, so every evening, the Ghost, Flopper, and I would pay a Ride Boy five bucks apiece to raise our respective awnings. I'd rather have kept the money.

"Would you stop moving around so fuckin' much? You're making me itch," Flopper yelled at Squirmy, a scrawny, thirtyish redhead who sported a brilliantly purple poison-ivy rash from ear to ear. It was like a full beard. He'd been scratching it nearly nonstop for the entire three days he'd been with the show.

Flopper moved the chunk of ice he was sucking from one cheek to the other. "I just gave you five bucks. Why don't you go to the corner drugstore and buy a bottle of calamine lotion with it instead of spending all your money on corn dogs and crap?"

"Now?" Squirmy asked.

"Finish raising the awning."

Squirmy did.

"Now split and don't let me see you again until your face is clear."

"You mean?"

"Don't come back here until the show leaves town."

Squirmy eyed the dirty five dollar bills he'd woven through his fingers, shrugged, and headed toward the Belgian waffle stand.

"What brought that all about?" I asked Flopper as I climbed into the trailer, careful not to smudge myself.

Flopper grunted and turned away. Although he fashioned himself after saintly Billy Graham, he succumbed frequently to dark moods. One wrong word could cause him to explode, so I left him alone and prepared to do business.

First, I checked the flash behind me to make sure it was all there, which wasn't always the case. Since the major prizes were never won, they were often borrowed by the agents and only haphazardly returned. Arrayed on three levels of shelving carpeted with crushed yellow velour was a variety of quality merchandise, at least relative to what the other joints displayed. A seventeen-inch Sony color TV was the centerpiece, flanked by GE portable radios, imitation Ginsu stainless steel knife sets, "Bolivia" electric clocks, Osterizer blenders, and a variety of knockoff wristwatches. Just two nights before, Flopper had used the blender to make a batch of ice cream daiquiris in his room.

That done, I extracted my game board from beneath the shelving. It was heavy and awkward to handle, an approximately three-foot-by-six-foot slab of varnished, ¾-inch plywood bordered on three sides by a three-inch-high plywood rim. The playing field was a grid of one-inch squares separated by thin strips of wood trim tacked down to the base. A number between 1 and 6 was hand-painted in black inside each square.

The game would unfold thusly: I'd hand the mark a cup wrapped in imitation brown leather. The cup contained six cat's-eyes marbles that the mark would toss onto the playing field. After each marble had settled into one of the one-inch squares, I'd add up the numerical values and check the total against a card placed at the side of the tray.

Across the top, the card read, "Play Football! 100 Yards or Over Wins!" Listed in rows underneath were the numbers 6 (the lowest value of the totaled marbles) through 48 (even though, in fact, the highest total a mark could throw was 6 times 6, or 36). Beside each of these numbers was a figure expressed in yardage. For example, if the mark threw a 40 when he tossed the marbles, he would gain fifteen yards. In order to win a valuable prize, the mark needed to gain a hundred yards or more after multiple throws. As an agent, my objective was to bring the mark swiftly and tantalizingly close to winning, to the point where greed made him short of breath, made it difficult for him to swallow, and he'd find himself wagering the vacation fund to win a portable radio by playing a game he barely understood and hadn't heard of until I'd waved him over and offered a free try.

Twisting, trying not to catch my sport coat's satin lining on a rough edge, I placed the board lengthwise beside where I would stand, the open side on the front counter facing the midway, the rear resting on the lowest of the display shelves.

In this position, the playing field was at eye level with the average mark, which made it difficult to see the numbers arrayed before him. Indeed, the Flat Store wasn't as indifferently constructed as it might seem. The raised floor of the trailer turned any Flattie into an imposing figure, towering over the player like a sentencing judge. The inexplicably heavy steel awnings, so difficult to raise and lower, could become nearly impenetrable shutters if the midway erupted in riot. The riveted, steel-clad walls afforded similar protection, and even if it was unlikely, pampered Flatties like me could console ourselves that while our fellow carnies were fleeing for their lives, we were safely ensconced in a fortress, perhaps blending ice cream daiquiris. The Flat Store was laden with so much armor that the truck towing it between towns strained to reach 45 MPH.

Tonight I had "last call," which meant I was in the third hole from the entrance to the carnival. The Ghost and Flopper would have first shot at the most appropriate marks making their way over the rocky, sandy midway, but since the Ghost had still not arrived and the Flopper was negotiating with another Ride Boy to bring him a bucket of ice cubes, for the moment I had the pick of the lot.

Each of the joints lining the midway zeroed in on the type of mark thought to be best suited for the game, one most likely to respond to the challenges and opportunities it presented. For example, a pair of men in blue jeans and work boots, beers hidden beneath their T-shirts, would be good bets for the Six Cat, a game that required baseball-throwing players to knock stuffed toys off a shelf. Similarly, a scrawny guy, a half-foot shorter than his hot date and anxious to improve his chances on lover's lane with a plush toy, could win by lofting dimes into plates at the Glass Pitch.

As the Fireman had schooled me, the ideal Flat Store mark was a middle-class businessman who didn't want to be on the carnival midway, who was perhaps only there because his wife was selling slices of pie for the Kiwanis Club. Or maybe he had a display of riding lawnmowers from his gardening shop down by the food tent, yet was intrigued by a game that didn't require concerted physical effort and was run by men in decent clothes who had recently showered.

No marks fit that description during the first minutes I turned my attention to the midway. I did, however, spot and pass on a biker and his "old lady" dressed in matching leather vests, their pet cockatiel perched on the biker's bare shoulder; and two sunburned guys in bathing trunks and flip-flops, one with a pair of giant, foot-wide sunglasses resting atop his head, the other with his hand rummaging inside the back of his trunks.

I tapped my Free Game card on the counter. About the size of a business card, it read "One Free Game, nontransferable, void after leaving stand." Of course, I gave one to every likely-looking customer. Choosing the wrong one could lead to disaster—small, hard objects thrown at my head, or an ambush behind the midway—so I had to be careful. If this was show business, the curtain was about to go up.

A couple approached. He was red-faced, fortyish, with gray

Bermuda shorts, shockingly white legs, black socks, dress shoes, and a purple Hawaiian shirt. His thin black hair was combed to conceal a bald spot. She, also fortyish, wore a turquoise blouse with matching shorts and turquoise canvas slip-ons. She carried a turquoise purse with a bamboo handle. Whether she dyed her hair or not was open to question, but it was a brilliant orange pulled back into a French roll. Both husband and wife were laughing. I figured they'd been drinking something other than bottles of Stroh's in the beer tent. More likely a couple of mixed drinks on the front porch of their cabin, or at a local lounge where they'd been regulars since the first afternoon of their vacation. It wasn't a good idea to play drunks—they could get belligerent—but this pair seemed like they might be gracious losers.

They were about ten feet away. I smiled at them broadly. "Say, get yours out in the parking lot?" I said with a ribald wink, waving the Free Game card in my hand. The husband picked up on the joke. "She didn't, but I did," he howled, looking at his wife. This was a good sign. I'd taken the correct approach.

"No, no, no. I'm talking about a card, like the one I have here. A Boy Scout is supposed to be handing them out in the parking lot." Lots of luck trying to find him.

"He was? Well, I feel discriminated against. Where can I file suit?" Hubby, the wit, curled his arm around his wife's neck, planting a wet kiss on her lips. I upped my estimate of his highball consumption to three.

"No need. C'mon over. I'll give you this one."

Hubby swayed toward the counter, pulling his wife by the hand. He looked at me with his mouth open and then pulled the card from my hand. "A lottery ticket," Hubby joked, handing the card to his wife who scanned it and wobbled, her right foot exiting her slip-on. I upped her to three drinks as well.

"Wish it was, for your sake." I faked a chuckle. "Actually, it entitles you to a free play on this game." I shouted in the direction of Flopper, "Don't pay the Boy Scouts tonight. They're goofing off."

"Gladly," Flopper answered, without looking my way.

I turned back to the couple. "See what happens when you try to help?"

Hubby was exploring both sides of the card, barely listening. "So where do I cash this in?"

"Right here," I said hurriedly, worried that I might lose him. "This game. The one I operate."

"Good. Gloria likes anything that's free."

"Can't blame her, can you, uh—"

"George."

"My name's Rusty," I told them. "You ever see one of these before?" I asked, gesturing toward the plywood game board.

"No. What is it?" Gloria asked, stepping closer to the counter, suddenly intrigued. She'd been eyeing the flash.

"It's called Play Football. Get a hundred yards or more and you win," I told her, stealing a glance over my shoulder as if I was about to say something I didn't want Flopper to hear. "And, listen, since you were nice enough to come over with George, I'm going to give you a Free Game card too. Just be sure you both hold onto them tight. Otherwise my boss will be wondering how you walked off with a bunch of prizes and didn't spend any money."

"What prizes?"

"Anything you see on the shelves, from teddy bears to electronics."

"I've already got my teddy bear," Gloria enthused, playfully hugging George.

I pointed a finger at the game board. "The object of this game is to roll the marbles I have in this cup onto the playing field, pot luck, all at once. Takes no skill at all." I demonstrated. "Then you total all the numbers in the squares and look at your scorecard to see how many yards you gain."

"Sounds simple enough," Gloria answered. Her tentative expression indicated she had but a vague idea of what I was talking about.

"Play ball," I said, handing the cup of marbles to her. Now, whatever station in real life George and Gloria held—no matter that they were more than twice my age, with more than twice the life experience and many times the money—their immediate future lay in my hands.

Gloria threw the marbles onto the playing field.

I counted rapidly. "Twelve, eighteen, twenty-eight. Check twenty-eight on your scorecard."

George looked at me, suspicious. "You counted awfully fast."

I laughed. "You're not the first customer to say that. So let's count the marbles again, all together this time." I picked up each marble individually and, in concert with George and Gloria, counted the number underneath, keeping a running total.

"Twenty-eight," George said when we were done, shaking his head. "The kid's right, honey."

Having cemented my reputation as a straight shooter, I replied in the way I always did at this point in the game. "I count them fast, but I count them accurate."

"You're a whiz."

"Surprisingly, I didn't get past the tenth grade."

"Well, I graduated from dental school and can't count that fast. Hope your scholastic career gets back on track," George said, extending his hand.

"Thanks for your encouragement," I answered, shaking his hand. "Now, look at your scorecard and see how many yards twenty-eight gets you."

George ran his finger up and down the card. "Twenty-eight is a blank."

"That means Gloria wins nothing." I turned to her. "Your luck's like mine, Gloria. All bad. How about we give George his try?"

"Sure. Win me a TV, honey," she urged him.

"Will do."

I handed the cup to George and, after vigorously shaking it near his ear, he tossed the marbles onto the playing field. As soon as they settled, I began my count—or more accurately, my miscount. On Gloria's roll, I had added the numbers properly in order to win the couple's trust. But from now on, I would miscount them into whatever number suited my purpose. I would inch George and Gloria ever closer to the game-winning hundred yards, yet leave them short of the goal line forever and ever.

It may be hard to swallow that reasonably intelligent people could be so gullible, yet my counting skills were rarely questioned during my Flat Store career. Even when they were, I had the perfect out: Simply put, it was impossible for a mark to score even a single yard unless I miscounted the marbles in his or her favor. Only if I deliberately counted incorrectly could the mark roll a number like 44, which netted a gain of fifty yards.

In other words, the highest score that could be obtained by a "natural" roll was 36—six marbles times the number 6. However, only the numbers above that—37 through 48—were assigned yardage on the scorecard. Therefore, even the optimum natural roll of the marbles—36—would result in a yardage gain of zero.

Why didn't marks notice this? Probably greed. Probably because everything happened too fast. Probably because they barely understood the game except that they'd earned ninety-nine yards in a matter of minutes, and how much more could it take to gain that extra yard and take home a color TV?

Problem is, that couldn't happen, that extra yard. It wasn't in the numbers, because once I'd led the mark to the goal line, I'd stop miscounting. That's right. Just when, for the mark, the direction of the game turned from impossibly easy to impossible, when he started to lose and was watching my every move, I was already home free. From this point on, the game board did the work for me. I could stand five feet away, allow the mark to count every marble for himself. It didn't matter. There was no way for him to win, no way for me to lose. I'd performed the sum total of my chicanery when the mark was gaining massive numbers of yards, when he or she had every incentive not to doubt.

I miscounted the marbles George had thrown. "Seven, nineteen, twenty-five, forty-four. Check forty-four on your scorecard."

George did as he was told. "Fifty yards," he blurted out.

"Well, shout hallelujah!" I said. "You aren't standing on a horseshoe, are you?"

"Doesn't feel like it," George answered. "But I didn't get a hundred yards, so I guess that's it. See you later, pal. Thanks."

"Tell you what," I interjected, "since you're my first customers tonight, I'm going to mark this last game of yours down as paid. That'll keep me from getting fired in case my boss notices."

"Wouldn't want that," George said, resuming interest.

"And since business is slow," I continued, "just hand me half a buck and I'll give each of you another game. I'll count the fifty yards you already have, which means you only need fifty more yards and the teddy bear is yours. In return, you need to do me one simple favor."

"What's the catch?" George asked, frowning.

"Just walk up and down the midway a few times, tell everybody you won the teddy bear here. A little free advertising for me."

"Honey, I'll tell the world!" Gloria enthused and pulled fifty cents from her purse.

"Make sure George agrees," I warned.

"Why not?" George shrugged. "Give him the money, baby." George had adopted what could be characterized as a cautious swagger. He appeared to be wary about being taken by me, yet seemed to relish the challenge of holding his own with a carny.

Gloria handed me a pair of quarters. George threw the marbles.

"Eleven, seventeen, thirty-eight . . . forty-two." I added. This was the same number I always counted the mark into at this juncture of the game.

George checked forty-two on his scorecard. "Twenty yards."

"That gives you seventy," I announced. "Now it's Gloria's turn to throw."

"We need a big one this time," George said, patting his wife's shoulder.

Gloria threw the marbles. I counted her into a twenty-eight.

"Twenty-eight says H.P.," George announced, confused.

"H.P.," I laughed. "That doesn't mean hot pants or a half-pint. It means House Pays. You double your money and get to roll again. Since you were playing for fifty cents, you get back a dollar." I pulled a dollar from my left pants pocket and laid it on the table in front of the couple.

"This is better than Vegas," George cracked a joke. That was good. He was enjoying himself.

"Let me throw," Gloria said, delicately extricating the cup from her husband's grasp.

The marbles flew across the board. "Six, thirteen . . . twenty-nine," I counted. "Hot damn—the bonus! Gloria, get yourself to the racetrack, because that's the luckiest number in the house. Now when you win, you don't take home a little old teddy bear. You win any of our major prizes." I swept my hand over the TV, the steak knives, the radios, and other fabulous merchandise.

"I could use a new blender," Gloria said.

"All you have to do is add a dollar."

George was taken aback.

"I add, you add," I explained. "Choose any prize, plus the bear." I smiled helpfully, trying to look like I was on their side. This was a tense moment, an important turning point. If George and Gloria stopped here, I would have been wasting my time. If they proceeded, there was a good chance I'd profit from their visit.

George eyed the dollar on the counter that he'd just won. He shrugged and pushed it toward me. "It's yours anyway," he said.

Gloria threw the marbles. "Eight, eighteen . . . thirty-six," I counted, and helped them find it on the scorecard. "Well, well, that earns you a teddy-bear prize and lets you throw again, free. No yardage is added." I lifted a freshly unpacked, green and white teddy bear off the back shelf and laid it gently on the counter before them.

"This is for you, dear," George said, offering it to Gloria.

"Isn't it cute?" Gloria responded, hugging the teddy bear to her breast.

She tossed the marbles again.

"Seven, twenty-one . . . forty-two," I said, glancing up as I did, pleased that George and Gloria were keeping their eyes on the scorecard, not on the playing field and my miscount.

"Twenty yards!" Gloria exclaimed.

"You're up to ninety. To keep playing, give me a buck."

"Here you go," George said, tossing a single onto the counter. Gloria threw the marbles.

"Twelve . . . twenty-eight. Golly gee, H.P. again. Remember

that one? You double your money. So here's another buck. Plus, you get to throw free again."

Gloria rolled. I counted her into a twenty-nine.

"This has got to be the luckiest woman in the world," I laughed. "Now two bucks wins you two major prizes when you hit that wonderful one hundred yards."

"Two dollars?" George asked.

"Yeah, I add, you add," I said and held my hand out. I needed to keep moving fast, not give them time to think, because that was the last thing I wanted two intelligent people to do. They'd ankle the joint if they started thinking.

"Here," George said, handing me the two dollars Gloria had just won moments before.

She rolled. "Twelve, thirty, forty." I counted.

"Five yards," George said, looking up from the scorecard.

"Gives you ninety-five yards. Still two dollars to play."

George pulled a couple of bucks from his wallet. I couldn't get a good look, but there seemed to be plenty more where that came from.

Concentrating hard, Gloria rattled the marbles inside the cup, as if the way she did so would affect the outcome. Apparently, she was becoming some sort of expert in the physics of marbles landing on a plywood board.

I counted. "H.P. again. Holy moly. Your two dollars gets you four and another free throw."

George added my two bucks to his and with a proprietary smugness straightened the bills into a diminutive stack. I noted his self-satisfied demeanor and filed it away to savor later, when he'd be upset and angry—probably within the next ten or fifteen minutes.

Gloria threw the marbles.

"Thirty-four," I exclaimed. "That's the same as twenty-nine. You get four prizes by investing four dollars now."

George pushed his tiny pile of four dollars my way. Gloria threw.

I added quickly. "Thirty-nine."

George scanned the scorecard. "That's two yards."

"Can you kick a field goal? 'Cause that's all you need. You've got ninety-seven yards."

George asked, "But it costs four bucks to play?"

"Right. For your chance to win four major prizes."

George pulled four singles from his wallet, his hand shaking slightly. He was playing with his own money for the first time since bellying up to the joint. "We only came here for a breath of fresh air."

"You may have to rent a Mack truck to carry home all the loot."

Gloria tossed out the marbles.

"Thirty-nine again. That's two more yards for a total of ninety-nine. You're making my heart palpitate. Another yard and the prizes are yours. Just four bucks to play."

George hesitated, then dove into his wallet. "Can you change a twenty?" he asked.

"Certainly." I did that quickly and handed the marble-filled cup to Gloria.

She raised the imitation leather container, shaking it until she said it was "ready." Then she let loose.

I counted George and Gloria into another H.P., then another bonus number. Now they could win eight prizes for the lowly price of eight dollars a throw. Little did they know how many Flat Store customers had experienced precisely such good fortune so many times before.

"Throw the marbles," I ordered Gloria.

"One more yard, boys," Gloria said as the marbles scattered across the playing field.

"Three, sixteen, twenty-seven. Find twenty-seven on the score-card."

George looked at the scorecard, then looked again. He blinked, avoiding eye contact with me. "No yards," he said, and took his wife by the arm. "C'mon, honey. Let's go."

Gloria shook him off. "Wait a minute," she said.

"That's what I say," I concurred. "You've got to be kidding, leaving with one yard to go. Man, that's like building a new house and not moving in. Like it says on the card, this game is non-transferable. We do that because some entrepreneur-types like to buy the rights to continue the game from a guy in your position for fifty or a hundred bucks. They consider it a crackerjack investment, because it earns them the chance to win ten times their seed money in prizes."

George caved in and gave me eight dollars. I was only mildly surprised. Few players walked away when they had only one yard to go. This time, he threw the marbles.

I counted him into a thirty-four, a so-called bonus number. Now George could win sixteen prizes for the sum of sixteen dollars each play. I warned him, though, that sixteen prizes was the maximum we allowed any single player to win.

"You're lucky there are a lot of bad teeth in Michigan," George said, breaking a twenty.

I counted him into a twenty-three. No yards. A loser.

Silent, stoic, George removed another twenty from his wallet. This was a good sign, his grim determination. Now he was chasing after his own money, trying to recoup his losses. From this point on, my primary responsibility would be to keep his anger from boiling over before he ran out of money. Emotionally, the game had him in a death grip.

I counted George into another teddy bear to give him something to show for his troubles. Then I led him into a number I called, on the spur of the moment, a "double bonus," which allowed him to win back the money he had lost plus the sixteen prizes at a cost of sixty-four dollars a throw. One more yard was all he needed to win.

George handed me a hundred dollar bill, I made change, and he threw the marbles.

"Four, seventeen, twenty-four. Damn, no gain."

I began to pick up the marbles. George grasped my wrist hard. "Let me count them first," he said, glaring at me.

I pulled away. "No problem. In fact, let's count them together," I said, trying to soothe the dentist turned badass. We added the numbers and twenty-four was, in fact, the correct total. "Like I said—I count them fast, but I count them accurate."

Gloria piped up. "Let's go, honey. We've lost too much already."

George stood his ground. "That's just the point. We're in too deep to quit now." He gave me another hundred dollar bill. I made change and, breathing heavily, George threw.

I began the count. George interrupted. "Let's do this together, young man."

"Whatever you say." I didn't care. There was no way the total, unless miscounted, would be anything but a loser. Sure enough, the number, twenty-seven, didn't gain any yards for George.

Gloria turned pale and walked out to the center of the midway. George leaned against the counter, wallet in hand. Then he took a deep breath and slid another hundred in my direction. He lost. Again. And again.

"You're cheating me somehow," he accused me.

"How could I? We're counting together."

Gloria returned. "I don't like this at all," she said. "We're decent people."

George and Gloria were now "hot," in carnival parlance. Time to get rid of them. I had more than four hundred dollars of their cash.

"Listen, don't spend your whole vacation fund," I advised them. Getting them to leave peaceably was just as important as hooking them in the first place.

"We already did," George said bitterly.

"Well, then, slow down. Because you never know what course this game will take. I had one guy who threw the marbles five times and went away with fifteen hundred dollars in prizes. On the other hand, there was this person who got stuck on ninety-seven yards and threw forty times before he gave up and walked away. It's all a matter of your taste and bank balance."

Gloria glowered at me. "Thanks for telling us after we got this far."

I shrugged, assuming the role of their concerned pastoral adviser. "It's up to you whether you want to quit or keep going. I'm just dispensing the facts. That's what I'm here for, to help explain the game to people like you. I'm what's known as a concessions consultant. I earn twenty dollars a day plus tips, and the only time I get tipped is when somebody wins. So believe me, it's also in my interest to have things come out right for you."

George paused a beat, after which he grandly declared, "Let me speak with your supervisor, young man."

"I'll see if he's available," I answered amiably. I rapped on the counter to get the attention of Flopper, who had crouched down to pour 7 Crown into an ice-filled plastic beer cup. He took a couple of quick swallows and stood up straight, a single ice cube distorting his right cheek.

"What's the problem?" he asked me.

"I have a customer complaint."

Flopper turned to George. "How can I help, sir?"

"We've spent a great deal of money on this game and have nothing but two teddy bears to show for it," George said.

"Thank you, sir, for bringing this to my attention," Flopper said graciously. "Let's analyze the situation together. On your current game: How many yards have you gained?"

"Ninety-nine."

"Frankly, sir, I'm astonished. You're so darn close to winning, I can't believe you're upset with my boy here." Flopper placed his hand on my shoulder and said sternly, "Son, you let these people play as long as they want in order to gain the yard that they need. If they win, we'll just have to live with it. Now, may I get back to what I was doing?" He dipped below the counter again and nodded at me, the ice cube working back and forth in his cheek.

I returned my attention to George, who was staring into space, lips pursed, apparently in deep dialogue with himself. I raised my hands, palms up. "I hope you don't think I'm trying to push you away."

"Actually, I do," George answered, smiling again, as if he'd caught me in the act.

"I'm with you, honey," Gloria agreed. "We must be close to winning. That's why he's trying to get rid of us."

George reached down and pulled a tightly folded bill from his sock. It was another hundred. "One last time," he said. "But son, you back away and I'll do the counting." Gloria nodded in agreement.

"Fine with me," I said, made change, and stepped away.

George tossed the marbles onto the playing field and counted carefully. He checked the scorecard. "No yards," he said, then as if resigned to his fate, started to leave, pulling Gloria away with him.

"That game is fake as hell and you're a crummy little shit," Gloria sneered at me.

"Don't leave yet," I said.

"Why?"

"I don't like my customers to go away mad."

"Too late, buster."

"Take this anyway," I said, shoving a four-foot-tall stuffed giraffe into her arms. A teddy bear swung from each of George's hands, so from all outward appearances, the couple were leaving as big winners. Hopefully, they would return straightaway to their cabin and not, full of righteous indignation, stop at the sheriff's office instead.

I turned my back to the midway and dumped the cash I'd won from them alongside the Bolivia clocks. For the first time in forty-five minutes, I felt the pent-up heat radiating from the sun-baked steel of the Flat Store. My temples were pounding. I'd sweated through my sport coat. Trembling, I counted out four hundred and seventy-eight dollars.

"Looks like the bad guy won again," Flopper said, peering over my shoulder.

I dragged a teddy bear over the disheveled cash, blocking it from Flopper's view. "Thanks," was all I could think to say. I clutched. Was Flopper spying for the Fireman and Jackie, keeping track of how much I earned? How much I kept for myself? Playing it safe, I shoved the entire amount into the cigar box that I'd hand to the Fireman at the end of the night. Then I hung my sport coat on a bent nail to dry, located my Free Game card, and went back to work. The northern sky was black and starry, with neon offering brilliant contrast, and marks, thick as mayflies, swarmed the midway. There was plenty more money to be made.

CHAPTER THIRTEEN

Never Trust an "A" Student

"Feeling pretty good about yourself, hey?" Jackie observed, dabbing a breaded shrimp in tartar sauce. Jackie, the Fireman, and I were in my room at the Sheraton Hotel in Flint, Michigan. It was the last stop on the Party Time Shows tour before Jackie and I left for college, although the season would continue for several weeks beyond. I had ordered the "55-Shrimp Party Platter" from room service to help kill time until my new silk suit from Five-Finger Discount arrived by taxi from Detroit. The round trip was a hundred and twenty miles, but the extra couple hundred dollars the delivery would cost me was an extravagance I brushed off like lint.

Success had gone to my head, and that was just fine with me. I had quickly become an adept Flattie, and had capped our week in Oscoda by winning big from a lieutenant colonel stationed at the nearby Air Force base. The more time I spent in the Flat Store, the more the money grew. It became harder to safely cache my winnings, which amounted to many thousands of dollars, and with too much money on hand I adopted the Flattie lifestyle of "degenerate" spending. Every week, I battled with the Ghost and Flopper over who could snag the best room in whatever town we were in. If the top hotel was a multistory affair, the goal was to be booked onto the top floor, and if we all wound up there, the competition was over whose room had the best view or largest number of operable bathroom fixtures. A Presidential Suite was, of course, the most desirable, and I trumped the Ghost and Flopper in Ypsilanti by paying the hotel superintendent a hundred bucks to paint a "Presidential Suite" sign and affix it to the door of my otherwise ordinary room. On the other hand, in some hardscrabble farm towns, where there was a single decrepit courtyard motel, the availability of a hot plate and small refrigerator were status symbols—as was close proximity to the ice machine, which allowed one easier access to the ice cream for his daiquiri. And every privilege required a bribe.

A multipage room service bill was also something to flaunt, although I gave up trying to compete with the Ghost. Wherever we stayed, he placed a standing order for the delivery of breakfast, lunch, and dinner, whether he was in his room or not. When he returned from the lot, he'd pick at the cold food or call to have it taken away.

Appearance was also a money pit. I went through Five-Finger Discount's apparel like Kleenex, sweating, ripping, and smudging clothes into ruin within days or even hours. But looking less than slick was not an option, particularly given my youth. Once, I bought a pair of real golf shoes with cleats. This won me style points, but the cleats were hell to walk on for twelve hours a day. That night I gave the shoes to Fred Fred, the Ride Boy, who left the show soon after to become a caddy.

There was also tremendous peer pressure to "signify," as the carnies put it, and exaggerate your lack of financial restraint. If one agent bought a round of drinks, for example, the next agent topped him by purchasing two while rewarding the waitress with a tip that was twice as large. At closing time, the table would often be covered with dozens of untouched cocktails, because no one could drink fast enough to keep pace with the ordering. In Birch Run, Michigan, I developed a taste for liver pâté, bought out the restaurant's supply, and ate nothing but pâté and Ritz crackers for two days. As a practical joke in the same town, Flopper ordered pickled pig's feet for the house, then smirked as a Ride Boy carried the huge glass jar around the tavern, placing a dripping foot in front of each patron.

One persistent truth, though, lampooned my personal swagger, making my Five-Finger Discount silks feel like rags: The success of the entire season hinged on whether I pried my year-end bonus from Jackie's lobster-claw grip. It wasn't so much the money, although by my calculations that had become a considerable amount. No, the cash in question, and who kept it, represented where Jackie and I stood with each other. Was I still his acolyte? Or was I now his equal or better?

Not that Jackie and I didn't enjoy good times together. Jackie had become much more relaxed since the Fireman had arrived. By installing the Fireman as his manager, Jackie had created a buffer between him, the Ghost and Flopper, and their grousing about his youth. What's more, with the Fireman looking over their shoulders, they began to earn more, or at least turn in more of what they earned. That had been such a plus, Jackie had handed Jimmy the job of managing all of his joints, down to the Balloon Dart.

It was a position the Fireman had taken on with relish. Every day, he patrolled the midway, hands clasped behind his back, offering pointed comments and criticisms. He performed surprise inspections and imposed fines if he found dust on the flash. And when he wasn't walking, he was watching with a pair of binoculars while seated conspicuously on a wooden folding chair in the shade.

With the weight of responsibility lifted from Jackie's shoulders, our friendship regained the shape of our high school days, with plenty of high-speed escapes to Detroit or Chicago for a taste of big-city pleasures. But now there was the issue of the bonus to be settled, which was why I had invited Jackie over to share the shrimp platter. He appeared as wary as I was, so I was not surprised that he was accompanied by the Fireman, who responded when I brought up the bonus.

"Let me tell you something, Joe College," the Fireman said, "since coming to this show, I've probably gotten to know Jackie better than anyone in the world except his bookie and a few loan sharks. I know what he's going to feel before he feels it, thinks before he thinks it, and when he's going to belch before he swallows his first spoonful of chili. And I can tell you something about this 'year-end bonus' jazz you bring up: Jackie would never make such a promise, because he knows no one in his right mind would expect him to keep it. I mean, what sort of scam you trying to pull here? Can you really tell me with a straight face that you believed Jackie would sit there with thousands of dollars of your money burning a hole in his pocket, then up and three months later give it back to you? From your standpoint, handing Jackie your money for safe-keeping was like you got knocked up, had a baby, and gave it to him for adoption. You can't come back later, after Jackie has burped it, changed its diapers, and taught it to say 'Momma,' hollering, 'Hey, man, give it back now or I'll call the cops.'"

"The money or the baby?"

Jimmy laughed and slapped me on the knee. "Go over and look at yourself in the mirror, because boy, are you hot under the collar. In fact, forget the mirror—you'd just steam it up—and open the window instead. We're reaching the boiling point in here." He paused, patted several pockets to make sure his various rolls of money were in place, then added with a dismissive wave, "Actually, I'm just funnin' with you, Mr. College. Yeah, Jackie promised you a bonus. That's true. But I'm his trusted manager, and I've advised him to make it available to you in the form of an Indiana Bust-Out."

"That better not be anything like a Georgia Gig Shot."

"It's not even like an Illinois Butt-Pop."

"That gives me comfort."

"The Bust-Out is another ancient carny ritual. Over the course of one day, starting at the Duck Pond and ending at the Flat Store, Jackie and you will work every game on the midway, side by side, in full view of each other. Come midnight, if you've brought in more money, you receive double your bonus. If Jackie earns more, he keeps the cash. As the highest-ranking agent on the lot, I will be the referee and keeper of your winnings. Any questions or comments?"

"What if I don't agree?"

"You got me. I didn't think that far ahead."

"Sure, I'm game."

The Fireman turned to Jackie. "How about you?"

Jackie pondered a moment. "I'll pass."

That startled the Fireman, which was apparently what Jackie wanted, because with a faint grin he added, "Of course I'm in."

Jimmy stood up, shaking breading from his trousers. "Well then, I'll see you boys 11:00 A.M. tomorrow at the Duck Pond."

Jackie followed him into the hallway, but not before turning to me and saying, "Thanks for the shrimp. Here's ten bucks for my share." He was gone before I could stuff the bill back into the breast pocket of his shirt.

A few hours later, after brooding about the Bust-Out and my chances, I left my room in order to voice my concerns to the referee. I found him napping in his kitchenette, the sales brochure for a deluxe Airstream slowly slipping off his lap.

★　　★　　★

News of the Bust-Out spread quickly along the midway. By noon, when Jackie and I had stationed ourselves in the Balloon Store/Duck Pond trailer, an excited crowd of agents had gathered around us to kibitz and make side bets; that is, until the Fireman directed all who wanted to keep a job back to their own place of business. His orders were followed with great reluctance. Apparently there hadn't been a Bust-Out in many years, most agents being unwilling to risk the reputations they had so assiduously inflated.

But, as Horserace Harry observed before retreating, Jackie and I were young and reckless enough to put our "dicks on the butcher block." Which didn't mean I was eager to proceed; I was revved up, yes, yet terrified at what was about to unfold. Jackie, on the other hand, was showing his usual surface calm, juggling three plastic ducks as we waited for the Fireman to give us the "go" sign. When Jackie ended his juggling act and began twisting several balloons into the shape of a giraffe, though, I sensed that he was trying a bit too hard to appear casual. It was encouraging to think he might have a case of nerves.

After the Fireman had successfully shooed away all the agents, he turned around to face us. I flinched. He'd been treating me badly, as he'd promised he would the prior night before I beat a hasty retreat from his trailer. "After all," he'd reminded me with a painful squeeze on the shoulder, "Jackie and I are so tight I feel like a bigamist. So don't look for me to be anything but hard on you during the Bust-Out. Jackie would expect nothing less."

Now, glaring at me before smiling at Jackie, he said, "Okay, boys, you know the rules. You'll be working every game on the lot, handing me your winnings each time we move on to a new joint. I'll put Joe College's money here in my right pocket and Jackie's in my left. At the stroke of midnight I'll total your bankrolls, and the guy with the highest take wins. In order to keep you both in nail-biting suspense, I won't make an interim count before then."

Jimmy, wearing a burnt-orange linen shirt over beige linen pants, then beckoned Fred Fred and a new Ride Boy called One Day with a wag of his pinkie finger. Fred Fred, an unlit cigarette in hand, had now been with the show several weeks. This made him the senior Ride Boy. One Day, so named because that's how long he was expected to last, was a local kid with freckles and muttonchops. He was finishing a grape snow cone and had purple lips. A secret smile on his face, the Fireman announced, "I'm assigning Fred Fred to Jackie and One Day to Joe College. They're here for one purpose only: to take care of your every need. Since you'll be devoting every moment to earning an income, they'll supply you with water, towels, clean clothes, and a pot to piss in, if you so desire. Any questions?"

"Can I take a broad break during the contest?" Jackie asked.

"Only if you want to lose valuable cheating time."

"How about a nap?" I inquired, trying to show that I, too, was relaxed enough for empty banter.

"I suggest you hold off until your golden years," the Fireman replied, "because every second counts in a competition like this, which if I ruled the Earth would be an Olympic sport. Now, if there are no further questions, I suggest we begin. Would somebody bang a gong or belch or something like that?"

"I've got just the ticket," Fred Fred said, grinning. He pulled a string of ladyfingers from his back pocket, straightened the wick, lit it, and tossed the firecrackers onto the ground. After several long moments, it became obvious to me that the firecrackers were not going to ignite. I stood erect, inhaled deeply, and began searching for my first mark.

"May the best man win," Jackie called out, stretching across the circulating ducks to offer his hand.

"Why?"

"Good point," Jackie answered, withdrawing before he made contact with me. I focused my attention again on the midway and hooked my first four-year-old mark.

Jackie and I were both wearing silk suits—his dark blue, mine silver—so we may have looked a little out of place, coaxing small fry into throwing a dart or picking up a duck. I didn't have a problem taking money from children. The younger ones especially got such a kick out of acting grown-up and handing money to me, a stranger, that winning a prize was merely icing on the cake. In that sense, it was quite touching, if not especially profitable, to see their eyes light up as they transferred their quarters into my possession.

Jackie was even more shameless, building tip after tip with his juggling act, then convincing the gathered mothers to give their entranced kids the chance to win a prize. The skills he'd developed years ago on the Free Show made him a formidable Hanky Pank agent, not that he'd ever admit it. When a school bus emptied nearby, he convinced the teachers and chaperones that the price of admission to the midway was a mere quarter, with a free game at the Duck Pond thrown in for good measure. Forty kids walked away with a piece of slum, one of them crying when he couldn't remove his index fingers from the Chinese handcuffs he'd won. After witnessing similar gambits for over ninety minutes out of the corner of my eye, I realized it was going to require hard labor to even keep within shouting distance of Jackie.

The next stop on our tour was the Cat Rack, a cavernous joint that required marks to throw baseballs and knock painted, two-foot-tall, sawdust-filled cats off a shelf in the rear of the tent. Jackie seemed invigorated, as if dropping his administrative chores and hopping back into a joint was therapeutic. I was flustered. I'd rarely worked the joint, and I lost valuable time and a few pieces of plush getting comfortable with the concealed lever that controlled whether the cats could fall from the shelf or not. Meanwhile, at his end of the joint, Jackie was again employing a very off-Broadway style of showmanship to pile up his winnings. He rang a cowbell to attract attention, told jokes to maintain the tip, and raced back and forth across the joint carrying a teddy bear piggyback when somebody won.

I was still fiddling with the hydraulic gaff when I glanced across the joint to see Jackie working One Day, who was in the process of losing the two dollars I'd tipped him for mopping my brow with a chilled, wet hand towel.

"Hold it right there. That's my Ride Boy you're beating," I shouted to Jackie.

Jackie grinned. "He has time on his hands. You're not keeping him busy."

I caught the attention of the Fireman, who had just given a well-dressed mark a Free Game pass for the Flat Store. "Jackie shouldn't be allowed to do that—play the game with One Day," I said.

The Fireman pondered for a moment, then stated, "I don't find it in the rules that Jackie can't go after your personal valet."

"Where's the rule book?"

"In here," Jimmy replied, tapping his forehead. "If you want a look, find a pick axe. Anyway, your two bucks was all One Day had to his name. That's not enough to affect the outcome of the contest. Look at the silver lining—if you were a bigger tipper, it could have."

I heaved a baseball at a stuffed cat, missing it. The ball hit the canvas, ballooned it, and dribbled to the ground. The Fireman was playing the role of Jackie's enabler a little too well.

The day had turned oppressively humid, thick, grimy clouds hanging low and immobile over the Flint skyline, as we arrived at the Nail Store. The joint was located alongside a giant oblong tent that the fair committee had dubbed the "Home Zone" and was filled with booths manned by anxious salesmen flogging everything from septic tank cleaners to kitchen remodels and miracle soaps. I handed my suit coat to One Day, exchanging it for a wet towel that I draped around my neck. Then, as I was wrapping a carpenter's apron stocked with gaffed nails around my waist, I sent One Day scurrying into the Home Zone with a message to spread.

Jackie, in the meantime, was munching on a pork barbeque sandwich that Fred Fred had brought him under a covered plate. He appeared supremely confident as Fred Fred finished tying the carpenter's apron on for him, then held a large paper Coke cup under his chin so that Jackie, his hands too busy with the sandwich, could take a few sips on the straw.

The Nail Store appealed, in the main, to overconfident professional carpenters and home improvement zealots. After all, the objective was to pound a finishing nail flush into a railroad tie with a single swing of a claw hammer. Right up their alley, although the task became impossible when the nail they hit had been altered to bend under the hammer's force. But any carpenter eager to impress his peers couldn't resist the challenge, so I wasn't surprised when One Day returned from the Home Zone trailed by a stout, resolute Sears hardware salesman carrying a state-of-the-art, oak-handled Craftsman hammer. The salesman asked me, "Is it true that you get fifty percent off on the cost of this game if you bring your own hammer?"

"Yes, sir, but for the next hour only. It's worth it to me, saving the wear and tear on my own hammer."

"How much?"

"One buck. One swing. Win a teddy bear."

"I'm game."

All Jackie could do was watch in frustration as I jacked Craftsman Fats up to five, then ten dollars per swing by enticing him with additional prizes, until he gave up a $357 loser. Fortunately, he was a fairly good sport about it, although I could understand why when he told me he could easily earn back that amount and more by cutting a few extra corners on a remodeling job he had lined up.

"Here's an extra teddy bear in honor of your positive attitude," I said, concluding the transaction.

Jackie never came close to a similar score, which allowed me to close the gap between us, although it was impossible to tell by how much. The Fireman deposited all of our winnings in his pockets without remark.

The Push 'Em Up Coke joint, where we gathered next, was a recent and intriguing arrival on the Party Time Shows midway. The game had, at first glance, three unremarkable components: a ten-ounce Coke bottle; a wooden cradle against which the bottle rested at a forty-five-degree angle, with the mouth of the bottle pointing toward the mark; and a barbeque fork with two long, sharp tines. To win, the player needed to push the Coke bottle into an upright position with the fork. If the bottle wobbled and fell over, he or she lost.

The gaff was the rare bottle, in which molten glass had settled and then cooled unevenly at the bottom during manufacture, rendering the interior of the base slightly lopsided and marginally heavier on one side. The barely noticeable defect allowed me to control whether the mark won or lost. If I twisted the bottle so that the heavier side was farthest away from the player, it would invariably topple over no matter how carefully it was pushed by the barbeque fork.

I'd often wondered, as I had with many of the games, what hardscrabble entrepreneur had noted the defect and devised a game to exploit it and make a few bucks, maybe even a family wage. What I knew for certain was that the gaffed Coke bottles were treated like valuable artifacts—which, indeed, they were in the right hands.

Therefore, I should have anticipated that Fred Fred would "accidentally" shatter my bottle on an iron tent stake when removing it from the velvet-lined box where it had nestled, leaving Jackie in possession of the only Coke bottle that worked.

"Don't hold me responsible for a Ride Boy's screwup," Jackie protested as an apologetic Fred Fred picked up the jagged pieces of the moneymaker.

"So what do the rules say about this, Mr. Referee?" I queried the Fireman, ninety-nine percent sure that Jackie had put Fred Fred up to it. In the near term, though, simply replacing the bottle had greater urgency.

"If there's not another gaffed Coke around, and I know there isn't, you'll have to forfeit this stage of the match," the Fireman said, with uncharacteristic discomfort.

Mentally riffling through my limited options, I asked One Day, "There's a party store up the street, isn't there?"

"Yeah, I think. That way." He pointed west.

"Come with me," I said, urging him along by the arm. With One Day in tow, I trotted off the lot to the sidewalk and raced ahead as best I could in my Italian loafers with slippery, brand-new leather soles. At the end of the first block, around the corner, I spied the party store—displaying, thank God, a Coke sign. I slipped One Day a five dollar tip, wove through an idle crowd of teenage boys (most of whom One Day acknowledged), and entered.

The proprietor was solidly built, with silver hair arranged atop her crown like a powdered sugar donut. She eyed me with suspicion.

"How much to buy all your Cokes?"

"All? No sell all. Police not allow such nonsense goings-on, probably," she grudgingly replied in a thick Polish accent.

"I was born in this country. I can assure you my request is not illegal."

Again, she gave me a thorough once-over. Just when I was about to bolt in search of another store, she exhaled through her teeth and announced, "You wear nice suit, so I believe you. To take all Coke, one hundred dollars. But if police arrest me, I kill you."

"Dubja," I replied, which I hoped was Polish for "thank you." When she snatched away the hundred I held before her, I sensed that my one-word Polish vocabulary had passed the test. I flung open a cooler door, removed several six-packs of Coke, and directed One Day to do the same. Then, to Sugar Donut's consternation, I scooped a bottle opener from the top of the battered cash register, hustled outside, flipped over a paint bucket turned trash receptacle, squatted on it, and began emptying Cokes for a better view of how the bottoms were shaped.

"No spill. No spill. Ruin sidewalk. Police come," Sugar Donut shrieked, hurrying toward me with surprising speed despite a rolling, arthritic wobble.

"I beg to differ. Police not come. But your wish is my command, anyway," I said, her protruding apron now inches from my face. A foaming river of Coke wound across the sidewalk and into the gutter. Desperate to continue, I nodded at the boys still loitering near the party store and asked One Day, "Are they friends of yours?"

Assessing them, One Day licked his upper lip, only now beginning to lose its snow-cone purple. "All except one," he concluded.

"Hey guys," I shouted to the boys, "how about this for a deal? I'll pay you one dollar for every Coke you can drink. Enough to cover your dental bill with money left over for—I don't know—say a few boxes of Milk Duds."

I didn't have to ask twice. One Day's friends rushed over and began guzzling Cokes almost as fast as I could open them. In turn, I examined each empty and gave the drinker a buck from my personal bankroll, so that my Bust-Out winnings would not be affected.

Soon, dozens of empties littered the sidewalk and, to please Sugar Donut, I assigned One Day to place those bottles back in the six-packs and stack them neatly inside the store.

My drinking team began to lose its enthusiasm after about ten dozen Cokes, and my spirits were headed south when I held the next empty against the sun in my sticky right hand and was wowed by a classically lopsided bottom, ideal for use in Push 'Em Up Coke.

Thrilled, I ran the entire distance to the joint, defiantly flashed the bottle at Jackie, placed it carefully in the wooden cradle, and picked up the barbeque fork, ready to do business.

"Well, nobody can say you aren't trying," Jackie said, looking somewhat shaken by my return.

Sweat-soaked and wheezing, I called in my first mark. I earned $227 from him and a hundred or so from a few others before the Fireman announced that it was time to turn in our winnings. Glimpsing Jackie's fat bankroll, I knew I hadn't made as much as him. But as he'd observed, I was trying.

Maybe it had something to do with surviving my Push 'Em Up travails, or maybe something to do with the rhythm of stealing I'd fallen into by that point, but around the six-hour mark of the Bust-Out I miraculously left my physical body to soar high in the clouds above the midway. Okay, it was more like ten feet above the row of tents in the vicinity of the Smashed Sandwich; still, it was a mar-velous vantage point. I saw Jackie and me working below, traveling from one joint to the next, with the Fireman placing my winnings in his right pocket, Jackie's in his left. And that wasn't all. Up and down the entirety of Party Time Shows, tips built and dissolved as the Ghost, Philadelphia Phil, Horserace Harry, and the rest of the crew did their best to transfer wealth from the unsuspecting to those who were "with it." I hovered there for hours, drinking it all in, until Fred Fred successfully lit a string of ladyfingers to mark the last stage of the Bust-Out, the Flat Store, and I plunged back into my corporeal self.

"This is it, boys. The final stop," the Fireman said as Jackie and I took a breather behind the steel-clad trailer. "How are you both holding up?"

"I've never felt better," Jackie answered, changing from his suit coat and dress shirt into an orchid print Hawaiian shirt, as if he was already preparing for his festive victory party.

"Let's do it again," I added. Shirtless, I poured a giant cup of ice water over my head, gasping at the cold. Then I shook the remaining glob of crushed ice into my hand and rubbed it under my arms.

"If you're so hot, why don't you crawl into an ice machine, for god sakes?" the Fireman chided.

"I needed reviving, that's all," I answered, accepting a towel from One Day. I had been feeling a little wobbly, possibly from the rapid pace of activities, possibly from the eight or ten Cokes I had consumed in my search for a trick bottle. But my ice bath, which still had me shivering, was the tonic I required. I dressed and flung open the door to the Flat Store, where Jackie was already introducing a mark to the game. He wasn't resting on his laurels, Hawaiian shirt or not.

The midway was elbow-to-elbow. A regional tribute to agriculture had just broken up, and swarms of farmers—as well as local and state officials—were making their way to the parking lot from the Home Zone, where several hundred wooden folding chairs had been set up in a cleared area at the far end of the tent. My pulse quickened; a few affluent farmers would be a nice catch. But not one person stopped. From the grim, determined faces and hot-headed pushing and shoving, I gathered the meeting had not gone well.

I leaned against a large Daffy Duck spoofer, lifting one foot and then the other in a futile attempt to ease the ache. Over time, the passing crowd thinned to a workable level. A well-dressed mark approached and I bolted to the counter, only to have Jackie nab him first, along with what appeared to be his wife and three well-scrubbed kids.

Ticked off, I was surveying the immediate vicinity for a likely prospect when Jackie's mark abruptly left him and walked my way. It was against protocol, and an embarrassing slap in the face, to call in a mark who had turned down another agent. But Jackie and I were at war, so I asked the man, "Excuse me, but where did you buy that nice suit?"

The mark, with sandy hair and brown, horn-rimmed glasses, smiled and said, "Brooks Brothers, in Detroit.".

"And such a great-looking family. You're lucky."

"Why, thanks. How nice of you to say that," he answered, drinking in the compliment. He seemed to take great pleasure in being buttered up. I decided to melt a few more creamy pats on his head before moving on to more important matters.

"I believe in giving credit where credit is due. I just wish my own upbringing had been as good as the one I'm sure your children are having."

"I can only hope they think that," he smiled, throwing an arm around his wife and winking at one of his young daughters, who was eyeing the Daffy Duck spoofer.

"Oh, she wants it. I can see that." I bent down and said to the daughter, "You'd like to have Daffy to sleep next to in bed, wouldn't you, cutie pie?"

"Uh-huh." The girl nodded shyly and retreated to the protection of her mother's skirt.

The mark chuckled. "Well, looks like I can't leave the premises without something she can hug tight."

"And don't forget the other kids. And me," said his wife, a sweet-faced blonde.

"Oh boy," the mark said, shaking his head, "looks like I have my work cut out for me now." Reaching for his wallet, he looked up at me, "So how do you play? This is a game, isn't it?"

"Yes, it's called Play Football and Win. Accumulate one hundred yards and receive your choice of valuable prizes."

"Sounds interesting. I used to play football myself, once upon a time. How much?"

"Tell you what, since you've been so nice, I'll give you the first game for free. And because your family is so charming, I'm presenting you with this special deal: When you win, all three kids and your wife get to pick out the stuffed animal of their dreams."

He wagged a playful finger at me. "I should warn you that I'm a lawyer and I'm going to hold you to that."

"Oh really?" It took a few seconds for me to regain my composure. I looked over at Jackie, who was smirking at my discomfort.

"Yup." He slid a business card across the counter, plainly pleased at the opportunity to reveal his status. "I'm a federal attorney at the Detroit field office."

I nearly choked. Whatever pressure I'd been feeling increased tenfold. Split-second visions of arrest and incarceration sped through my mind. Abruptly, the fear diminished and was replaced by a sense of resolve, even enthusiasm. It would look good on my resumé if I beat a federal official for a nice piece of change. In certain circles, anyway.

So I played the attorney for all it was worth, complimenting the assured manner with which he tossed the marbles, urging him on to victory as he piled up the yards, presenting each of his children with free miniature plastic whistles, sharing the family's highs and ultimate loss of $214 like it was a steak knife piercing my ribs. But the fed took the defeat with dignity, as befitted a man of his stature.

"I can't believe you're smiling when I'm near tears," I said to him, wiping my brow.

He shrugged his shoulders. "The government pays me well, so I have no real worries. Anyway, I'm philosophical about such things. You know, there's always a lesson to be learned. Like in this case—I just found out that it's sometimes cheaper to buy toys at Sears Roebuck than—" He looked around, then turned to me. "What's the name of this place?"

"Party Time Shows."

"Just do me one favor," he asked, gesturing to his now-impatient wife to wait for a moment, then drawing closer to me and saying conspiratorially, "You're a pleasant young man and a fine salesman. You have my card. Contact me sometime. Our office can always use another energetic intern. But in the meantime—don't tell anyone about my losses tonight. Wouldn't look right in the *Detroit News,* if you know what I mean."

"Sure do," I said with all the sincerity I could muster when it was nearly impossible not to leap with joy at the beautiful score. "Tell you what. You've been such a trouper that"—I untied the rope that held Daffy Duck to a post, then stepped to the rear display counter and scooped up three teddy bears—"I'm going to give you the prizes you wanted so badly and thank you again for being such a devoted father." After handing the plush to his wife and kids, I shook the fed's hand.

"And thank you for being so understanding," he said, almost apologetically, and gathered his family and left. I waited for them to melt into the crowd before letting out a triumphant whoop.

"You think this is a pep rally?" Jackie said angrily. "You don't jump up and down after beating a guy. There are other marks watching. We're not supposed to be thrilled because they lose."

"Hush up now, Jackie," the Fireman said, rushing in to stifle further conflict.

"You see all the flash he gave those people? Why don't we loan
them a semitruck to take it away?" Jackie said, heaving a pink-and-
white teddy bear just over my head. Struck by the impulse to throw
something back, I grabbed a blender off the display.

"Cool down, both of you," the Fireman intervened. "Take a
walk, Jackie. Play the Cat Rack. Throw a bunch of baseballs down
there. And who knows, you might win a prize."

"I'll stretch my legs," Jackie replied. He jumped out of the Flat
Store, strode to the opposite side of the midway, and turned around
to stare at the joint, still angry.

The Fireman watched him until he was apparently satisfied that
Jackie wouldn't storm back. "He'll get over it even if he has to find
God first. By the way, did you know that was a big-time federal at-
torney you beat up on?"

Cocky, I replied, "I think he left happy."

"He better be as giddy as a lobotomy patient, or you're going to
be wearing striped pants."

"He thanked me."

The Fireman chuckled. "My golly. Did he fix you up with his
wife, too? She was a knockout." He peered down at his watch.
"Well, look here. It's midnight. The Bust-Out is over. Let's count up
and declare us a winner before your buddy the fed changes his
mind." He whistled sharply, waving Jackie back to the trailer.

"Sorry about going overboard with the guy," I apologized.

The mix of 7 Crown and Sen-Sen in his breath warming my
ear, Jimmy replied, "Don't be. It was a real good move. Stealing him
took the wind right out of Jackie's sails."

I'm sure I appeared to be in a state of shock as the Fireman me-
thodically counted our winnings on the lower Flat Store display

shelf. My mouth had even gone temporarily numb after twelve hours of seducing, haranguing, and consoling. Still, my thinking was clear and acute.

Ten minutes later, Jimmy, looking down at the yellow legal sheet he'd been scribbling on, announced that Jackie had earned the impossibly high sum of $2,183.65. There was no way I could beat that number. But I did; my earnings totaled $2,586.87. I refused to react, concerned that if I started shouting with glee, Jackie would change the rules of the Bust-Out.

Either Jackie wasn't bothered by the loss, or he held his emotions in check like me. "Don't spend this all on one horse," he said, withdrawing a huge roll from the inside pocket of his double-breasted blue blazer.

I accepted the money. The bills strained against a half-dozen industrial strength rubber bands. Brimming with nervous energy, I tossed the roll from hand to hand like a football.

"That's over fifteen thousand dollars," the Fireman said, patting me on the forearm. "I expect to see it in the collection plate this Sunday." He backed away, the tension between Jackie and me appearing to cause him discomfort. "Listen, I know you boys have some things to settle now that you're both going off to college, so I'll leave you alone for a while to cry on each other's shoulders and otherwise get all emotional, like the end of *Gone With the Wind*." After wiping a smudge from a teddy bear's eye, the Fireman left.

Jackie and I didn't utter a word for an uncomfortably long time. Increasingly self-conscious, I was coming up with an excuse to exit when Jackie asked, "So when you leaving for school?"

"Tonight," I answered, surprised at regaining my voice.

"Tomorrow morning for me." Then, for the first time since handing over my bonus, he made eye contact. "You did well. I thought it wouldn't be close."

"Hey, thanks," I replied, suddenly thunderstruck by a sort of winner's remorse, a regret that I had beaten the only guy I'd ever looked up to. Now what did I have?

Another long silence. It dawned on me that, after holding an unceasing conversation for years, there was nothing more for us to say. But, as I began to walk away, Jackie called after me, "Hey, I always knew you were H.O.ing. Don't worry about it."

The carbonated bubbles in my stomach began an alarming rolling motion. "Why didn't you fire me, then?"

"Everyone holds out. But, I figured because of us being friends, you'd steal less than the others. You know—guilt. And I was right. I crunched the numbers. You were relatively honest."

I took that as a backhanded compliment. And with that, Jackie and I parted, without a word about keeping in touch, dropping a line, or hitting the race track. I knew that was for later, or perhaps not at all. One thing was certain—we'd had enough of each other to last a long while. Our friendship had outlived its usefulness.

I strolled well past the shuttered and silent tents, leapt over a runny ditch, and veered left on a path through a thicket of forsythia bushes, where my motorcycle and the Fireman were stationed. There, after a tense wait for the sound of footsteps, I paid him the fifteen hundred bucks I'd promised for his cooperation the night before. When toting up my take, the Fireman had seeded it with another thousand that I'd given him to slip into my cash pile, if needed.

"Congratulations. You won," the Fireman said, slipping a common paper clip over his money.

"In a manner of speaking."

"Stop your sobbing right there. You thought of a way to come out on top that Jackie didn't. You know what happened? The guy got too full of himself. He believed too strongly in his own natural ability. True, fair and square, Jackie did beat you. But you won. You out-conned a born con. Start patting yourself on the back instead."

"Thanks for the pep talk. I feel better already."

"Good, because I'm not doing too bad either. You delivered quite a blow to Jackie, and the less sure he feels about himself, the more he'll feel he needs a savvy partner like me."

"Now I know why you—"

"Listen," Jimmy interrupted, "there's one thing I wanted to ask you before you ride off into the darkness and crash your motorcycle into a telephone pole. How does one go about becoming an 'A' student?"

"Well, I don't know if I should reveal this. It's a secret every academic achiever holds close to his or her chest. But if it'll make you any happier, I'll tell you—we cheat."

The Fireman nodded sagely and flashed me the "okay" sign. I fired up the Triumph and left for college.

Twenty-four hours. That's how long it was before I dropped out of the University of Michigan, although I remained on campus for a couple more weeks, soaking up Ann Arbor's classic college-town atmosphere in the event I never again was a student. There were a number of reasons why I quit. For one thing, I'd scheduled two consecutive classes that were a mile apart, with ten minutes to run to the second. In my advanced English class, the professor told us we could earn a grade by completing a project of our choosing—including, but not limited to, building a tree house. And the cafeteria didn't serve 13-Inch Foot-Longs.

The primary reason, though, was that I just wasn't ready to sit in one place long enough to underline passages in textbooks. So one day I simply vanished, without notifying my roommate or the dorm supervisor, or whatever in the hell the grad student who completely ignored us was called. Without any idea where I was headed, I wound up at Detroit Race Course; using my Alabama driver's license, I purchased a reserved seat on the clubhouse level, played the Daily Double, won $247.50, and escaped before losing it all back to the track. Then, on impulse, I headed south of Detroit to Ecorse, a gritty suburb. There, along the banks of the Detroit River, Party Time Shows was in full swing, visible waves of heat rising into the towering elms. I kept my distance across the street, making certain I would be lost in the arriving crowds. I spotted the Fireman trotting toward the Flat Store and a single Airstream—like Jackie's, but also like the model the Fireman had been contemplating—parked among many lesser trailers in the back. Over the next ten minutes, there was no sign of Jackie. Nervousness about being spotted made me flee before discovering whether he was at Wharton or relaxing inside his air-conditioned home away from home.